John Whatmore was bor[illegible] Surrey, though his journ[illegible] Africa. He currently work[illegible] *ian*. He has experience o[illegible] Tiger Moth biplanes, but [illegible] – is camping. His trips i[illegible], after which he took the bike by bus [illegible] through the Everglades swamps and the Florida Keys, and several cycle-camping trips to Maryland and Virginia. He is a graduate of the Open University.

JOHN WHATMORE

The CTC Book of Cycle-Touring

GRAFTON BOOKS
A Division of the Collins Publishing Group

LONDON GLASGOW
TORONTO SYDNEY AUCKLAND

Grafton Books
A Division of the Collins Publishing Group
8 Grafton Street, London W1X 3LA

This revised edition published by Grafton Books 1986
in collaboration with the Cyclists' Touring Club,
Cotterell House, 69 Meadrow, Godalming, Surrey,
GU7 3HS, telephone (048 68) 7217.

First published in Great Britain by
David & Charles (Publishers) Ltd 1983
under the title *The CTC Book of Cycling*

ISBN 0-586-06559-8

Printed and bound in Great Britain by
Collins, Glasgow

Set in Times

For Jeannette

—

Contents

	Introduction	ix
1	Choosing the machine	1
2	Gearing, clothing and accessories	14
3	Exploring in town and country	28
4	Wild tracks and the camping scene	47
5	Abroad with a bike	66

GAZETTEER OF CYCLING ROUTES
Introduction 91

England
The West Country 94
Southern England 114
The Midlands 139
The Welsh Border 148
East Anglia 155
Peaks and Pennines 160
The Lake District and the Isle of Man 173

Wales
South and Central Wales 180
North Wales 187

Scotland
The Borders 194
The Lowlands 197
The Highlands 198

Northern Ireland 203

The Shetland Islands 207

Bibliography	209
Appendix: Gear Tables	212
Acknowledgements	216
Index	217

Introduction

I was aged eight when the cycling bug bit. England was in the grip of the Depression of the mid-1930s, and in our terraced house near the centre of Birmingham there was little money for luxuries. I did, however, have an elder brother who owned a bicycle, and even at that age I realized that he had a rare possession. He brought back jars of sticklebacks from a stream some miles distant, and armfuls of bluebells and catkins which were put in jam-jars on the windowsill, and in the autumn he collected pounds of blackberries.

He knew of another world beyond the chimneypots, far from the waste ground on which we boys played. I nagged at my parents with the determination that only a child can show, complaining that 'you can get a second-hand bike for fifteen shillings' and seeking the support of my father who had been assistant secretary of the Birmingham and Midland District Association of the Cyclists' Touring Club during World War I before illness ended his cycling. Although the money must have represented much of the housekeeping for a week, they agreed that if I could find a bike for that sum, I could have it. I rushed out of the house that summer evening and walked for miles among the back-streets of Birmingham looking for a second-hand shop that might have a bike.

With the luck that the gods sometimes bestow on the very young I came across what could truly be called a junk shop. It was really more of an extension to a back-street house, with rusting bedsteads and tin trunks littering the pavement, but among it all, wonder of wonders, was a bicycle! Rust had long since obscured the maker's name, it had only one brake and the saddle was misshapen, but to me it looked wonderful. On being asked how much it was, the shirt-sleeved shopkeeper replied, 'Oh, you can have that for fifteen bob.' Of such moments are happiness made. I ran all the way home and returned with the money, and I think that from that moment I lived in a dream world.

My elder sister, although she could not ride herself, taught me to do so by holding me up until I could wobble along the roads on my own, dodging the trams and trying to avoid getting the front wheel caught in the tramlines, which I soon discovered spelt disaster for the unwary. From that day life changed. I found that it was possible to tie a fishing rod to the machine and, with care, to suspend a jam-jar of frogspawn from the handlebars.

War came and the blitz destroyed our Birmingham house. We moved to the comparative rural delights of nearby Sutton Coldfield which has a large area of wild parkland studded with lakes and streams, a place where rare wildflowers grew and where, it was rumoured among us boys, there was even a spot where the sundew plant that eats flies could be found, though I never discovered it. The possession of a bicycle – a rather newer one by now – meant that I could leave home in the early mornings of the long summer holidays and be in that wild park in a quarter of an hour to spend the day in the heather, or fishing, or collecting butterflies.

The invasion of Europe by the Allied forces came in June 1944, and with my bike I had a ringside seat. A dozen miles from my home was an aerodrome, used for repairing damaged Lancasters and Spitfires, and I had already become a familiar sight sitting there on the cycle watching the aircraft take off and land. But in that summer of 1944 a new kind of air traffic appeared. I packed my sandwiches and set off on the bike as Dakota aircraft, emblazoned with the black and white stripes that marked them as Allied invasion planes, took off for France loaded with paratroopers, later returning with the fuselage doors still open and the remains of the static lines used in the drops still dangling from the doorways.

The first job meant some financial independence, and one of the first things I bought was a new cycle. It seemed only logical then to join the Cyclists' Touring Club and learn how to do things properly. Over the years I have had good cause to thank those riders of mature years, for what they taught me and for the way they put up with us younger members who in excess of enthusiasm would 'burn up the road' in what we imagined to be true racing style. They would patiently explain by the side of the road why a tyre should be put on this way rather than that, and if they grumbled among themselves that we had no road discipline, they were still ready to help out with the loan of equipment to lads who could not afford to buy it. I recall one husband and wife who regularly turned out on a tandem in all weathers. That was thirty years ago, but I met them again recently, still riding the same tandem and not looking so very different. Cyclists go on for a long time!

When I was honorary secretary of my local district association of the CTC I would frequently be approached by middle-aged people who said that they wanted to return to cycling, and the reason was usually the same: they found that the best times of their youth were spent in the saddle of a bicycle among good friends. Now more and more are returning to the sport. They are very welcome.

1

Choosing the machine

Cycling is a huge subject, and like other sports and pastimes it yields up its delights most readily to those who are prepared to take the trouble to learn how to do it properly. At last the cloth-cap image that dogged cycling in Britain for so many years is disappearing. Let's bury it for good. The modern cycle is not the poor relation of the car, nor is it a toy suitable only for youngsters until they can afford their first motor vehicle. It is one of the most efficient machines ever devised, and more than ever it has a place in our modern world.

There have been few inventions in the history of mankind that have brought more benefits at lower cost than the bicycle. Its efficiency as a converter of energy into forward motion is phenomenal: it is virtually silent, does no harm to the environment and provides the rider with exercise that can give him a fresh outlook on life, and all at little expense. Its speed is such that, on a summer evening, it is possible to exchange greetings with people working in their gardens, yet the enthusiast can manage a hundred miles a day or more, and whole continents are regularly crossed by long-distance tourists. The bicycle can be transported by plane, train, ship or car, usually at little or no extra cost, and is then ready for instant use anywhere. Truly, the cycle is a marvellous machine.

A belief has grown up that the car is an enemy of the cycle, but this is an attitude that must change. Even on our crowded city roads there is room for both, and the cycle can be a wonderful piece of additional equipment for the motorist. Anyone who has attended cycle rallies on the Continent is likely to have been surprised by the number of cyclists who arrive by car with gaily coloured machines on the roofs of their vehicles. After a journey, perhaps half way across France, the motorists will park their vehicles and take to the byroads on their true 'transport of delight'.

Without the need for registration, taxation or compulsory insurance, the cycle is one of today's great bargains. Not everyone wants to become a dedicated tourist, or to race, or to join the hundreds of club-runs which take place every Sunday throughout the country. For many families it is sufficient to keep a cycle in the garage as a work-horse. There it is available, particularly if it is a unisex machine of the type which is enjoying enormous popularity, for quick shopping trips, for the commuter to use to reach the local station, or for the youngster to pedal to school. For whatever reason it is used, there is no doubt that it will repay its initial cost in a matter of months by the savings made in petrol and fares, and maintenance costs are extremely low. Today, folding cycles are available that will fit in the boot of a car, or that can be kept in the cupboard under the stairs of a small house or in any other odd space. Nor is the weather a problem with modern waterproof clothing – and it is not difficult to look great on a bike!

In fact, it is estimated that between eight and ten million people in Britain now cycle regularly, and with the continual rise in petrol prices, this figure will certainly increase. Nor is Britain alone in experiencing a bike boom: in Germany more bicycles than cars have been sold in recent years, and that is in a country not known for being cycle-conscious. Indeed, there are so many advantages to owning and using a cycle that the committed rider is usually amazed that more people do not follow his example. About the only disadvantage is the danger from other road-users, and that can be reduced with care and practice. Regular riders are not unmindful of the dangers, but they find that the all-round vision available to the cyclist, and his ability to hear traffic approaching from behind, go a long way towards keeping him safe. Also, a cycle has wonderful manoeuvrability which makes riding, even in the most crowded streets, much safer than might at first be imagined.

When it comes to purchasing a cycle, no one has yet managed to better the small- or medium-sized shop where the dealer really knows his trade. It will be necessary to pay rather more than at a cut-price warehouse which sells cheap imported machines, but it is as true in the cycle industry as anywhere else that you get what you pay for, and a good cycle will last for many years.

If going to a 'cheapy' warehouse, consider the machines there carefully. Ignore for the moment the bright colour and the thin coating of chrome that make a cycle look superficially attractive, and study the component parts as an engineer might. Look first at the small things. Are the mudguard stays fastened to the frame by a brazed-on fitting, or are they merely secured by a cheap clip? If the latter, trouble may follow. Similarly, what about the fittings for the pump and lights? Next, look at the frame itself; examine the lugs – the heavy metal castings joining the tubing which makes up the frame. This is a sure way to tell a good machine from a poor one. If they look heavy and clumsy, the rest of the frame is sure to be made of similar material. Finely machined lugs are expensive and will be used with other high-quality materials on a good cycle. Try the brakes: is the action smooth and positive, or does it all feel rather tin-like? Those brakes must stop the cycle and rider, often with a load on the machine, under any conditions. Do they give confidence? Finally, look at the pedals and wheel hubs. Are the parts well machined or are they merely stamped from thin metal?

So, return to the local cycle dealer. The range of machines will seem rather confusing at first, but they can be divided into three basic types: those intended for use around town; junior cycles; and touring machines. There is a fourth class, the thoroughbred racing machine intended for competition work, but for the moment it is only necessary to recognize that this specialist end of the market exists and concentrate on the other three.

About-town machines

There has been a revolution here in recent years with the introduction of the small-wheel unisex cycle. With a wheel diameter of 20in or less, the rider is closer to the ground than on the conventional machine. The designers have ensured that he sits in an upright position, with a good view all around, and the absence of a top-tube, often wrongly called the crossbar, means that hopping on and off is easy. The tyres are wide to give maximum comfort, and there is usually a chainguard to keep oil off dresses or trousers. A large luggage basket can be mounted on the front of the cycle, and a saddlebag at the rear. An alloy prop-stand makes parking the machine even more easy than usual. Gears are almost always of the hub type, that is all the working parts are enclosed within the rear hub, out of the weather, and they are generally trouble-free, any problems being confined to the maladjustment of the control cable. Most manufacturers offer a choice of either a three-speed gear or merely a single speed.

Having discovered a ready market with the small-wheel machine, the designers went one better and produced the folding version, which sometimes has its own carrying bag. Folding cycles are hardly a new idea as they were tried by the armies of France and Austria at the close of the last century, and in World War II paratroopers on both sides were equipped with them. Nevertheless, the folding cycle has caught on and has made a big difference to city cycling. The essential problem was to design a hinge fitting that would be strong enough and reliable, so that the cycle could be folded in seconds. Although the designers intended these machines to be used mainly on relatively short journeys, there are already indications that they should be taken seriously as touring machines. While cycle-touring in the Middle East, I met a middle-aged English cyclist happily using such a machine which he lifted into buses and taxis. Having brought it out by air, he planned to ride it back from Israel, using ferries to take him through Cyprus and Greece, and so across Europe. I hope that he made it home safely.

An alternative to the small-wheel cycle is what is sometimes called the lightweight roadster, a sturdy cycle of conventional design usually available as a man's or woman's model. This type of mount has the advantage of being more versatile than the small-wheel machine, and it probably has a longer life. One of the disadvantages of the small-wheel cycle is that its wide tyres cause more drag on the road surface and so its efficiency is reduced. This is not really a problem on short journeys, but where longer rides are likely to be the rule, the conventional cycles are swifter and probably have the edge in general efficiency. They are normally available as three-speed or five-speed machines, and the gearing may be either the enclosed hub type or the derailleur, that is the mechanism where the chain is 'derailed' from one sprocket of the freewheel block and moved to another of different size.

Junior cycles

What has been said so far applies equally to machines intended for youngsters. Scaled-down versions exist of the unisex machines, the roadsters and for that matter touring cycles, of which more in a moment. Dawes, for example, make a small-wheel machine which features an extra low centre of gravity for additional safety, a gear ratio chosen with young legs in mind, and reflectors on the pedals. One of the problems when choosing a cycle for a growing boy or girl is to get the correct size. It is tempting to choose something just too large so that it will last longer, but this is asking a son or daughter to start off into traffic not just on a strange machine, which in itself is an extra hazard to the inexperienced, but on one which cannot be properly controlled because it is too large. Not only is it gambling with the youngster's safety, it is also loading the dice against him.

Fortunately, there is enough room for adjustment in the saddle-pillar and handlebars to allow for several years of growth. It is really a matter of keeping an eye on the bike and rider over the months and making sure that the simple adjustments are made as the youngster grows. Nevertheless, it is necessary to know how to choose the correct size of frame from the start. Because we are not all built in exactly the same proportions, these figures can only be a guide, but the fine adjustment can easily be made after the rider has become used to the cycle.

The golden rule is that the rider must be able to straddle the cycle, with both feet on the ground, with at least 1in (25mm) of clearance above the top-tube (remember, we don't call it the crossbar!). This is the minimum inside leg measurement for the appropriate frame size as recommended by the Dawes cycle company:

29in (74cm) (inside leg)	18½in frame
30in (76cm)	19½in
30½in (77cm)	20in
31½in (80cm)	21in
33in (84cm)	22½in
34in (86cm)	23½in
35¾in (91cm)	25¼in

The frame size is the distance from the centre of the bottom-bracket spindle to the top of the seat-tube. The inside leg measurement, by the way, is the distance from the crotch to the base of the heel in stocking feet. Now for the fine adjustment, assuming that you have the correct-sized machine. Get someone to hold up the machine, or if you are alone lean against a wall. While wearing shoes, put both *heels* on the pedals and rotate them backwards. If the saddle height is correct, it should be possible just to keep the heels on the pedals at the lowest position. This means that when the cycle is ridden normally, with the balls of the feet on the pedals, the leg will be just slightly bent at the bottom position. Adjusting the handlebars is more of a matter of feel. Start with the bars just slightly lower than the top of the saddle, and adjust later to give what is found to be the most comfortable position. In both cases, make the adjustments in small steps: ½in (12.5mm) extra saddle-pillar is enough at one time.

Touring machines

We now enter the world of serious cycling. The ideal touring machine is one which will be comfortable to ride, yet responsive; light yet strong enough to carry a heavy rider, and perhaps camping gear, over the roughest terrain. It can be expected to have ten – or occasionally even fifteen – gears. It will have dropped handlebars, not because they give a sporty appearance but because they allow at least three riding positions. Choice of the ideal touring machine is complex and often a matter of personal preference. The machine may be produced in a factory on a mass-production system or it may be made to measure by a specialist hand-builder. Either way, there is a wide variety of choice.

The frame

The conventional frame is usually referred to as being diamond-shaped; in fact it is composed of several triangles, one of the strongest geometrical forms. You will find this frame illustrated on page 8, together with a diagram showing the names of the various parts of the frame.

The characteristics of the machine, that is whether it is lively or more comfortable and sedate, depend largely on the geometry of the frame. To understand something of what it is all about, we start by considering the frame angles and recognize that this is only part of the equation. The other factors include fork rake, bottom-bracket height, chainstay length and top-tube length. There are two angles that primarily interest us: that at the junction of the head and top-tube, and that where the seat-tube and top-tube meet. The steeper these angles are, the shorter will be the wheelbase and the more lively and responsive the machine.

However, there will be a price to be paid as such a cycle will be less comfortable – something to be considered carefully on a machine meant for touring. For most purposes, the best compromise comes when both angles are 72°, usually referred to as '72 parallel'. If you are interested in having a really sporting machine, perhaps wishing to combine some racing with short fast runs, a degree or two steeper in the head angle would give you what you want. An elderly rider, looking for greater comfort, might prefer several degrees less in both angles.

If the machine is mass-produced, you will have to accept what the makers give you, and this is likely to be about 72 parallel, with a wheelbase of about 42in (106.5cm). But if you cannot stipulate what angles you want, then it might be wondered why you should bother with the technicalities at all. Isn't it all rather academic? There are two reasons why you should take the trouble: the first is that if you are to take cycling seriously you need to know why a machine should have

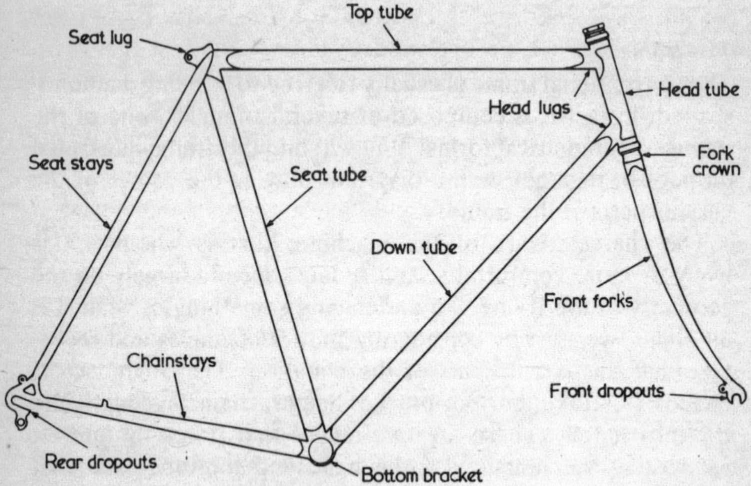
Top tube
Seat lug
Head tube
Head lugs
Fork
crown
Seat stays
Seat tube
Down tube
Front forks
Chainstays
Front dropouts
Rear dropouts
Bottom bracket

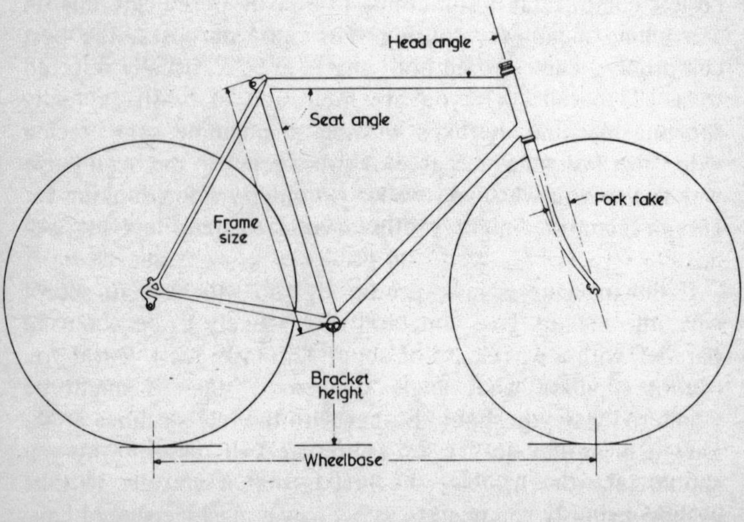
Head angle
Seat angle
Fork rake
Frame
size
Bracket
height
Wheelbase

certain handling qualities, and the second, when having a frame hand-built to suit a personal build you can certainly stipulate exactly what is wanted. Even though it may not be the intention to go to the expense of a hand-built frame, the standards that can be achieved by this method ought to be known so that you will have a better idea of judging quality when it comes to choosing any cycle.

One of the country's top frame-builders, John Connell of Loch Ewe Cycles, who builds machines in Yorkshire, says that the difference between the hand-built machine and one from a factory can be compared to a mass-produced motor car and one built by Rolls-Royce. No matter how good the engineering on the mass-produced article may be, it can be matched by the specialist and further improved by the skilled human touch. The hand-builder can incorporate almost anything you want. Stops and guides can be brazed on to the frame to neaten the fitting of brake and gear cables. Chain hangers, lamp bosses, dynamo fittings, eyelets for panniers, or brake bridges can all be added during building. Chroming, either decorative or hard engineering chrome for added protection, can be applied. More important, the frame will be built to suit your requirements, giving a machine that will exactly suit your physique, one that will be a joy to ride and which, with care, will last almost indefinitely. It would not be too much to expect to pass it on to your grandchildren!

John Connell says that if you want a hand-built frame you should, if possible, visit the builder and look around his workshop to see the methods used. These are the points he advises you to look for. Accurate fitting-up between the tubes. This is important because without a good fit-up the braze will not run completely round the joint and up into the inside of the tubing, forming a fillet. A fillet on the inside of the tube, plus one between the tubing and the lug, gives a very strong and durable joint. The setting up of the lugwork is important. As lugs are manufactured in only one or two angles, it is necessary to change the angles to suit the frame configuration. Check to see that this is done before the frame is brazed up and that the modified lugs fit neatly around the tube with no obvious gaps.

Filing of the lugwork should be done carefully with no filemarks on the tubing due to file slips. The transition from lug to tube should be small to avoid stress concentrations at the interface. Low temperature brazing rods should be used: the really low ones have at least 30 per cent silver content. The lower the heat input, the smaller the heat-affected zone and the smaller the section of the tube which has its yield point reduced. That is, it will stand higher stresses before becoming permanently bent. A common place for the frame to fail is at the down-tube just below the bottom head lug. Next, check how the extras are brazed on. Again, these should be done at low temperature. If the builder is adding extras which are small and have thin sections, you can be sure he is doing them at low temperature – high temperatures would melt them. Finally, attention to detail. Are all the sharp corners chamfered? For example, the inside of the slot running down the seat-tube should be chamfered to minimize scoring of the seat-pillar. Are the tubes filed and degreased before brazing, thus ensuring that the braze runs up to form a fillet?

Choosing a good builder is something of an art in itself. Designing the perfect machine is a two-way process between customer and craftsman. The good builder will take measurements of such details as the distance between the rider's hip-joint and knee-joint, his arm length, shoulder to hip length, and so on. He will prevent the customer waking up in a cold sweat at night convinced that he has asked for the wrong-sized frame with a technical specification that will never result in a cycle that feels 'just right'.

The builder will also want to know whether mudguard clearance will be required. Pure racing machines, of course, do not use mudguards and the wheels, owing to the short wheelbase, are too close to the frame tubes to allow them to be inserted. He will want to know how much luggage will be carried (camping gear perhaps?), for tourists carrying a heavy load will need a stiffer frame than those engaged in light touring. Similarly, a rider with a powerful sprint will need a stronger frame than will a smooth pedaller. Many cyclists prefer to order only the frame and assemble the finished machine from parts they choose at leisure, though the builder will do this if asked. Building up a bike yourself is half the fun of the game.

So much for the thoroughbred, but perhaps it should be shouted from the rooftops that there are few journeys that can be made on an expensive machine that cannot also be managed on a factory-produced cycle. Generations of cyclists have made epic journeys across Europe, Asia and America on appalling roads using whatever machines were available. The thoroughbred may be a machine to plan – or yearn – for, but let us not be too influenced by equipment. The sport of cycling is about riding where you will, in as near to complete freedom as is possible in the world today. Provided the machine is well maintained, it will go almost anywhere with a high degree of reliability. The limits of a journey are imposed by the ability and physical fitness of the rider, not by any shortcomings in the machine. So, recognizing that a hand-built machine may be the ultimate, and the standard by which others are judged, we acknowledge that the factory-built cycle is no mean thing and proceed to look at it in detail.

Wheels

The first choice here is between alloy and steel rims. It may seem that steel rims are stronger and more likely to remain true, though this is not necessarily so. The strength of the wheel lies in how well it was built and whether all the spokes are still correctly tensioned rather than in the inherent strength of the rim. The main advantage of alloy rims is that they are lighter, and this is more important than it first seems, for wheels comprise moving weight and a reduction there is of much greater advantage than the same amount of weight saved, say, in the frame. Also, in wet weather, the braking is more efficient with alloy rims than with steel. With the latter, the moisture between the brake-blocks and the rims reduces the stopping-power to a greater extent, though this can be partly overcome by using rims with roughened surfaces or by fitting special brake-blocks, some of which are made of leather. Alloy rims tend to be more expensive.

The choice between hubs divides itself into large flange or small. The difference is that with the large-flange hub the spokes will be slightly shorter, and this will give a stiffer, more responsive wheel, but it will not absorb shocks so well. The popularity of the large-flange hub originates in a fashion in road racing where it makes sense to choose a more lively wheel. Also, many people feel that the large flange gives the wheel a more attractive appearance. The large-flange hub has the extra advantage that if a spoke breaks in the rear hub on the sprocket side – which is where they do break owing to the sheering force being greater there – it is just possible with some ingenuity to replace the spoke by the side of the road without removing the freewheel block, a task for which a special tool and quite a lot of effort are needed. Spoke breakages other than close to the freewheel are easily dealt with.

There is some controversy over spoking. Until recent years, the British tradition was to have 40 spokes in the rear wheel and 32 in the front. Now it is the practice to have 36 in each. Not everyone is happy with the change, the critics saying that as the rear wheel carries most of the weight it should have a larger number of spokes. Others disagree, pointing out that it is not the number of spokes that determines the strength of the wheel. Some add that, in any case, a machine laden with touring gear should have some of the weight over the front wheel to achieve a better-balanced bike.

Three-cross spoking is adequate for general cycling, that is where the spokes cross each other three times, though if camping gear is to be carried with a heavy rider it is worth having the rear wheel built on the four-cross pattern. A wheel which is not misused, such as by riding over pavement kerbs, should last for years. Spokes come in three types: rustless, chrome and stainless. It is sometimes claimed that chrome and stainless spokes suffer from being brittle, and that the rustless are cheaper and stronger, although they do not look as good. Spoke breakages are a curse and if they happen more than very occasionally something is wrong. They almost always go at the hub end, and it may be that the hub is of a cheap design without the spokeholes being countersunk, so the edges of the hole eventually cut the spoke. Sudden stamping on the pedals can also exert terrific force on the spokeheads.

If you are having wheels built up by a specialist you should tell him the purpose for which the cycle will be used. If building your own – not beyond the ability of the enthusiastic amateur – match the spokes carefully to the hub, for if the spoke gauge is too narrow, the spoke will be able to move in the hole, resulting eventually in broken spokes. Grease on the spoke-heads can also help reduce breakages, and it is a good idea, when having wheels built, to ask that small brass washers be used at each spokehole in the hub. The best hubs are machined from one piece of metal, while the cheaper ones are built from three separate pieces. The present fashion is to have quick-release fittings. This practice became popular because racing cyclists use them: it makes sense for them to do so because it saves time on a wheel change. However, solid spindles are stronger, simpler and much more secure. The track-nut cannot be beaten as a means of ensuring that the wheels stay put!

Brakes

The choice is often one of sidepulls or centrepulls. In practice there is not a great deal to choose between them, though sidepulls are lighter and slightly less complicated but the leverage is theoretically not as great. One advantage of side-pulls is that they do not get in the way of the saddlebag as the centrepull rear brake can do. It is much more important to obtain a quality set rather than debate the relative efficiency of the two mechanisms. If you are having a bike built, it is well worth considering having cantilever brakes; the bosses for these should be brazed on during building. The extra leverage that can be exerted makes this a very efficient system.

Brakes sometimes have a habit of squealing, often due to road film building up on the wheel rims. To cure it, try dipping a cloth in white spirit and thoroughly cleaning the rims, If this does not work, roughen the brake-blocks with a coarse rasp, and if that fails, change to a softer brake-block – red are usually less hard than black.

2

Gearing, clothing and accessories

With modern variable gears no hills and few mountains need be feared. In fact, the short, sharp hills that are experienced in English country lanes, such as the 1 in 6 variety, are often steeper than the gradients in the Alps and Pyrenees. In the case of the European mountains, the climbs go on much longer but the way the roads are engineered in a series of zigzags makes the gradients relatively gentle. The secret of long-distance touring is not to be over-geared, especially when heavily laden. A bike that seems fine with its high gears on a Sunday run may be hopeless when loaded with camping gear for a mountain tour.

It is a sad fact that most touring cycles are sold with far too high a gear ratio. Complaints to a dealer are likely to bring the response that the dictates of fashion are that unless a ten-speed machine has a top gear of about 100in it will not sell well. What nonsense this is. There are no times when one *needs* such a high gear, but what is needed is plenty of really low gears. Even one as low as 28in can be achieved on a ten-speed machine by using a small chainwheel (or chainring) of only 30 teeth in conjunction with a largest rear sprocket of 28 teeth. The tiny chainwheel may cause surprise among many riders, but after a long day in the hills they are likely to be more appreciative.

When our Victorian great-grandparents rode their high Ordinaries – Penny Farthings if you like – one revolution of the pedals, and therefore of the large wheel, carried the rider along a distance equal to the circumference of the tyre. The maximum size the wheel could be was governed by the length of the rider's legs, and it became standard practice to express the gear size as the diameter of the wheel. Later, with the introduction of the chain, it became possible to develop a 'Safety' bicycle with its smaller wheels and to achieve different sizes in gears.

The size of a particular gear is expressed in inches. If, for example, the chainwheel has 40 teeth and the chain passes over a sprocket (on the rear wheel) with 20 teeth, then a cycle will travel two revolutions of the wheel for each complete revolution of the pedals. Let us assume that the cycle has 27in wheels. Twice 27 is 54, so we say the cycle has a 54in gear. However, it is necessary to recognize that the distance travelled by one revolution of a 27in wheel is not 27in; that is the diameter. The distance travelled will be equal to the circumference of the wheel, which is about 85in. Nevertheless, the calculations are based on the diameter of the wheel and so we stick to the definition, in the example, of a 54in gear.

To arrive at the size of any gear resulting from combinations of chainwheel and sprocket size, there is a simple formula. Divide the number of teeth on the chainwheel by the number of teeth on the rear sprocket and multiply the answer by the size of the road wheel (in inches). In the case of a chainwheel with 40 teeth, and a rear sprocket with 18, fitted to a cycle with 27in wheels, we get: $^{40}/_{18} \times 27 = 60$. That is to say the cycle has a gear of 60in. There is, in fact, no need to do the arithmetic; it is simple to read the answers for any combination of chainwheels and sprockets from a gear table (see Appendix for the tables for 26in and 27in wheels).

Similarly, the process can be reversed. If a cycle has, say, a 40 tooth chainwheel and what is wanted is a gear of about 50in, the gear table shows that it will be necessary to fit a 22 tooth sprocket which would give a gear of 49.1in.

Many an old cyclist has been heard to murmur the adage 'As little bicycle as possible', meaning you can't beat a single fixed gear and no 'gadgets'. But the purpose of variable gearing, which is very reliable today, is to make more efficient use of the energy we expend. A variable gear is not an accelerator, but when used correctly it allows a steady, rhythmic pedalling to be maintained. Theoretically, if the rider is going uphill, the lower gear that he uses will enable him to keep pedalling at the same speed as he did on the flat, though the cycle will travel more slowly; downhill the opposite applies. But let us not be too purist about this: we are not machines and will certainly expend more energy going uphill than we do on the flat. It will be necessary to 'put a bit more effort into it'. But that steady rhythm is something that should be aimed for, as to acquire it is to gain a big advantage on a long ride. The classic example of rhythmic riding is provided by the older club rider who has developed the style over the years and who can cover considerable distances in a day, never seeming to hurry yet arriving at the tea place less fatigued than someone, perhaps younger, who has 'burned up the road' in a series of fast sprints.

The best rhythm is certainly achieved by riders who still prefer the single fixed gear, that is without a freewheel. Indeed, before World War II this was the normal type of gear for many experienced cyclists as it gave wonderful control of the machine and a feeling that it was part of the rider. Retarding pressure on the pedals instantly slows the machine and gives it a responsiveness that has been lost with multi-geared cycles. Such was the degree of control that a fixed wheel gave that in some clubs a newcomer who turned up with a freewheel might be taken quietly on one side and told that next Sunday he would be expected to turn out on a 'single fixed' to make him less of a danger when riding in a tight group. Those days are gone, but many racing cyclists enjoy fixed-wheel riding during the winter training sessions when the rapid pedalling keeps them warm – and track racing is always conducted with fixed wheels. For tourists, the absence of those delicious long downhill swoops swings the balance against fixed wheels, but for city riding the degree of control given by the solid sprocket among the slow-moving traffic could mean that they enjoy a comeback. They are, however, really for the experienced cyclist and unsuitable for upright machines.

Multiple gearing on the modern cycle is divided into the derailleur type, where the chain is moved from one sprocket on the freewheel block to another of different size, and the hub gear, such as that manufactured by Sturmey-Archer, where all the working parts are enclosed in the rear hub.

Derailleur gears

Changing gear with this type of mechanism is only possible when the pedals are being turned. The correct procedure is to ease the pressure on the pedals and gently ease the control lever forward or backward so that the chain, relieved of its tension, will be able to move to the next sprocket. It is a mistake to try to move the chain across several sprockets at once as this causes unnecessary distortion in the chain and wear in the gear-shift mechanism. On climbing a hill, the change-down must be made well before the point where the rider is struggling; if it is left until this stage, the rider will be exerting heavy pressure on the pedals to keep the cycle moving, and either the gear mechanism will fail to make the shift to the larger sprocket, or it will do so only with difficulty and with the danger that some of the sprocket teeth will be broken. When caught in the wrong gear halfway up a hill, it is far better to dismount, raise the rear wheel, and while gently turning the pedals, ease the gear lever so that the shift mechanism moves the chain on to a large enough sprocket to enable the climb to be continued from stationary – this will usually mean bottom gear.

The gear mechanism is exposed to all weathers and it is in a position where it readily picks up road dirt which soon becomes mixed with the oil, and so the moving parts suffer. The derailleur mechanism, perhaps more than any other part of the cycle, requires regular attention. It should be wiped over carefully, preferably after every long ride and certainly every time it has been used in wet conditions. A spot of oil should be applied at each of the pivots which control the movement of the chain guide cage and wherever there is movement between one surface and another, as well as a drop on the small adjusting screws. Remember to wipe off the surplus oil, otherwise it will attract road dirt. With a new machine, the cable operating the mechanism may stretch slightly after a few weeks. An adjuster is provided near the cable end for taking up the slack.

Front changers

With the popularity of ten-speed machines, the double chainwheel (or double chainring) has become almost standard for touring cycles. What has been said already about keeping the mechanism well oiled and clean applies equally to the front change mechanism, though being in a position where it gets less road dirt, and because its range of movement is smaller, merely covering the gap between the two chainwheels, it is less likely to give trouble. A word of caution about using ten-speed machines: chains designed for derailleur gears are flexible, allowing them to be run somewhat out of line, but their life will be increased considerably if they are run with a minimum of distortion. It is inadvisable to run the chain from the left-hand chainwheel to the extreme right-hand (smallest) sprocket, or from the outer ring to the inner (largest) sprocket, as this 'cross over' results in too much distortion in the chain. It will not do much harm for a short while, but try to avoid it, particularly when applying considerable pressure such as on a steep hill.

Hub gears

Hub gears have mainly been a feature of about-town cycles, largely because the range of gears has been restricted. At one time, only three gears could be employed compared to the five or ten available with the derailleur system. Now hub gears can have a range of four or five. The hub gear has two clear advantages over the derailleur: its working parts are totally enclosed and protected from bad weather, and the chain runs permanently in line. Though it has never really caught on with serious tourists generally, it does have its advocates who are strong in the praise of the reliability and smoothness of the transmission. The mechanism may seem complicated (the system of gearing makes the hub revolve faster or slower than the sprocket), but it is well within the capabilities of the amateur mechanic to replace worn parts – and these are often more easily obtained than are spares for derailleurs, where wear can mean that the whole unit has to be replaced. The principal makers of hub gears in Britain, Sturmey-Archer, point out that gear changing may be done while the cycle is moving or stationary. When it is moving, pressure should be eased off the pedals, but pedalling should continue and the control lever should be moved smartly to the next position. When changing gear while the machine is stationary, the pedals should be eased backwards.

Lovers of roughstuff riding frequently prefer the hub gear as it is less likely to be damaged by becoming entangled in the undergrowth. It is possible to double the number of gears available by fitting a double chainwheel and a front changer, adding a jockey arm to take up the slack in the chain which occurs when moving from the large chainwheel to the smaller, though perhaps this robs the hub gear of some of its advantages.

Handlebars

Dropped handlebars are usual for touring machines as they give more flexibility in riding style. It is pleasant to have the hands comfortably positioned on the brake lever hoods for much of the time, giving a semi-low riding position. When battling into a headwind, or when making a special effort to put on speed, the hands can move down to the 'on the hooks' position, which will make better use of the lower back and thigh muscles. If an upright position is wanted, perhaps to see a view over a hedge, or just for a change, the hands can be moved to the centre of the top of the bars near the handlebar stem, and the back can be more erect. Some riders have no desire to 'get down to it' and prefer a flatter type of handlebar. There is plenty of room for personal preference, but whatever shape of bars is preferred, they should be wider than the rider's chest, otherwise his upper arms will constrict his chest, making breathing more difficult and generally cramping him. Large riders may find the deep wide bars made popular by some of the 'giants' (in both senses of the word) of the Tour de France particularly suitable.

Saddles

It is often said that no material has been produced which makes a better saddle than top-quality leather, and there is good reason for this claim. However, it does need looking after, takes a long time to break in and can be ruined if it gets wet and is then allowed to lose its shape. A new leather saddle should be treated with a preservative such as Brooks Proofide or neat's-foot oil – the latter acts more quickly but has to be warmed before use, and until it is thoroughly absorbed by the leather (some days) it will stain clothing. A saddle bought in advance could be given several moderate applications of neat's-foot oil both underneath and on top, and then be allowed time to soak it up thoroughly; an application of Proofide, well rubbed in with a soft cloth, will equally ensure that the saddle will last, wear in well to the rider's shape and be extremely comfortable.

Saddles made of synthetic materials are often cheaper, though it is wise to get one from the top end of the market. They are slightly lighter than leather, do not require a lengthy breaking-in period, are more weather-resistant and will not easily lose their shape. They are often made of a pliable nylon base with a high-density foam cushioning. Where the pelvic bones meet the saddle, the base is more flexible. Whichever saddle is chosen, it must be wide enough to support the bones of the pelvis. About-town machines often have a saddle of man-made material resting on a bed of springs. This is quite adequate and comfortable for short journeys, but the large number of springs means that much of the power used in pedalling is absorbed by the springiness of the saddle instead of being translated into thrust at the pedals.

Saddlebags

Anyone out for more than just a short ride has to carry his equipment somehow. Even for a day's ride there will be tools, puncture-repair outfit, spare inner-tube, spare sweater, cape or other waterproof equipment, map, food and probably a camera. The one place it should not be carried is on the rider's back. To wear any sort of heavy rucksack is folly as it is both uncomfortable and unsafe. An exception can be made for the musette, a light bag slung across the shoulders. While it is a handy place in which to keep small quantities of food or a map, if it becomes too heavy the straps dig into the shoulders and it begins to irritate. A better plan is to wind the strap of the musette around the saddle-pillar and allow the bag to rest on top of the saddlebag where it will be readily accessible.

The best way to carry things on tour is in a saddlebag, though for a ride about town on a shopping machine there is much to be said for a basket firmly attached to the handlebars. Saddlebags come in a variety of sizes and are usually made of nylon or cotton duck: the former is lighter and more water-resistant, but the latter retains its shape better when not full. Either will give good service and the choice is largely a matter of taste. A surprising amount of equipment can be packed into a saddlebag after a little practice, but as they are not always as waterproof as the makers suggest, it is a good idea to pack all the articles into plastic bags of the sort that can be bought at any supermarket. This not only keeps the contents dry, it also keeps them cleaner and more accessible.

Handlebar bags

These have become more popular in recent years, a trend which has spread to Britain from the Continent. Provided that no more than a few pounds is put in them – the manufacturers give the recommended weights – they will not affect the steering. In fact, some weight on the front wheel balances the bike better than having everything at the back. They are particularly useful because small items, such as a bar of chocolate, can easily be taken out without stopping. Some designs have straps on the top to hold a map.

Panniers

Panniers probably provide campers with the only way in which to carry all their equipment, and tandem riders, too, find that they are the best way to contain the double load of luggage. They are available for either front or rear wheel fitting. Usually, those intended for the front are smaller as too much weight would affect the steering. They are attached to frames which must in turn be bolted securely to the cycle. In choosing a set, it is important to be sure that your heel will not catch the bottom of the bag when pedalling: some designs are cut into a slight wedge shape to avoid this. A particular point to watch for is that the fastenings between the bags and the pannier frame are of good quality, for if they break it may be almost impossible to refasten the heavy bags securely again, and on rough ground they can take a great deal of strain. Panniers also have the advantage that the weight is kept low; even a heavily loaded machine can be a positive pleasure to ride if the weight has been well distributed between the front and back of the cycle. A touring machine complete with lights, bags and equipment for a non-camping tour of two weeks or more need not weigh more than about 42lb (19kg) in total – the cycle probably weighs about 30lb (13.6kg).

Lights

Dynamo or battery is the choice. A dynamo costs rather more to start with, and there is some drag on the wheel with most sets, though there are now more expensive designs on the market which reduce this. For anyone making regular use of the cycle at night, the dynamo is almost certainly the better choice, if only because of the high cost of batteries, though the design of the battery-operated rear lights is such that they give a much brighter light provided the battery is not nearly exhausted. It is inadvisable to buy a cheap dynamo if a considerable amount of long-distance night-riding is planned. One disadvantage of the dynamo is that the lights will go out if the cyclist has to stop – for example, on the crown of the road while waiting to make a right-hand turn against oncoming traffic, which is just where he most needs to be seen from both front and behind. One can buy dynamo sets which incorporate a battery which can be brought into use for just such an occasion, though this obviously adds to the weight of the equipment. Otherwise, the safest course is often to halt at the side of the road by the turn, wait for a suitable gap in the traffic, then proceed to make the turn carefully from the side of the road.

Clothing

The enemies of the cyclist are wind and rain. Cycling is by its nature an active occupation, and the cyclist generates plenty of body heat. The problem is to regulate the heat so that it is not lost owing to the wind blowing through unsuitable clothing, or because the clothing has become wet, either by direct contact with the rain or through condensation which occurs when perspiration cannot escape naturally through the weave of the material but instead builds up in tiny droplets of moisture on the inside of the garment. On all except the most perfect summer days, some form of wind-resistant jacket is usually needed in Britain – wind-resistant rather than wind-proof because some of the excellent 'training tops' have a weave which deliberately allows the air to pass through. They are particularly suitable for the serious rider who uses a lot of energy. They are usually made of acrylic material and are very warm, though on cold, windy days many riders slip a sheet of plastic, or even newspaper, inside the front of them to prevent the wind causing heat loss.

Training tops come in bright colours and look particularly smart with black close-fitting trousers, usually called training trousers, which are ideal for both men and women. The trousers have tapered legs and zipped ankle fastenings, and the better ones also have a chamois seat insert. In fact, whatever form of trousers or shorts are worn, it is desirable to have some form of double seat both for the greater comfort it gives and to prolong the life of the garment, as the wear at the seat is considerable. 'Plusses' are still favoured by many riders as they give more freedom at the knees; the modern fabric of the training trousers enables them to 'give' at this point, though perhaps they are less comfortable when wet.

A spin-off from the racing scene is the jersey – again in bright colours – which comes in short or long sleeve versions, the latter being more suitable for general use. They have a small zip at the neck to increase ventilation and to make them easier to slip on and off quickly, and up to three pockets at the back, intended for tucking food into during a race, but just as handy for the touring cyclist. A particular advantage of these jerseys is that they are very long, for it cannot be too strongly emphasized how vital it is to keep the lower back covered, otherwise muscular troubles will certainly follow. If the garment is allowed to ride up at the back while the cyclist is perspiring, he will soon have a cold area exposed to the wind, and a sudden exertion can easily lead to a pulled muscle in just that part. Cycling is healthy and, with common sense, a wonderful exercise for the back, but it is asking for trouble to let the muscles of the back get cold and stiff.

Shorts give a feeling of freedom like no other garment. They can be bought as acrylic racing shorts, usually in black, or in heavier worsted fabric, intended to give years of use. As with 'longs', chamois inserts or double seats are desirable. It is traditional to wear white ankle socks with shorts, and certainly nothing else looks as smart.

Shoes made specially for cycling are of thin leather, very supple and laced up to the toe. There is a fashion for those intended for racing to have holes drilled in the uppers to keep the feet cool, but in Britain at least, there is little advantage in this. Feet do not get particularly hot during cycling – in winter the problem is to keep them warm – and perforated shoes should be avoided for touring or general use. Most lightweight dealers seem to stock cycling shoes that are mainly intended for racing; to get a pair that are suitable for touring, make sure that they have a fairly thick heel as it will be necessary to walk in them as well as cycle, and racing shoes wear out very quickly if they are subjected to much walking. Cycling shoes are expensive, but they do make a big difference to comfort. If they are found to be too expensive, trainers are a good alternative, and for use in wild country where there is likely to be a considerable amount of clambering over rocks or through mud, they may be preferable. Such lightweight footwear as plimsolls or tennis shoes is best avoided. There is no need to buy too much specialist equipment at first. Unlike some sports, such as mountaineering or hill-walking, where particular equipment is necessary to ensure safety, the cyclist can make do and buy something better when money permits.

The garments that have been mentioned so far have largely been designed as a result of experience gained in cycle-racing where bunches of gaily coloured riders thrill huge crowds on the Continent. Cycling is a fun sport, and bright colours are now universally accepted as *de rigueur*. Their main advantage, of course, is that brightly clad cyclists are readily seen by other road-users. There can no longer be any real argument that to stand out clearly on the road is essential: forget any idea about aesthetically-pleasing greens and browns in the countryside and go for the brightest jackets and sweaters you can find. The cyclist is vulnerable, and while the sport of cycle-touring is not a dangerous one, the number of accidents which do take place each year make it essential for any road-user to be clearly visible – or in the case of the cyclist, stand out like a beacon. It should be shouted from the housetops that bright colour is a lifesaver. Mountain walkers, climbers and yachtsmen have all long been converted to their 'international orange' high-visibility gear: we should be right up there in the forefront. Additional safety can be gained by the use of reflective tape on saddlebags, panniers, or anywhere else on the rear of the cycle, giving the motorist that much more chance to see the rider when his mind is diverted by other traffic problems.

In this northern European climate of ours, a jacket is needed on most days, or at least it should be stowed handily in the saddlebag. The jacket forms the 'shell' of the cyclist's clothing; that is, it keeps the wind from blowing through the woollen garments he or she may be wearing beneath, and will also keep out light rain. The essential requirement for a good cycling jacket is that it be long enough to protect the lower back when the rider is stretched forward with hands on the lower part of the handlebars. If a gap is allowed to form between the bottom of the jacket and the cyclist's trousers, be ready for some acute backache! Jackets designed for golfers and walkers may seem tempting but they are usually too short. There are plenty of specialist manufacturers of good cycling jackets, and it is a wise investment to buy the proper garment. While selecting one, make sure that there are plenty of pockets, and wherever possible they should have zips fitted or some other means of ensuring that nothing falls out of them. Five or even seven pockets is not unusual on a good cycling jacket.

The more expensive jackets are now often made of Gore-Tex which largely overcomes the problems of condensation forming on the inside of the jackets. Gore-Tex is waterproof but allows the perspiration to pass through the fabric: in other words, moisture can pass out through the garment but rain will not come in. The disadvantage of this type of fabric is its relatively high price, but there is no doubt that it is a great asset to the cyclist. Jackets made of this fabric are likely to be well designed, as a manufacturer is unlikely to use expensive material for a second-grade product.

For many years the waterproof cape has done good service, and for the tourist or general rider it probably has not yet been bettered. If the size is chosen carefully, it will fit neatly over the rider and saddlebag, and also cover the handlebar bag if fitted. It will also keep the hands dry, and it can actually be pleasant to ride all day in the soft rain, the pattering of the raindrops on the fabric being an agreeable sound when the rider is warm and dry inside, for a cape gives a surprising amount of warmth. It is true that capes tend to billow up in a high wind but, except in the worst conditions, this can be controlled by tucking your thumbs through the loops of the tapes which are normally fastened to the inside of the cape, and if necessary by sitting on the back of it, though this does leave the saddlebag unprotected. If there is much gear-changing to be done, it is usually enough to use only the left-hand tape loop, leaving the right hand free to operate the gear-shift mechanism. The tapes should never be tied down to the handlebars as this would be dangerous in the event of a fall or the need to scramble off quickly. Capes are usually made in yellow fabric, but there are still a few black ones on sale; the latter should be avoided, as on a dark, wet night a cyclist completely enveloped in a black cape becomes almost invisible. One manufacturer has produced a cape with a fitted hood. Normally a hood is dangerous as it restricts vision, but in this case the design is such that the hood is cut away to give unrestricted vision to the sides.

However, there is no doubt that a cape does slow a cyclist, and for those hard-riders determined to get in the maximum number of miles, whatever the weather, nylon jackets with overtrousers of similar material are available. Again, these are a spin-off from the racing scene. They are colourful and smart and are equally suitable for the about-town rider who is frequently hopping on and off the machine and who would find a cape restrictive and cumbersome.

Some form of headgear is necessary. Even in dry weather it makes the cyclist feel much warmer. In rain, the sou'wester works well but is hardly flattering. A woolly hat for both sexes, or a tweed cap for men, keeps out the rain for surprisingly long periods, though they eventually become sodden. Nylon caps are available which pack into a very small space, and these are quite effective, though the rain sometimes tends to run down the neck. All in all, rain is not a problem provided the rider can keep warm, and garments that have become slightly wet dry quickly in the airflow created by the cyclist.

Wet feet, however, can be a curse. The forward part of the ankle catches the spray from the front wheel in rainy conditions, the socks become wet and the feet cold. This can be reduced by fitting a mudflap to the front mudguard, though it does not entirely solve the problem. Waterproof overshoes which cover the ankle are quite good, though if the rain is really heavy any moisture reaching the sock above the overshoe soaks down into the shoe. Most overshoes are made of light fabric which will not stand up to a great deal of walking. Take what precautions you can – but carry a spare pair of socks to change into!

Even in dry weather, the feet can get cold: some people suffer more than others. Again, it is the ankle which is in contact with the cold air which causes the trouble. Fleece-lined boots are available, but perhaps the best solution is to get off and trot briskly up a hill whenever your feet seem to be getting cold. That gets the circulation going and costs nothing. A pair of woollen gloves is essential on a cold day. Once the circulation speeds up and your hands become warm – with the feet they are the last part of the body to do so – they can easily be slipped into a jacket pocket.

3

Exploring in town and country

It isn't fashionable to love large cities. Books, magazines and television programmes all make great play of people who have escaped from the dismal streets of great conurbations to a cleaner, simpler life. When William Blake wrote about the dark satanic mills of England he had a point. They contrasted starkly with the green and pleasant land that he saw beyond the fringe of the cities, but that was 200 years ago, and anyway it is debatable how pleasant rural life was for most people at that time. In the Depression years of the twenties and thirties, many unemployed found relief in cycling away from the dole queues and the disillusioned groups of men who stood on the street corners waiting, not for work for there wasn't much hope of that, but just waiting because there was little else to do.

It is not surprising that cyclists out for the day tend to look for their enjoyment in the countryside, but the urban scene also has much to offer. In many towns, to turn a corner or to travel a few hundred yards from one street to another can bring a complete change in the mood of the place. Anyone who has house-hunted in London or other large cities knows that property values at one end of the street can differ markedly from those at the other end. It is not only a matter of being at the fashionable end of the street; the style of the houses, size of the gardens, width of the road and the type of shops can change rapidly, giving the street a completely different character. In the city we have so many different architectural styles in public buildings, houses, shops, churches, pubs, cinemas, bingo halls, and enough history to keep anyone happy. This is not to denigrate the rural lands of Britain, which compare well for sheer beauty with any in the world, but to emphazise what too often we fail to see: that any city, however smoke-grimed, can be a great place for a day's ride, and without any need for long-distance riding. We need to rekindle our enthusiasm for cities and to look at them through fresh eyes. Of course, there are long, dismal roads where there is little of interest, where the sameness of the scene is depressing in a way that must be numbing for those who live there. But it is not all like that.

The way to find something new in one's own town is to turn down any narrow street or alleyway that has previously been passed by, for even if it is marked 'no through road' there may still be a way through for the cyclist. It is a safe bet that there are a dozen streets within a short distance of any city-dweller's home that he has rarely travelled along or even looked at properly. We are creatures of habit and travel the same route each day to work or to the shops or bus stop. It is a revelation to take a bike and spend an afternoon just enjoying the urban scene, with a saddlebag or bar-basket to hand because combing the back-streets for bargains in odd shops is half the fun.

To demonstrate this, let us take a morning ride in the borough of Mortlake, in south-west London. Most people say that there is nothing specially attractive about Mortlake, but the Ordnance Survey map shows that there are roads and pathways by the side of the River Thames, so it seems unlikely that it will be totally uninteresting. The starting point is the brewery, an unlovely building at the junction of several busy streets and just the sort of place cyclists usually avoid, but a closer look shows that it has a pair of ornamental wrought-iron gates, well worth stopping to look at. Within a few hundred yards, along the High Street, there is a pub called the Charlie Butler, named by the brewery after one of their draymen, and on the pub sign is a painting of Charlie. Can any other brewery drayman ever have had his portrait on an inn sign? After another hundred yards comes the Church of St Mary the Virgin, worth a stop if only to look at the unusual tower, which is built of stone at the base and brick at the top and capped with a wooden 'lantern'. A walk inside, with the cycle safely locked to the church railings, brings the cyclist to a plaque showing that the tower was built by King Henry VIII in

1543. Perhaps many of us had not realized that kings built churches, or thought that Henry was more likely to have knocked them down. There was no mention in the church of another oddity: a Norman arch standing alone in the churchyard and looking like the upended jawbone of a whale. A mystery, perhaps, to enquire into later. Opposite the church is a pair of Georgian houses of the sort which, while built for the ordinary people, are now sold for astronomical sums. On one, above the yellow-painted front door, is a large plaster cast of an angel. Another small mystery to ponder on along the main road for the few hundred yards that it takes to reach the path along the Thames.

One should mentally thank the burghers of Mortlake or whoever it was who planted daffodil bulbs along the river, for they make a fine sight among the grass. Hammersmith Bridge next comes into sight giving a reason for getting out the camera in order to photograph the colourful emblem on the bridge; a quick ride over then brings the rider on to the other river-bank to start the return ride. Georgian buildings and rowing clubs abound here, and a wealth of old pubs. Can there be a better site for an English pub than beside a river? Riverside pubs seem to have a special character and are rarely bad. Other things that seem almost to grow here are unusual signs. One building, the headquarters of the William Morris Society whose members are supporters of the traditions laid down by that fine old Victorian reformer, bears an old sign in gilt lettering urging the passer-by to drink a toast to the health of the Hammersmith Socialists. On the same building a stone slab relates that the first electric telegraph, 8 miles long, was constructed on the site by Sir Francis Ronalds in 1816. Over the door of a pub, tucked away in an alleyway, is another, which reads:

> When you come inside to drink
> Pause a little while and think
> Children may not come inside
> (Although an awful lot have tried)
> Come inside yourself we plead
> But keep your dog upon a lead

The narrow, sometimes traffic-congested road twists alongside the river, slipping between the houses and the old boats moored at the water's edge. The route is frequently interrupted by stretches of urban parkland bearing 'no cycling' notices. No matter, to push through makes a pleasant change, and those who want to sit quietly in the gardens, or to stroll through them, have a right to do so without having to glance over their shoulders to see whether they are about to be run down. All at once, after slipping past a house that has a figurehead of a ship in the front garden, the quiet road comes into a roar of traffic at the busy intersection of Hogarth roundabout, one of the noisiest in London. But even here there is a track, the remains of an earlier road which has become too narrow for modern traffic but which allows the cyclist to avoid the main road and slip into an oasis formed by a square of old houses. Yet another plaque (blessings upon whichever society or council it is which puts them up) tells us that this square was mentioned by Thackeray in *Vanity Fair*, and was the garden frequented by Becky Sharp. Across the road is Chiswick House, open to the public, but a visit there would take a whole afternoon itself.

The main road back to Mortlake is busy but not uninteresting, and the run is not yet over. Near the starting point of Mortlake Brewery is the grave of Sir Richard Burton, the Victorian explorer who, in 1858, set out with Speke to find the source of the Nile. Burton, as befits a man who dressed as an Arab and became the first non-believer to reach Mecca, is buried in a huge stone tent in the Roman Catholic cemetery there. A box of leaflets, placed by the grave by the local priest, tells the story of Burton's controversial travels and adds, with a touch of refreshing candour, that Burton, who was married to a Catholic, was received into the Church only on his deathbed, in fact probably after he was actually dead! For those who take a delight in tomb hunting, an iron ladder has been let into the side of the stone tent, over which fly the banners of Islam, and a glass panel is set into the top of the tomb, with the gilded coffins of Burton and his wife on view, surrounded by mementoes of their travels. It is said that camel bells hung inside will give a warning of anyone who tries to enter.

From that dusty relic of a former age, the cyclist can return to the bustle of Mortlake, and the cyclometer will have clocked up just 10 miles. Perhaps it is luck to choose a route so full of interest, but would it have been any less fascinating along, for example, the Bridgewater Canal from Manchester or any other industrial route? The art is to use one's knowledge of an area to find the most interesting rides.

Riding for safety

In an ideal world, this section would be unnecessary. If everyone used the roads with due consideration, good manners and an appreciation of the problems and limitations of others, the accident rate would fall dramatically. But we live in the real world and we must learn to survive in it as it is. Riding safely in our urban environment calls for an awareness of the dangers and then the taking of steps to avoid them. The cyclist is at particular risk because he travels at a different speed from the main flow of traffic and because, unlike the motorist, he is not inside a vehicle which provides a degree of protection in an impact. However, the cyclist has the advantage of largely unrestricted vision and, most important, he has the ability to hear vehicles approaching from behind – this is something that the motorist lacks.

The *Highway Code* gives the basic advice for cyclists, but it is by developing a sense of anticipation for what is about to happen that the cyclist learns to avoid an accident. After an accident the phrase 'It all happened so quickly' is often heard, or 'I couldn't do a thing about it'. While it seems like that at the time, there were probably quite a few seconds in which something could have been done if the road-user had seen the dangerous situation developing. A look at some of the danger spots on city roads serves to show how common sense and foresight allow the hazards to be reduced.

Intersections

An intersection is probably the place at which the cyclist is most at risk. A common danger is caused by a vehicle pulling out of a side road into the path of an oncoming cyclist. Often, the motorist simply does not see the cyclist. The first indication that a stationary car at a junction is starting to move comes from a glance at its wheels, which can be seen starting to rotate valuable seconds before the body of the car can be observed to be moving. This gives the cyclist enough warning to allow him to take avoiding action, perhaps to swing into the road the car is leaving, or to brake. Sometimes a shout will bring a driver to a halt; ringing a bicycle bell rarely has much effect.

Roundabouts

The danger situation is most likely to occur when wishing to negotiate the roundabout and turn right. A motorist intending to turn right will approach the roundabout in the right-hand lane and stay in that lane until he moves to the left lane to leave the roundabout. If a cyclist adopts this course, he often finds, when about to move to the left lane, that a fast-moving vehicle is coming up behind and from his left, and to turn into its path is to court disaster. Nor is he in a good position to halt in the right-hand lane close to the island. The experienced rider can deal with the situation by careful anticipation, but the *Highway Code* gives cyclists the option of remaining in the left-hand lane of the roundabout throughout the manoeuvre, and at busy times, or at any time for the inexperienced, this is probably the safer alternative. It is still necessary to beware of vehicles which may cut in front of the cyclist at each exit point.

Traffic-choked streets

The almost classical accident occurs when a car door is opened in the face of a passing cyclist as he rides along a line of parked cars. It happens so frequently that it must be one of the most common forms of cycling accidents. At the least it can result in bruising; at the worst the rider can be thrown to the ground in front of oncoming traffic. As the cyclist passes the parked cars, it takes only a moment to glance along the line and note the ones which have someone sitting in the driving seat. These are the potentially dangerous cars: if possible they should be given a slightly wider clearance; if it is not readily possible, at least the rider is forewarned that the door could possibly be opened.

Bad road surfaces

Heavy lorries can ruin the surfaces of old city streets. Potholes occur most readily just where the wheels of lorries constantly pound the surface, and also at the side of the road where the action of rainwater helps to break up any damaged surface. It is the legal responsibility of the local authority to maintain the roads in a safe condition, but it is often some time before they make the necessary repairs. A letter to the local council office pointing out that a particularly dangerous spot exists often has good results. A cyclist is normally expected to ride well to the left of the road, but to keep too close to the kerb can mean that he is too closely confined by overtaking traffic to be able to avoid an obstruction. While it is a matter of riding according to the conditions, it is sometimes better to be another foot or two out from the kerb to allow enough room to avoid, say, a sunken drain cover.

Rural rides

The earliest British roads were worn by the tread of the feet of travellers, though there were relatively few of these, over many, many years. The Ridgeway, one of Europe's oldest roads which was in use during the Old Stone Age before even Stonehenge was built, runs high along the ridge of southern England because the thin soil did not support forests which would bar the passage of man, and there were fewer bogs or areas of dense undergrowth than in the valleys below. Man has always sought the easiest routes for his journeys. So it was with our system of lanes. Medieval Europe – though many British byways date from well before this period – had a large number of small communities under the dominance of a manor. In the day-to-day business of life, journeys had to be made from rude dwellings to the strip fields, to the lands of the manor, to the church, or to draw water from the communal well. There were restrictions on taking the easiest way – for example, it was not permissible to trespass on tilled land – and this caused the tracks to change course suddenly. A secondary path might branch away to reach the crossing point of a stream or a piece of land where the right had been granted for the collection of wood or the grazing of animals.

The carts which were used to move the produce about the lord's lands churned up the paths in winter so that they became impassable, and new paths would be worn, perhaps just a few yards to one side, perhaps further away. Within a few years the course of a path might have changed again, but always paths were created by necessity, sometimes abandoned, and often in later years used again. We have a heritage of lanes which we should value. To travel along them is to pass along ways created by long-forgotten ancestors, and though their names may never be known, they have left their marks. The drovers' roads, or drift roads, have wide verges where the cattle were allowed to graze on the long journeys from farm to market, and many villages and market towns have a Goose Green where the birds were either sold or kept overnight. The straight tracks of the Roman roads, many of which are main roads today, stand out clearly on the Ordnance Survey maps, often with stretches missing, though sometimes a green track will follow the line of the old road exactly. The Roman roads followed a course sighted from beacon to beacon and many were stone causeways capable of being used in all weathers. By contrast, the medieval roads were merely tracks, impassable for much of the year, for there was little demand for long journeys.

It is on these roads, or at least the descendants of them, that cyclists can ride at will across Britain. It is doubtful if anyone has accurately estimated how many thousands of miles of byways exist in Britain, but they give the opportunity to discover a quieter land, away from the motorways or other busy roads. Indeed, the cyclist has much to thank the arterial roads for as they 'drain off' the heavy motor traffic from the lanes.

G. K. Chesterton captured something of the delight of the system of English lanes when he wrote his poem *The Rolling English Road*:

> Before the Romans came to Rye or out to Severn strode,
> The rolling English drunkard made the rolling English road.
> A reeling road, a rolling road, that rambles round the shire,
> And after him the parson ran, the sexton and the squire.
> A merry road, a mazy road, and such as we did tread
> That night we went to Birmingham by way of Beachy Head.

A first ride

Even a short ride needs a destination to give it a sense of purpose, and perhaps of achievement. It is pleasant to wander at will, but to aim for an old church, a castle, village, hilltop or even the site of an old battle (they are marked on the maps) gives the ride a structure. It also ensures that there will be some degree of planning, so that the byways likely to be most attractive can be chosen. To become embroiled in a series of arterial roads and battered by the noise of traffic hurtling past is frustrating, as a glance at the map would probably have shown a quiet road or bridleway nearby which would better serve the cyclist. Make it a short ride to begin with: 5 or 10 miles is enough for anyone who has done little cycling or who is returning to it after some years of driving everywhere. A long run is not necessarily more enjoyable than a short one, and it is easier to add a few extra miles towards the end of the run than to shorten it.

Let us assume that an evening run is planned. It is perfect summer weather (for the moment!) but take a waterproof, just in case, as it is comforting to know that it is there. A cape can easily be rolled up and strapped to the top of the saddlebag ready for instant use. On all but the shortest runs take some food, perhaps sandwiches or at least a bar of chocolate, as it is surprising how much energy is used up while riding. Long-distance cyclists guard against what they call the hunger knock, which is a form of exhaustion caused by too much exertion and too little food. When it strikes, the cyclist becomes more and more weary until it seems almost impossible to turn the pedals any more, and it leads to a growing disenchantment with all matters concerned with cycling. It isn't serious and can be cured by stopping for at least an hour and eating a hot meal, though not large amounts of meat which the body will not readily digest. However, there will be no such trouble on an evening ride.

Take a few basic tools, not a whole workshopful, just a puncture-repair outfit, tyre levers, a dumb-bell spanner (the sort that fits lots of different nuts), a small adjustable spanner and a pair of pliers. A roll of insulating tape is useful for fastening together things which come apart – such unorthodox repairs will suffice until they can be properly dealt with at home. Once on your way, the countryside is yours, it only remains for you to enjoy it.

Simple touring

When riding all day it is to your advantage to do it in such a manner as will cause the least fatigue. The balls of the feet should rest on the centre of the pedals; if the cycle is fitted with toeclips, these will ensure that the feet are kept in the correct position. This allows you to 'ankle' – just before the top of the rotation of the crank the heel is lowered slightly so that the foot can push forward against the pedal making a smooth circular pedalling action. Once acquired, this practice becomes automatic.

When cornering while freewheeling down a hill, ease the cycle into the line that you intend to take through the curve. If it is a left-hand bend, raise the left-hand pedal to the top of its stroke, and vice versa for a right-hand bend. This is not because there is a danger of the pedal striking the road, as it would be necessary to lean over a very long way for that to happen, but to give more control. Pressure on the lowered pedal will give greater balance in the curve. If travelling swiftly, keep plenty of weight over the front wheel so that both wheels have a good grip on the road, and watch out for loose grit or wet leaves. If vision is restricted around the curve, apply both brakes gently at the start of the descent as there may be a hazard just out of sight. Once the road can be seen to be clear, the brakes can be eased off and the speed allowed to build up to a sensible level. Descending swiftly and safely requires practice and at all times it is necessary to watch for any emergency, such as a dog running into the road or a car coming out of a driveway. But the joy of a long fast controlled descent, perhaps of a mile or more, is what makes up for the long haul up the hills.

When faced with a headwind, reduce the wind-resistance as much as possible by adopting a low position, though not so low as to become uncomfortable. Change down to a slightly lower gear if this seems to help. Headwinds can be more tiring than hills, and on a long tour it is advisable to avoid riding day after day towards the south-west as, in the summer at least, this is the prevailing direction of the winds in England. The run from Land's End to John O' Groats is much easier than the same trip in the reverse direction. In spring, there are more likely to be winds from the north or north-east.

There is no such thing as an average mileage for a day's ride, the great delight in cycling is the freedom it gives to do just as you choose. Twenty-five, fifty, seventy, one hundred miles a day – it doesn't matter what is achieved. What does matter is the enjoyment of the ride. If the weather is hot and you feel like resting, why not do so? Dismount and walk up a hill if it becomes too steep: no one is timing you. There are plenty of diversions for a day's ride: don't make it all work. Try spending part of a morning at a market, farm museum, jumble sale or country fête. There may be a flower show in a village marquee, an agricultural show, a steam railway, nature reserve or the gardens of a stately home.

Winter riding

On the summit of a track in mid-Wales stands a memorial stone to Wayfarer, the pen-name of a cycling writer whose descriptive articles in *Cycling* and the *CTC Gazette* during the first half of this century did much to popularize cycle-touring. The articles had such a following over many years that W. Robinson, who was Wayfarer, has become part of the folklore of the sport. In March 1919 he made a crossing of the Berwyn Mountains, which are really rugged hills rather than real mountains, though in March, when the snow is still deep in the narrow valleys, it is a formidable place. The article he wrote, which was published in *Cycling* in May of that year, did much to show what rides could be done, and even enjoyed, whatever the weather. It is on the route that he rode that his memorial stands.

The short winter days make cycling a brisker affair, but a simple pair of woollen gloves will keep the hands warm, and two pairs of socks, preferably woollen, will go a long way towards keeping the feet warm. There are hazards to be avoided, too. Ice can suddenly appear on country lanes where a farmer has hosed out his dairy or where a ditch has overflowed.

Perhaps the road was merely wet during the afternoon but by nightfall it may have frozen and become a danger for the unwary. Riding in thin snow along a country lane can be delightful, but on main roads if the snow has been heavy and is followed by a frost, avoid the ridges caused by the frozen slush at the edge of the road. Mechanical problems are even more annoying than during the warmer months, and it is not unknown for a derailleur gear to ice up and refuse to operate if slush freezes on it. Gentle hand pressure on the operating arm will usually free it.

But winter really is a good time, and it is still possible to find a pub or tearoom with a roaring fire. Such places should be cherished as they provide unmatched occasions for cyclists to meet. At least, after a long struggle through the snow, you will have grand tales to tell of the conditions in which you rode.

The longer tour

Packing for a tour of a week or more is simplified by dividing clothes into two groups: those to be worn while cycling and those for use in the evenings. Even if you hope to wear shorts for most of the day, some form of long trousers is useful in Britain. For both sexes, 'training bottoms' are ideal, and their elastic waists enable them to be pulled on readily over a pair of shorts. Two lightweight sweaters, one to wear and one to keep in the saddlebag as a reserve, are better than one thick one. A light shirt or racing vest, or a non-iron blouse for women, again with a spare, and a jacket, preferably with lots of zip-up pockets, complete the outer wear, plus of course the rainwear mentioned in the preceding chapter.

What non-cycling clothes are taken depends on how the evenings will be spent and the sort of accommodation planned: youth hostel, farmhouse, small hotel. But after a day's riding it is unlikely that many people will wish to do much more than wander at leisure around a strange town or merely chat with new-made friends, so clothing can be kept simple. A pair of lightweight shoes, such as moccasins, are worth carrying as they are pleasant to change into. The art is to travel light: if everything, including clothing, soap, towel, shaving kit, camera, tools and spares, will not fit into one large saddlebag, too much is probably being carried. In addition to the tools mentioned earlier it is worth taking a crank-removal tool if cotterless cranks are fitted to your cycle, as this device incorporates the special spanner needed to tighten the cranks should they work loose. A chain-link rivet extractor (or spare chain-link for those with hub gears) is always advisable as well as spare bulbs, tyre canvas, brake and gear cables, various small nuts and bolts and a short length of soft wire for securing odd jobs. A spare inner-tube will avoid the need to repair punctures by the side of the road, as it is far easier, and more efficient, to repair a puncture at leisure during the evening when the task is less likely to be skimped. It is also worth taping a couple of spare spokes to the seatstay; even though the rider may not feel able to replace spokes and retrue a wheel himself, it is sometimes easier to persuade a repairer to tackle the job at once if the correct-sized spokes are to hand. There is no need to worry about the things that might go wrong on a tour; experienced cyclists ride thousands of miles without serious problems, and if something mechanical does go wrong, it is surprising how helpful people can be. The sight of a stranded cyclist seems to bring out the best in them, and any 'real' cyclist will stop and help if he sees a rider in trouble, often to the point of dashing off to obtain some much-needed spare.

Map-reading

Pick up almost any book on map-reading and, even if it is meant for beginners, it will soon become complicated. The difference between deviation and variation of the compass, or between true north, magnetic north and grid north, or grid bearings, magnetic bearings and cross-bearings can bring a glaze to the eyes of anyone trying to work it all out. Navigation, in its full sense, is a complex science. Even the books that deal with map-reading for the rambler usually assume at some stage that the walker will be in difficult country where lives may depend on his ability to navigate safely, and so the instruction tends to be detailed. Fortunately, cyclists, even if taking to the roughstuff tracks, rarely need to take compass bearings to establish their position. Almost always they will be on a road or track which can be located on the map, and will be able to see the way ahead without the compass calculations that a walker in rough country might feel to be necessary. Mist and hill fog, however, can introduce an element of uncertainty. The roughstuff enthusiast, therefore, should always carry a map and compass and know how to use them.

It is always worth while slipping a map into the saddlebag even before a short ride as its regular use soon reveals features that would otherwise be missed, and the practice this gives ensures that the map can easily be read in unfamiliar territory. The maps most commonly used by the cyclist are the 1:50,000 Ordnance Survey series, and those published by John Bartholomew and Son Ltd at a scale of 1:100,000. The Ordnance Survey maps cover an area 40km (25 miles) by 40km, and those by Bartholomew about 100km (62 miles) by 60km (37 miles). The scale 1:50,000 means that 1cm (⅓in) on the map represents ½km (⅓ mile) on the ground; 1:100,000 means 1cm (⅓in) on the map to 1km (⅔ mile) on the ground.

These maps respectively replace the Ordnance Survey 1in to the mile and the Bartholomew ½in to the mile series. For those who like to think in imperial measure, the 1:50,000 maps are about 1¼in to the mile, and the 1:100,000 a little under ¾in to the mile. The main difference that the change to metric has brought is that the slightly larger scale has enabled the map-makers to show detail more clearly, and in many cases to add features that could not previously be shown.

Every map starts to go out of date as soon as the surveyors pack up their instruments and move on. Buildings are demolished, woods cut down and ferries cease to run. While map-makers allow for these changes when they are known in advance, there is always the occasion when minor detail on the ground does not fit the map, though this is rarely a serious problem. If the map does not quite agree with the scene, then it is much more likely that the cyclist is not quite where he thought he was!

The scale of 1:50,000 will show a large amount of detail. In addition to all roads, bridleways (which cyclists have a legal right to use) and footpaths are shown. Maps on this scale also show woods, quarries, antiquities (such as Roman villas or tumuli), historic houses, country parks and sufficient detail of churches to help fix a position. The 1:100,000 scale will give less detail, but all the minor roads are shown as well as footpaths and bridleways, though the scale does not allow the makers to differentiate between these last two.

Ordnance Survey and Bartholomew maps have quite different ways of indicating the rise and fall of land. The former use contour lines, and the latter a colour system. It is not a question of one being better than the other; on a relatively large-scale map such as the 1:50,000 there is more room to be precise, while the smaller-scale map still provides an excellent guide by the use of different shades.

The contour line system

A contour line links all the points which are the same height above sea-level. There is a 'vertical interval' between the lines of 50ft (15m). Therefore, the closer the contour lines are together, the steeper will be the slope, and the further away they are the more gentle will be the incline. In addition, and of great advantage to the cyclist, as the road rises and falls the high and low points are marked as spot-heights, which makes it very easy to see whether a particular stretch of road is going uphill or downhill.

Maps are published in colour and so give more information than appears in the black and white version depicted in the illustrated section, but it can still be seen that travelling along the road east from Singleton, in the South Downs, the rider will be cycling along the valley between steep hills, steeper on the left than the right. Levin Down, on the left as seen by the cyclist, is a rounded hill with a steep south-facing slope. There is a wood near the top (green on the map). The road climbs gently to 63m (206ft) just before the village of Charlton, then climbs again to 98m (321ft) 1 mile east of East Dean. Following a downhill stretch to the spot-height marked 87 (285ft) after Ide's Barn, the road climbs again to the point marked 97 (318ft), descends a little, and then climbs once more to the 108m (354ft) mark shortly after joining the A285. At Singleton, the church with a tower is clearly shown on a byroad to the south of the village with a footpath climbing up into the Downs from it. The village also has a post office and an inn. The road running north climbs steeply to 80m (262ft) at Cucumber Farm. Farms which are named on the map are a handy way of confirming your position as frequently the name of the farm appears on the gate.

Where a particularly steep gradient occurs, it will be marked on the map as a black arrowhead. Gradients of 1 in 7 to 1 in 5 have a single arrowhead; those of 1 in 5 or steeper have a double arrowhead. The arrow points down the slope. If these symbols appear frequently, it tends to mean exciting country – often a case of hanging on to the brakes on the way down and then sprinting out of the dip before the momentum is lost.

Colour coding

Bartholomew maps indicate the height of the land by tinting the lower levels in shades of green, through ochre to darker browns on the higher land. There is a different shade for every change in height of 50m (164ft). Names of farms are given, small rivers are plotted, and it is quite easy to identify woods and even small buildings in rural areas. These maps have an advantage over the Ordnance Survey in that not so many sheets need be carried on a long tour.

Finding your position

This is readily done by identifying some features of the landscape, and a compass is a great help. First you should 'set the map', which simply means having the top of the map pointing north so that all the features on the ground are seen in their corresponding positions on the map. For example, a church on your left hand will appear on the map to the left of your known position. Strictly speaking, the compass will indicate magnetic north; this is not quite the same as the lines on the map – which are called grid lines – but as it is not intended to plot a compass course, the difference can be ignored.

All you need to do is to identify some easily recognizable features, perhaps a stream running alongside the road just before a church with a spire, or a railway bridge close to a crossroads. The point is to have more than one feature with which to confirm your position: a railway line may cross several roads in the area where you are. If you are sitting on a railway bridge, look around to see what is visible. There may be a T-junction ahead, or a line of electricity pylons, or a wooded hill. The more features that can be related to the map, the more certain it is that you will discover your correct position. This method is much more accurate than simply looking at the map and trying to identify the roads you believe you have come along.

A most useful compass is the oil-filled Silva type, popular with orienteers and ramblers. It is cheap and comes with detailed instructions should you wish to learn the art of taking accurate compass bearings. But compasses can be deflected by metal objects, so it should be held away from the cycle. Some machines cause more interference to a compass than others. Walk a few steps away from the cycle with the compass in your hand, and see whether it is being affected to any great extent. Even in towns a compass is useful. When winding through twisting streets it enables a broadly accurate direction to be maintained – a great advantage when trying to find the way in a strange city.

Estimating distance

When planning a tour at home it is possible to use a small map-measure, a little wheel which when run along the proposed route gives the distance in either miles or kilometres. Otherwise, a piece of string can be twisted along the roads to be taken, or a pair of dividers used. These methods tend to underestimate the distance slightly. When on the road, try to have something handy that can be used, perhaps a piece of string that has knots at predetermined distances. One literal rule of thumb is to know the length of the top joint of your thumb – on an adult man it is about 1½in (3.8cm), which is just over a mile on an Ordnance Survey map. It is simple to place the thumb on the map and read off the miles.

Estimating time

An experienced cyclist who is fit will probably travel at about 17 miles an hour, but he will not *average* that. Stops made to look at the map, slowing down on hills and pauses in traffic all play havoc with average speeds. In hilly country a given distance can take up to half as long again as the same journey in flat lands. What is gained by the swift descents does not make up for the slower pace going up hills, and a head-wind will slow a rider more than he would expect. It is worth while timing yourself on a variety of runs and in different conditions. When allowing for meal stops it may be found that an average over the day of 10 miles an hour is all that has been managed. One of the reliability rides that club cyclists sometimes indulge in is to ride 100 miles in eight hours, which is only an average of 12½ miles an hour. But most entrants find that, having stopped for a half-hour lunch break, it needs all their efforts to get back on time! Some clubs have competitions for speed-judging, the object being to ride out and return along the same course in exactly the same time for each leg without, of course, using a watch. It isn't as easy as it sounds.

The National Grid

Ordnance Survey maps are marked with a series of thin blue lines right across the sheet, forming the National Grid reference system. By plotting a six-figure map reference it is possible to identify any spot on the map to an accuracy of 100m (328ft). This is very useful because youth hostels, for example, which are sometimes hard to find, give the grid reference number in their handbooks, or friends planning to meet at a particular crossroads may make certain which one is meant by agreeing on the grid reference. Each side of the box formed by the blue lines is 1km (1,094yd). To plot a map reference proceed in the following way.

Let us say that you intend to give a map reference to enable a friend to meet you at a particular T-junction. Take the west edge of the kilometre square in which the T-junction lies and read the figures in the margin at the top or bottom of the map – they are the large figures printed in blue. Assume that the number is 40. Next, estimate the number of tenths eastward in which the road junction lies: if it is halfway to the next blue line, as accurately as you can estimate it, it will be five-tenths. We now have the first three figures of the grid reference: 405.

That was called obtaining the Easting because it was estimated eastwards. Now for the second half of the reference you obtain the Northing. Take the south edge of the kilometre square in which the T-junction lies and note the large blue figures in the margin on the left or right side of the map. Let us say the figure is 28. Again estimate tenths, this time northwards. If the junction is almost on the top blue line, it may be said that it is nine-tenths of the way there, so the second half of the reference is plotted as 289. The six-figure reference number for that T-junction will then be 405289.

With practice, it is very simple to plot these references, and the Ordnance Survey maps include examples on the inside cover. The main point to remember is that the large blue figures are read off the top or bottom margin before they are read off the side of the map. If you fail to estimate the tenths accurately, all is not lost. To estimate six-tenths where it should have been seven will give an error of only 100m (109yd) – not likely to cause anyone to go to the wrong place.

The object of map-reading for the cyclist is not just to get from one point to another in as short a distance as possible, but to do so by a route that will give the greatest enjoyment. With a little practice it is possible to select lanes or bridleways which will keep you well clear of busy roads, or to choose a route which will avoid steep hills.

4

Wild tracks and the camping scene

Running from near Stonehenge eastwards across a spine of high ground and crossing Wiltshire, Berkshire and disappearing into the Chiltern Hills is the Ridgeway, the green road, possibly Europe's most ancient way, which was mentioned in the previous chapter. Even before Britain was an island it was used by people migrating from Europe; once it may have reached right across East Anglia to the sea, and almost certainly it connected with other ancient ways. Its significance in creating the land that much, much later was to become England is immense, but we can only guess at the lives of the people who first trod it during the Old Stone Age, at their customs and religious rites. The green track that stands out so clearly today was one of the ways by which change came to these islands. The Romans arrived, trod the ancient way and in their turn left; the Saxons no doubt used it, and King Arthur may have moved his troops along its windswept way from Wessex.

Today, the lonely unsurfaced track, wide enough for a vehicle to pass along, has changed little. Sometimes the Ridgeway consists of smooth turf while in other places it is rutted with boggy patches, and brambles often obstruct the way. J. R. L. Anderson, in *The Oldest Road: an Exploration of the Ridgeway* (Wildwood House, 1975), says:

> Where the track runs on the bare, high Downs above Marlborough and Wantage you can go for miles without seeing a human habitation: it is unbelievably remote, and the sky reaches down to the land to make a horizon, something rarely found in our modern urban landscape. It is like being at sea – you sense that there is something different in the quality of your surroundings, and suddenly it strikes you that you can see the true horizon. It is infinitely refreshing, to both eye and spirit.

Then there is the journey in time. You are no longer shackled within three generations – your own, your parents' and your children's. You walk in the footsteps of three hundred generations, seeing the same rounded hills, the same sky, tripping, it may be, over the same stone that stubbed a human toe ten thousand years ago. In our time-bounded life it is good to move out of time, to feel that all the human politics, triumphs and disasters of ten thousand years – or twice ten thousand years – have left the road you walk unchanged. Often it must have seemed to your shadowy travelling companion that human life was in such a mess that it simply couldn't go on – yet the road runs on, and you, their two or three hundred times great-grandson, are there to tread it. This adds a useful perspective to time-foreshortened life.

For the seasoned roughstuff cyclist, the Ridgeway is not a particularly difficult road. The path is well marked and it is even signposted with blue flashes painted on trees and bushes where there is any doubt about its true route. If ever there was a haunted road, this must be it; although only a few miles away people are shopping in the modern towns or going about their everyday lives, the loneliness of the Ridgeway, with its huge skies, distances it from ordinary activities. At times of coming storms, the black gathering clouds heighten the effect, making it an awesome place, despite the continual song of larks in summer and the profusion of wildflowers that grow on land largely unsullied by weedkillers.

In its length of 50 to 80 miles, depending on where you consider it now ends, it passes within a few miles of many urban areas but always manages to stay remote from them. Wales has old drovers' roads which are far wilder, the tracks through the Yorkshire hills are much steeper, and Scotland has routes on a much grander scale, but none quite brings the sense of the remote past so close. It is something to marvel at that anything as old as the Ridgeway has survived so long unchanged. It is possible to cycle the length of the route, slipping and sliding over the chalk and forcing a way through the mud with the back wheel spinning. There are places where one could spend the night, perhaps in a pub at a small town under the Ridgeway. Though not particularly a believer in superstition or the supernatural, I do not think that I would wish to camp on those lonely uplands.

Such are the attractions of the wild tracks of Britain, and there are a great many of them. Interest in roughstuff is growing as more and more people try to escape from the crowded roads. Enthusiasts have their own organization, the Rough-Stuff Fellowship, which was set up in 1955 with a handful of members and now has several hundred spread all over the country. Several local groups exist which hold occasional runs and social events, but members are mainly linked by a magazine in which details of wild routes are published, and in which members recount their experiences, not only in Britain but also in Europe and further afield.

The tales told by roughstuffers are many. One, which helps to show the spirit of companionship pervading the sport, concerns two young lads who were riding a tandem on a tour of the Lake District. They had been told that there was a short cut from Patterdale to Keswick over Helvellyn. So there is, but whoever told them presumably did not know that they had a tandem with them! They finally pushed it to Striding Edge, which is no mean feat in itself, but were then faced with an impossible descent. But in the best tradition, help was at hand for they met by chance half a dozen roughstuff riders. Even they could not get the tandem down, so they did the next best thing and took it to pieces. Wheels, mudguards, lamps, saddlebags and even the oily chains were taken off and carried down. Finally, the frame followed and the whole lot was reassembled at the bottom!

Roughstuff riding has probably been with us for as long as bicycles have been invented. Even from the earliest days, there were riders who left the roads and turned on to the tracks with a sense of adventure, a desire to see both what lay beyond the well-known thoroughfares and what this new creation, the bicycle, was capable of doing.

The first documentary evidence comes from 1890 when a man called Amos Sugden took a bike weighing 50lb (23kg) over the Styhead Pass in the Lake District, and even he did not claim to be the first to do it, though the number who beat him over the Styhead must have been very few. The next recorded episode was in about 1910 when a member of the North Road Club, Vernon Blake, took his machine not only over the Styhead, but also over Black Sail and Scarth Gap all in one go, and then went for a ride to fill in the rest of the day! Even with the lightweight equipment of today, that would be an achievement.

World War I came, and after it the tattered remains of the youth of Britain looked for an escapist recreation. They wanted to forget life in the trenches and the horrors of the Somme and Passchendaele. Cycling boomed, and again some of the riders turned off on to the tracks where they found adventure without fear or danger. The days followed in which the writer Wayfarer preached the gospel of roughstuff to all who would listen, by magazine articles, talks and lantern-slide shows. Roughstuff became respectable, but the rides were still 'set pieces'; the new sportsmen were expected to achieve the crossing of well-known mountain routes – pass-storming, they called it.

After World War II, the nation's youth again returned to cycling, and once more the sport of roughstuffing took on a new life, but this time with a difference. From articles in the cycling press of the time it is obvious that riders were finding their own routes everywhere from Land's End to John O' Groats. Some were wild, dramatic rides, others more pastoral, seeking out corners of Britain that had been a sort of dream during the long war years. So the sport developed, and in 1955, at the Black Swan in Leominster, the Rough-Stuff Fellowship was formed, not to control the sport but to help individuals pursue their passion.

One of those men was Alan Mepham, who later explained to members of the Pedal Club just what roughstuffing meant to him. It is worth quoting him at some length as he sums up so well that essential spirit of freedom and adventure behind the sport. This is what he had to say:

> This phrase roughstuff must conjure up a lot of interesting visions in the mind of the non-cyclist, but even in the wheelers' world it is still all things to all men. To some it is a form of self-inflicted mental and physical cruelty which no right-thinking man should be called on to endure. To others, it is something very wonderful, the gateway to another Britain.
>
> Perhaps I can dispel a couple of myths about it. The first is that to make a success of roughstuffing you need to be something of a

mountain goat. This is quite misleading: there are many tracks in this country that are quite easy going, quite level and rideable throughout without a great deal of effort. The second myth concerns the ideal machine. Regrettably, it just does not exist. Any machine that is properly built with well-constructed wheels, with reasonable equipment, and kept in good order, will do the job.

I find it difficult to convey the magic, the lure and the magnetism of roughstuff as I see it, and to describe properly the sheer breathtaking beauty of what I see around me when I am engaged on some roughstuff venture. I think only Shakespeare could describe this sort of thing, and his graphic and beautiful references to the countryside sprinkled through his works are ample evidence of this. You have only to read his two beautiful descriptions of dawn: one by Horatio on the battlements of Elsinore, and the second by Romeo as he leaps from the bed of Juliet. Then there are the remarks on the open air life by the exiled duke in *As You Like It*.

When my father bought me a bike on my fifth birthday, in 1928, and taught me to ride it the same afternoon, he introduced me to a pastime that was to dominate my way of life. He gave me the key to freedom, the key to the world, the key to paradise. Like most roughstuffers, I am a great lover of the countryside, but to me it's more than that, it's a passion, an obsession. I'm well aware that I live in the most beautiful country in the world and I love it in all its moods and all its seasons. I'm also a climber, of modest pretensions, and a fell-walker, but the bike is my first love, the one and only endearing love of my life and perhaps my only real love. So there you have it, the love of a bike wedded irrevocably to the love of the countryside. There you have the conditions in which roughstuff is possible, the germ which makes it come true, perhaps even makes it essential.

Somebody asked me about six months ago what I had got out of forty years of roughstuffing. I found it difficult to reply because there is no pat answer. I think that, basically, roughstuff gives me solitude. I like solitude, but I love something else: I love loneliness. To some people, loneliness is terrible, but it holds no worries for me. I like it. Solitude is very wonderful, but it can be shared: loneliness is very personal and it is golden. I think there comes a time when, like the psalmist of old, you must lift up your eyes to the hills, for it is in the hills and mountains that you see nature at its best. It's there that you see the most beautiful scenery, the far-reaching views; you see the countryside, nature, beautiful, awesome, rugged, grand, even brutal, but always breathtaking.

I'm never happier than when I'm up in the mountains, tucked up under the sky. Many a time I've struggled up some mountain track, over loose scree and boulders, up the inevitable one-in-two or one-in-three gradient, sweating and swearing, and I've asked myself,

'What in hell am I doing here?' Then, all of a sudden, I've turned some corner, reached some vantage point, and there, spread at my feet, has been England, my England, and I don't need to ask the question any more; I know what I'm there for and what it's all about.

Or again, you ride some ridge track, with the country falling away on either side, and you ride on the roof of the world, on the wings of the wind. That's what roughstuff is all about. Regrettably, though, it is also about a lot of damned hard work, buckled wheels and smashed gears, and even a handful of broken ribs here and there. But you could probably get that on a main road, anyway.

I think the germ of roughstuffing, what it really means to you, is sometimes revealed in a fleeting moment, in adversity. Some time ago I was roughstuffing along the Ridgeway, and the day was particularly bad. I was soaked, and the wonderful views that you can see from there were denied to me. It was misty, murky and half dark. The track was soggy, and wet chalk is not the happiest, nor the safest, surface on which to do your roughstuff. After thirty miles and several hours, it was getting on for teatime, and I had had enough. I cursed my luck and turned off, descended by the White Horse of Uffington, and, as I did so, there appeared a line in the sky just as though somebody had ruled it off with a straight-edge. Below the line it was blue; above the line it was black, and over the next twenty minutes or so this black line rolled back like somebody rolling back a canopy. And then it was all clear blue and the sun shone. The sun is of benefit to any roughstuffer, but this day had been particularly wet and the hedgerows were sodden. Then in the sunlight I saw a million diamonds and I reckon that made my day; that was my reward which made the effort worthwhile.

On the second occasion, I was going over the Styhead Pass. It was a terrible day, wet without raining, a specialty of the Lake District, and I went from Borrowdale to Wasdale in low cloud, thick mist, black skies and a howling gale. I was going towards Wasdale, cursing my luck because I know the tremendous views you can get in that area. It is, indeed, my favourite corner of the Lake District. After about an hour, the wind tore the sky to pieces, and in a flash it was all clear blue and the sun shone gloriously. I stood stock still with this tremendous horseshoe of mountains around me. I knew them all by name and they were like familiar friends to me. I looked out towards Wastwater and it was fantastic. No matter how many times I see that view it never fails to take my breath away. And all of a sudden it was gone. The sky closed in and I never saw any more all day. I went on down the pass and at the bottom there was a car parked by a hotel, and the driver looked at me rather pityingly, as they very often do, and I thought to myself, 'Don't pity me. Up there about an hour ago was England. You missed it and I was there.' And I reckon that was the reward for my effort.

Camping

Cycle-campers owe a debt of gratitude to the backpacking fraternity for the wide variety of good lightweight camping equipment that has come on to the market as a result of the rise in popularity of that sport, because camping gives freedom to the cyclist in a measure that few other people possess. He has the advantage over the walker that he can cover about five times as many miles in a day, and carry rather heavier loads without difficulty. The cyclist can afford to choose a camp site in some wild spot and then cycle several miles to a town for the evening, or to pick up supplies, should he wish to do so. Freedom is his, and that must be worth something today.

A two-man tent with inner and outer skin, which now usually replaces the rather heavy older style tent and flysheet, need weigh no more than 6lb (2.7kg) and still be large enough to store saddlebags in the rear bell-end, leaving the front extension free for cooking in if the weather is really bad. Such tents often divide conveniently into two, so that the weight can be shared.

Unfortunately, low weight comes at high cost, for there is a great deal of skilled labour involved in making a light tent that can be guaranteed to stand up to the wildest weather. It is even more true of tents and sleeping bags than of most things to say, 'Buy the very best you can afford.' A well-made tent will look after its occupants and last for years, and still have a high resale value when the cheaper article has been discarded. But that advice must be qualified by the caution that equipment should be chosen according to the job it will be asked to do. There is no point in buying a mummy-type down-filled sleeping bag of the sort designed for the most extreme mountain conditions, and costing a high price, if it is only to be used at low altitudes in the summer. Most manufacturers of tents and sleeping bags indicate in their catalogues the sort of conditions that their equipment is designed to withstand. Choose according to the worst conditions that are likely to be met, remembering that gales can sweep the English lowlands in summer. In the mountains, even during the summer, the nights are often cold, and it is folly to trust yourself in them at other times of the year with equipment that was never meant to stand up to the conditions occurring there.

For many years, down was considered to be by far the best filling for sleeping bags, followed in descending order of desirability by a mixture of down and feathers, feathers alone, and finally synthetic materials. While that still largely holds good, new synthetic materials are now on the market which are claimed to be as warm as down and which retain their insulation properties when wet better than the natural materials. They are also rather cheaper, though they have the disadvantage of being more bulky and of slightly greater weight.

The method of construction of a sleeping bag will also dictate how warm it will be. If the stitching of the quilting goes directly through the bag, cold spots will develop as there is less filling at these points. Slant pleating is used in the more expensive bags to overcome this problem. Some bags have a short zip which is not there to enable the camper to get in more easily, but to allow the bag to be unzipped for ventilation in warm conditions. Bags intended for very cold conditions have no such arrangements and can be too warm on hot nights. Zips on cheaper bags have a habit of coming undone during the night. If a bag is not warm enough, it is possible to purchase a special inner lining which will increase its insulation properties. A simple sheet lining will also increase warmth, and keep the inside of the bag from becoming grubby.

For a good night's sleep, it is necessary to have something between yourself and the ground. An airbed works well and gives a high degree of comfort, but it is usually rather heavy. A good quality airbed, that is one made of fairly weighty materials, weighs nearly 4lb (1.8kg). While that may be acceptable if a base camp is to be used, it is too heavy if you intend to move on each day and take everything along. Mats made of synthetic foam material have become firm favourites with backpackers as they weigh virtually nothing. They are made in various lengths, and it is not necessary to have one that is full length, as for most conditions the legs do not need to be protected. Some experimentation is needed to find the best way to carry the mat. If the shorter length of mat is chosen, it is possible to roll it tightly around the top-tube, fastening it with a strap, though there is still the difficulty that the knees tend to brush against it. If this proves to be too much of an irritation, it may be possible to strap it along the top of the rear pannier frame, under the saddlebag.

Most people put the mat under the sleeping bag and on top of the groundsheet, but the surface of the groundsheet provides little adhesion, and during the night the mat tends to slip from underneath the sleeper. If the ground is not muddy, it is worth slipping the mat underneath the groundsheet from outside the tent. The insulation properties of the mat are excellent, though it cannot be claimed that it adds greatly to the softness of the bed. When camping truly wild, heather or bracken makes a good 'mattress' under the groundsheet, and its insulation is so good that a mat is not needed. Another possibility is to dispense with the mat and buy from a toyshop one of those inflatable plastic airbeds meant for use in a swimming pool. They pack up very small and work reasonably well, though their strength leaves much to be desired. Nevertheless, they are worth experimenting with.

The modern lightweight tent is usually constructed of a nylon outer tent, which will keep out any rain, and a cotton inner tent with sewn-in groundsheet. The intention of using cotton for the inner tent is to reduce the problem of condensation. The moisture which evaporates during the night remains on the inner surface of the outer tent, where it does no harm, and it soon dries in the morning sun.

The diversity of lightweight tents on the market increases each year. Tents intended for mountain use, where high winds can be expected, are often designed with A-poles for greater stability, and this gives the added advantage that entry to the tent is not obstructed by a pole, though the A-poles do mean that the tent will be slightly heavier than a single-pole model. The wedge-shaped tent is enjoying great popularity and can be obtained with A-poles or with a single pole at the front. In either case, there is usually a small pole at the rear. The wedge shape gives the advantage of reduced wind-resistance, so the tent is less likely to be knocked down in a gale, particularly if it is pitched end-on to the wind.

There is also a move towards dome-shaped tents as they make better use of the available space, though these are often rather heavier than their wedge-shaped counterparts and, for carrying purposes, are best divided between two or three cyclists.

A two-man tent can weigh from about 5lb (2.2kg) upwards, while the lightest single-man tent on the market weighs about 4lb (1.8kg). From this it can be seen that to reduce the size of a tent does not proportionally reduce the weight. A few extra square feet of nylon add little to the weight yet provide much more space. While the lightest tents are excellent for spending the night in, and then moving on, if you intend to spend longer in the tent, perhaps because of bad weather, it is well worth while carrying the few extra ounces and having a tent that will not be cramped. The front extension, which provides a porch under which extra baggage can be kept, is, as already mentioned, also intended to be a cooking area, but it cannot be too strongly emphasized that cooking should only be done with the greatest care. The ground is unlikely to be smooth, and if a pressure stove flares up on first being lit, as they often do, it can instantly set fire to the nylon, leaving the camper in an extremely difficult position from which to get out of the tent. If cooking within the extension has to be done, some form of flat stone should be placed on the grass to give a level surface, and the stove should be lit clear of the tent until it is running normally. The greatest care should be taken that saucepans on the stove are not so heavy that they overbalance.

Pressure stoves are powered by paraffin, petrol or gas canisters. Petrol is more easily obtained than paraffin abroad, otherwise there is not much to choose between them. Stoves which use gas canisters, such as Gaz, are cheaper to buy and cleaner, with cartridges available throughout Europe, but they take longer to boil water, and in a wind much of the heat can be lost unless there is a good wind-shield. In fact, a simple wind-shield is essential whatever type of stove is used. It is easy to make one by taking a short length of deckchair canvas about as wide as the height of the stove, and pushing four wire tent-pegs through the material so that it can be made to stand up around the stove.

Whatever is taken, it is necessary to have it loaded on to the cycle so that a balanced machine results, with the weight as low as possible. A cycle that has all the weight over the back wheel will not have sufficient front-wheel grip when cornering on downhill stretches. Fitting front panniers, with the tent in one side and the sleeping bag in the other, works well, provided that the weight can be kept within the limits whereby the steering is not adversely affected. Front panniers are usually smaller than those intended for the rear for that reason.

This could be the basic camping equipment for any length of tour:

Tent (two-man)	6½lb (2.9kg)
Sleeping bag (feather and down)	3½lb (1.6kg)
Petrol stove	2lb (0.9kg)
Spare petrol in metal container	½lb (0.2kg)
Nest of cooking pans	1lb (0.4kg)
Plastic folding water-bottle	½lb (0.2kg)
Total	14lb (6.2kg)

To this must be added knife, fork and several spoons, dishcloth, several boxes of matches, teabags, dried milk and small quantities of cooking fat in resealable tins, but the basic weight of the camping gear need not exceed 20lb (9kg), and much of that can be divided among two people.

It is not normally worth taking food from home, except for some light emergency rations, as it is too heavy. A couple of string shopping bags, however, are invaluable as they can be tucked in anywhere, weigh almost nothing, and when you are shopping for food, can hold almost anything and be tied on to the outside of the saddlebag for the final mile or so to the camp site. If the tent and sleeping bag (in a plastic bag to keep it dry) go into the front panniers, this leaves the saddlebag for the cooking gear and spare clothing. The tools, spare tube and small first-aid kit go in one side pocket, and the camera in the other, preferably protected with foam padding. The poles for the tent fit under the flap of the saddlebag.

Camping is something of a battle of wits – yourself against

the problems of weight and bulk. In the ounce war, much of the fun is in doing without items that motor campers would consider essential, yet maintaining a high degree of comfort. The essentials are to be dry and warm; chairs and tables are not for the lightweight enthusiast, but a conveniently placed rock or log can make a great back-rest against which to relax at the end of the day and look at the view, well fed and with the knowledge that you will be warm and snug at night whatever the weather. The true lightweight enthusiast envies no man.

Youth hostels

There are more than 260 youth hostels in England and Wales, run by the Youth Hostels Association, the membership card of which is valid all over the world. There are 150 hostels in Scotland and Ireland, nearly 3,000 on the continent of Europe, and several hundred more in the countries from Iceland to Japan. Hostels exist to enable people to enjoy and explore the countryside, and they seek to provide simple, cheap accommodation at the end of the day in an atmosphere of friendly self-help. They have dormitories, washing facilities and a common room. Most provide meals at reasonable prices, and all in England and Wales have a fully equipped kitchen where members can cook their own food. Perhaps the greatest attraction is that they provide a meeting place for people who are seeing the country usually, but not always, under their own steam, that is by walking, cycling or canoeing, though more and more the transport used is bus, train or minibus.

Youth hostels are certainly not only for the young, though it is best to be young at heart. In England and Wales the only age restrictions are that members under twelve years must be accompanied by a member of at least eighteen years of age. Switzerland and Bavaria place a maximum age limit of twenty-seven years, but for the rest of the world there are no upper age limits; pensioners are sometimes the keenest and most experienced travellers in youth hostels.

Many youth hostel buildings are of considerable interest, ranging from a shepherd's hut to a Norman castle in England

and Wales and including farm buildings, watermills and mansions. Some were built as hostels, but most are conversions. In size they range from a dozen beds to more than 300. Hostels are graded according to the facilities they provide, the majority being either standard or simple grade. The latter are sometimes only a converted barn in the mountains, but many experienced hostellers find that these provide the 'best' type of accommodation as the spirit of comradeship is greater than in the 'superior' or 'special' grade hostels, where there may be central heating and perhaps separate family accommodation. As hostels are for active countrygoers, they are closed during the day, usually opening at 5 P.M. The rule under which members had to move on after three nights has now been changed and, subject to space being available, the warden may allow hostellers to stay longer.

Emphasis is on self-help, and before leaving, members are expected to perform some domestic duty to help in the smooth running of the hostel. This may range from sweeping out a dormitory to chopping wood, but it is unlikely to take more than fifteen minutes or so and, as no domestic staff are employed, it keeps down the cost of hostelling. The address of the Youth Hostels Association (England and Wales) is: Trevelyan House, 8 St Stephen's Hill, St Albans, Herts AL1 2DY. In Scotland, the national office is at 7 Glebe Crescent, Stirling FK8 2JA. The Youth Hostels Association of Northern Ireland has its headquarters at 56 Bradbury Place, Belfast.

Bed and breakfast accommodation

Britain is singularly fortunate in the number of farmhouses, seaside guest-houses and other private houses which readily provide overnight accommodation for travellers at reasonable prices. The Cyclists' Touring Club provides a handbook for its members which lists many of these, including details of the charges. The cooked British breakfast is enjoying a reputation among visitors to this country, largely as a result of the breakfasts provided by these establishments. Bacon, eggs, fried bread, toast and marmalade, with pots of coffee or tea, is something that is not found in many countries, and Scottish landladies often add honey and oatcakes.

Family cycling

One of the great things about the sport of cycling is that there are no barriers of age or sex except those which we impose ourselves. There is room for all, and this particularly applies to families who wish to cycle together. Between the wars, many cycling clubs had family sections. Tandems, with or without sidecars, were the order of the day. Child-size bicycles or adult machines with kiddie seats all turned out, and the ride was conducted at a modest pace and ended with a communal tea. Today, there are fewer family sections, although they do still exist in some of the larger clubs, but there are welcome signs that family cycling is making a comeback. On any summer day small family groups can now be seen out riding. They often avoid club membership, preferring to set their own pace, stopping at will and altering their plans to cater for the needs of the younger members of the family.

With the resurgence of family cycling, the tandem has found a new popularity, and anyone who has one tucked away in the garage from the 1930s probably has something of a collector's piece. There is an intimacy about tandem riding: the couple are close enough to be able to talk easily, though there needs to be a harmony about the relationship. Just to change gear, for example, the rider on the back must ease the pressure from the pedals as the partner in front makes the gear change. Tandems are faster on flat roads or on downhill stretches than are solo machines, but much of the advantage is lost when going uphill. They can easily reach 40 miles an hour when going downhill, and though usually equipped with a hub brake in addition to the two normal rim brakes, the extra weight means that they take some stopping.

Sidecars, trailers and kiddie seats

Babies from a few weeks old can be taken out in a sidecar or trailer, and when they are a little older, from about fifteen months, it is possible to use a kiddie seat, that is a seat fixed firmly to the frame behind the saddle.

It is not an unusual sight at a large rally to see several machines, either tandems or solos, fitted with sidecars or trailers on which the word 'BABY!' is emblazoned in large letters as a warning to other road-users. It is seen more often on the Continent than on the more crowded roads of Britain, and in Holland, basketwork carriers for toddlers are a common sight.

Many parents will be wary of trusting their offspring to the busy roads when even a minor spill could put the youngster at serious risk. Everyone who sets foot on the road is at risk, but how far we are justified in exposing very young children to the dangers is a matter for each parent to consider. Conversations with parents who regularly take out very young children suggest that they find the child benefits from the fresh air, and with commonsense riding they feel that the risk is no greater than, say, pushing a pram through a crowded city street. What is important is to ensure that the kiddie seat, or whatever trailer or sidecar is used, is really well designed and fastened to the cycle in such a way that it cannot work loose.

The Cyclists' Touring Club publishes plans for its members for building both a sidecar and a two-seater trailer, though it points out that some technical competence is necessary. It says that a family with a great deal of experience of touring with babies gave their child a first ride at the age of ten weeks. They found that they hardly noticed they were pulling a trailer behind their tandem and the traffic gave them a wide berth. The baby seemed happy in the trailer and was often sent to sleep by the motion. It was not necessary to carry large amounts of baby items for an enjoyable day out. By using a disposable nappy inside a terry-towelling nappy, one nappy could last for a day's journey.

The cereal-based baby foods mixed in the morning and carried in plastic containers kept fairly warm and were light to carry, although a spare meal was always taken in case of breakdowns. The lying and sitting positions needed to be varied during the day, and reins could be used when the baby was sitting up. A long lunch break and a short afternoon break were necessary and the daily mileage was limited to a maximum of 45 miles. Enough clothes for two adults and the baby could be packed into two panniers, saddlebag and the trailer for a holiday of up to ten days.

The CTC advises that warmth is an essential factor to remember – the child sitting there is immobile with a cooling wind blowing past and will feel the cold a lot more than the person pedalling the cycle. A track suit is usually necessary even on the hottest days. The family mentioned above used a padded suit, intended for use with a pushchair, when the child was on the kiddie seat, and found that this kept him warm. They say that he has never suffered from cold – in fact, he seems to be far more healthy than his contemporaries who have the use of a car.

Adventure cycling for boys and girls

The Youth Hostels Association (Trevelyan House, 8 St Stephen's Hill, St Albans, Herts, AL1 2DY) runs cycling adventure holidays both in Britain and on the Continent. The South Downs, North Yorkshire Moors, and Wild Wales are examples of seven-night tours which are available in Britain, while Holland is a favourite country for touring on the Continent. On some holidays, cycles are supplied; on others, those taking part are expected to bring their own. They need not be lightweight, but they should be in good condition. Overnight accommodation is usually in youth hostels. There are also a number of private companies providing cycle-touring holidays, and their addresses can be found in the cycling press. Distances covered are usually only moderate, well within the capabilities of any reasonably fit person, and plenty of time is allowed for exploring interesting places along the way.

Another possibility for making a family holiday more interesting is to take along a couple of cycles for the children. This works particularly well on a camping or caravan holiday. If the family are taking their own caravan, it is not difficult to put the cycles inside it during the journey to the holiday site, and these are then ready to give the younger members a chance to explore the area – perhaps a trip to a more distant beach or to some other place of interest. A couple of folding bikes do not take up too much space on a car roofrack when it is considered how useful they can be.

There are usually a number of boys and girls who cycle to school regularly; with a little luck a member of the teaching staff may be found who will help in forming a school cycling group. Weekends can then be arranged, staying at youth hostels, and sometimes the school's minibus may be pressed into service if it has a large roof-carrier for all the bikes.

The older rider

There are a variety of clubs for older riders, some providing regular rides, others linking members by post and a club magazine. The Autumn Tints, the Fellowship of Cycling Old-Timers, the Forty-Plus CC are just three. The names and addresses of the secretaries appear in the cycling press. Subscriptions are very low and not only do the clubs provide a link between members, many of whom can no longer ride regularly, but the magazines serve to build up a historic record of early cycling which would otherwise be lost.

One of the largest magazines is the *Fellowship News*, published quarterly by the Fellowship of Cycling Old-Timers. Its members, who range in age from fifty to over a hundred, reminisce over past events, discuss current fads and fashions, and air their memories, opinions, hopes and fears. The magazine carries illustrations by the most famous cycling artist of them all, the late Frank Patterson.

The cycling artist

If anyone captured the pleasures of cycling in the first half of this century, it was Frank Patterson. His delightful line drawings of the English countryside, or the rugged hills of Scotland or Wales, appeared on the pages of *Cycling* from about the turn of the century, and in the *CTC Gazette* from 1925 onwards. Patterson, who lived for about forty years in a sixteenth-century farmhouse in Sussex, was a master of light and shade, using only fine lines to achieve his effects. An art critic might say that he made full use of space: what an observer of his pictures would experience would be a feeling of being in them, for he was able to convey the warmth of the summer scene

that he was drawing, or the chill of the rain in some desolate glen. A lifetime of cycling until his death in 1952 had given him an intimate knowledge of the characters of the country folk he drew. The scenes he portrayed were invariably happy ones: tea on a summer's day, a chat with a cottager, always the scene was idyllic. Perhaps the view he gave of rural England was not a very balanced one, for even the poverty of a cottager's life was given a charm that was not always justified, but Patterson was not setting out to be a social reformer, only to express the delight that could be found cycling around the British Isles, and in that he succeeded like no one before or since.

The Mountain Bike

One cannot leave the topic of off-road riding and cycle-camping without a final mention of the Mountain Bike, or All-Terrain Cycle to give it the correct name, which has made its presence felt in the past few years. These machines have an exceptionally strong though responsive frame, wide, tough tyres with deep treads, flat, wide handlebars and up to fifteen gears. When they made their appearance from the United States, they were greeted as mere toys, but there is now no doubt that with the development that has taken place in their design they are a serious machine equipped like nothing else for riding in wild places. Their low centre of gravity also makes them ideal for carrying heavy camping gear, and despite the increased drag caused by the broad tyres they are increasingly being used as touring machines in the wilder parts of the world. It does seem that with this versatile machine cyclists who love the wild places have a specialized, if rather expensive, cycle that will open up new areas. Their continued development will be watched by all cyclists.

5

Abroad with a bike

Cycles are normally accepted free of charge within the 44lb (20kg) baggage allowance on regular international passenger services, including Apex and standby bookings, though not usually on charter flights. This opens up the whole world to the cycle-tourist, and it is now common to see cycles being loaded on to planes to Europe and North America, and there are signs that the more adventurous are also leaving their wheel-tracks in the Far East, India, Africa, the Middle East and South America.

The rules governing the carriage of cycles varies between individual airlines, and their interpretation sometimes differs from one official to another, so that the result is sometimes confusing. Nevertheless, the ability to take a bike abroad free is such a valuable plus that it is well worth while sorting out just what is involved. The golden rule is to be sure before buying a ticket that the airline knows you will be taking a cycle and that you know of any particular conditions relating to packing it that may be required. Though airlines usually say that they will 'generally accept' bikes, they sometimes tend to take refuge in warnings that restricted baggage space on certain aircraft may result in cycles being unacceptable on a particular flight. However, cyclists who have taken their machines seem to have no more horror stories than other air travellers.

Regulations on flights between Britain and the United States and Canada are rather different from elsewhere and perhaps more onerous, though the airlines serving these routes are well used to the carriage of cycles. On the transatlantic routes, a different free baggage allowance is in force from that applying to the rest of the world and airlines may make a charge if the dimensions of the cycle, when added together, exceed 107in

(274cm). In other words, it is the size and number of the articles of baggage which count, rather than weight. The old regulations under which bikes had to be packed inside cardboard containers or plastic bags have largely disappeared on international flights owing to the huge cargo space that is available on modern airliners. However, it must be emphasized that this relates to the longer-haul routes, and it is essential to check with the airline before buying the ticket just how they want to handle the cycle. The author travelled without any problem from London to Miami, but on trying to put the bike on an internal flight it was a case of 'Sorry, no bike box, no flight'. It is not impossible to obtain a suitable box in a strange town – tour all the local bike shops; they receive their new machines in cardboard boxes and they are usually happy to give away any still littering their premises. For peace of mind, however, insist that the airline gives you a letter when you make your booking stating that the cycle is acceptable for the particular flight without further payment and as part of your luggage allowance. Armed with this you are in a strong position at the check-in desk if a baggage handler looks suspiciously at your bike and reaches for his rule book. While charter flights do not normally take cycles as a matter of course, if the plane is likely to be only partly full, say during the off-season, they will often allow them on. Anyone negotiating for a seat on a half-empty plane can to advantage try a little arm-twisting by saying that purchase of the ticket is dependent upon the bike going too. It's surprising how often this works.

Almost all airlines ask for the handlebars to be 'folded flat', that is turned in parallel to the top-tube, and for the pedals to be removed, all of which makes it easier for the machine to be stacked in the aircraft hold. The handlebars can easily be turned by slacking off the bolt in the centre of the handlebar stem, and, if necessary, giving it a gentle tap. On many machines, the bolt takes the form of an Allen key fitting, so it is vital to arrive at the airport with the correct size of Allen key. Removal of the pedals can be more of a problem; if they have not been taken off for some time they may have become over-tight where the spindle enters the crank, so free them off before leaving for the airport. A special pedal spanner makes the task easier, but remember, *the left-hand pedal has a left-hand thread*; the right-hand pedal has the conventional right-hand thread. Airline officials often ask that tyres be deflated because luggage holds are not fully pressurized and they fear that the tyres may burst at high altitudes. There is some controversy over this as damage can be done to deflated tyres and tubes through the vibration of the cargo deck. The best answer is to deflate the tyres only partly.

Strictly speaking, the airline is entitled to weigh all the luggage that you take on board, but in fact they do not usually weigh the one item of hand-luggage that goes in the cabin, the only stipulation being that it is small enough to fit under the aircraft seat. A saddlebag will easily do so, so it usually does not get weighed, allowing more than enough baggage weight for the cycle and any other bags you may be taking. Some airlines, however, accept only two pieces of luggage free through the check-in, say the bike and one pannier. The other pannier goes as hand-luggage, but anything in excess of this would be charged for. With a tandem, it is always necessary to find out before buying a ticket whether the particular airline will accept it.

Airlines, generally, are selling seats on their planes in intense competition and do not raise unnecessary objections. Experience with officials at check-in points shows that they are more interested in getting all the baggage on the aircraft as speedily and efficiently as possible than in looking up the regulations to see whether a cycle is acceptable. I was once stopped at a Middle East airport by an official – but he only wanted to buy the machine! Cycles should always be taken directly to the airport, not to the air terminal, and arrive well before the advertised time.

Strangely, there seem to be more problems in taking a cycle by train in Europe than in flying with it halfway round the world. In France, and similarly in most other European countries, the cycle has to be registered to its destination. This means that the state railway takes responsibility for it; railway staff will load and unload it, and you will not have access to it until it reaches its destination. If you are fortunate, it will travel on the same train as you and be available shortly after arrival. If it is handed in well before departure, it should be waiting at the destination. However, in practice things do not always go as smoothly as that, and it is by no means unknown for the machine to arrive a day or more after the owner. This is a particular problem if you have to change stations in Paris. In such a case, it is often better to register the cycle to Paris, collect it, ride it across the city and register it again to its final destination.

It is simplicity itself to take a bike across on one of the many car ferries from England to France, Belgium or Holland. Usually, all you need to do is buy a ticket and ride to the ferry terminal at the port from which you wish to leave. Cycles are often put at the head of the car queue and you merely cycle up the gangway, tie up the machine in a convenient corner of the car deck and are first into the restaurant or bar. On the short crossings to France, many companies make no charge for cycles; on the longer routes a charge is made, though it is fairly modest.

The remainder of this chapter is a brief survey of cycling opportunities and conditions in Europe and North America.

France

France has a greater variety of scenery than any other country in Europe; there are a large number of distinctive touring areas, though this does not mean that delightful countryside cannot be found outside them. Many of the more attractive areas of France now have routes which are specifically recommended for cyclists, usually keeping the rider well away from busy main roads. These are charming routes, clearly marked with a small sign depicting a bicycle, and often the local tourist office can supply a pamphlet explaining all the cycle routes in the area. These routes are becoming so popular with both overseas tourists and French cyclists that it is not long before one comes across other cyclists, and so the routes also serve as an introduction to others riders of like mind. The better-known areas are:

Normandy

This is a really great area for a first tour abroad, not only because it is so near to Britain but also because of the variety of the scenery. The cycling is really easy with lots of small towns in which to linger and some of the best food in France. The attractions range from the sandy beaches of the Channel coast to the rocky cliffs and wooded valleys of Swiss Normandy, but the impression of Normandy that most often remains with the cyclist is the typical green hill country with narrow deserted roads studded with farms, abbeys and orchards. The roads often wind beside small rivers giving the impression that England must have been much like this before the coming of the motor car.

A good area for a first ride is to cross to Le Havre and, strictly avoiding the main road, head for the Pont Tancarville. This is achieved by taking any of the tiny roads north of the lorry-choked route. They are marked as cyclists' or scenic routes, and will bring the rider directly on to the toll bridge. But cyclists go across free, so ride slowly over, enjoying the view of the Seine estuary stretching for miles on either side. Once over the river, work west to the little town of Honfleur with its old harbour. There is an excellent camp ground right in the town.

Other towns well worth visiting are Lisieux, Rouen, with its superb cathedral, Bayeux for the tapestry, and the slightly seedy but still aristocratic Deauville. For a really easy and pleasant ride, follow the valley of the Orne south from Caen – again, specific cycling routes are signposted.

The Contentin Peninsular, south from Cherbourg, is equally good, with a very fine coastline. St Lo makes a good centre and has a very active cycling club where a warm welcome is likely.

Brittany

Brittany has two coastlines, one on the Channel and the other on the Atlantic, and it is its coastal scenery that is its first attraction. It has 3,500 km of cliffs and sandy beaches, and those facing the Atlantic are touched by warm currents. Palm trees and magnolias are a common sight along this shore, though do not expect constant sunshine as this is an area where drizzly days and lots of cloud are common. St Malo makes a good starting point and has much more character than most Channel ports. The old walls around the town make a good walk and give some fine views.

The area is divided into Higher and Lower Brittany, and paradoxically Lower Brittany, the western part, is the more hilly. The inland countryside varies from quiet farmland and pasture to moorland and wooded hills, but everywhere there is interest: calvaries appear in quaint villages or at crossroads, festivals are common and wild life and flowers are abundant. As with Normandy, there are plenty of minor roads marked as cycling routes. Generally the roads in Brittany are quiet and there are gravel surfaces on some of those that carry little traffic. One spectacular route follows the Emerald Coast to Quiberon, while inland the Nantes–Brest canal towpath provides an interesting route.

Loire Valley

The most popular section of the river for touring is between Angers and Gien. The countryside is gentle with a soft landscape of fields, trees and vineyards, while the real attraction is the extraordinary wealth of châteaux. As the area is so popular, it is worth considering visiting it out of season.

Dordogne

A fascinating region with scenery which is green, hilly or often bizarre with great limestone rocks, ravines and caverns. The earliest European traces of man have been found in the caves, and a visit to one is a 'must'. If the tourists are too thick on the ground, try the area north of Dordogne and south of Gueret with its many minor roads on which to explore the lovely hilly countryside.

Massif Central

The mountain gradients are gentle but long, and there is a good network of minor roads on which traffic is light. This is desolate country with gorges and deep valleys and is a good area for a strenuous tour. Outstanding features include some extinct volcanoes in the area of Le Mont-Dore and Puy-de-Dôme, though cyclists are not allowed to ride to the summit of the latter.

Alsace and Lorraine

The main attraction is the Vosges mountain range, which is possibly the least visited range in France, but not the least interesting. The Route de Cretes runs for miles along a high ridge with wonderful views. The region is well wooded and the hills have characteristic rounded summits known as 'balloons'; in many respects it resembles the Black Forest of Germany which lies on the other side of the Rhine. The slopes used for wine-growing have given rise to the Route de Vin, from Colmar to Molsheim, which passes through rolling countryside with much wine-tasting along the way.

Jura

An upland plateau between Burgundy and the Swiss frontier, with pine forests, deep valleys and waterfalls. The Col de la Faucille, north of Geneva, gives a view across the whole Mont Blanc range, regarded by many as the finest in all France.

Alps

The numerous high passes of 6,000ft (1,830m) or more provide fine high-altitude cycling. The Alps run for 250 miles from Geneva almost to the Mediterranean. In the north are the chalet houses of Savoy with its Alpine vegetation, in the centre the square stone farmhouses, and in the south the parched, scrub-covered Mediterranean Alps with small villages clinging to their slopes.

Côte d'Azur and Provence

The Riviera between Cannes and Menton is marred by crowds during the summer, and the heavy traffic and an excess of commercialism make it desirable to incorporate a visit to this area in a tour of Provence, which is rich in scenery, art and Roman history. The terraced hills of vines and olives are surprisingly unspoiled. Attractions include the 2,000ft (610m) deep Gorge-du-Verdon, said to be the finest in Europe, and the Camargue, a wild nature reserve by the Rhône estuary.

Pyrenees

The barrier between France and Spain incorporates 250 miles of high mountains with many minor roads that allow the cyclist to get away from it all. There are numerous fine passes, the highest of which is the Port d'Envalira which leads from France to Andorra, the tiny republic in the centre of the Pyrenees. Roads in the mountains are generally well surfaced.

Paris

This can be a dangerous place for the cyclist, much more so than London or any other British city. Early morning is the best time to use the roads, otherwise signal clearly, especially on roundabouts, and don't dither but know where you want to go. French drivers assume their right of way but expect you to do as much. Sightseeing is best done on foot. Versailles is also very busy with heavy motor traffic at peak times.

Belgium

Much of the interest in Belgium lies in the fine old towns, and there is an exceptional wealth of art treasures. Nevertheless, much of northern Belgium is dull from the point of view of the cyclist. Some of the most interesting areas are:

The Ardennes

This is the most popular cycle-touring area of the country, and lies in the south-east quarter. It is renowned for its wooded hills, cleft by deep valleys and deep, fast rivers with castles and picturesque villages. A special feature are the limestone caves and grotto systems. The gradients make cycling strenuous.

The Campine (or Kempen)

This is an area which is much less fertile than northern Belgium generally, and so has not become a chequerboard of fields but remains a wilder area of bogs and heathland where reed-fringed ponds and sandy knolls are scenic features.

The Meuse Valley

The area above Namur is especially scenic with an abundance of quaint villages, ruined castles and abbeys, and has been compared to the Rhine Gorge. The valley is flanked by wilder country, reached by climbing the tributary valleys.

Scheldeland

The land bordering the River Schelde has lush, pastoral scenery, and though it has no claim to outstanding interest, its quiet charms provide a pleasant contrast both to the Campine and the northern plains.

A marked route

For those wishing to follow a waymarked cycle route, passing through picturesque areas of Belgium, there is the Grande Randonnée No. 5, a 100 mile tour which starts at Bergen-op-Zoom in Holland (25 miles from Flushing) and finishes at Bokrijk in Belgium. The route is marked with red triangles all the way (black at the start and finish). There are plenty of camp sites along it.

Holland

The existence of a unique network of cyclepaths, often chosen to follow the most attractive routes from one place to another, coupled with the friendliness of the people, makes Holland an ideal country for cyclists. There are more cycles per head of the population here than anywhere else in the Western World. The industrial areas are around Rotterdam, Amsterdam, The Hague and Utrecht, but Dutch cities do not sprawl and you are soon out in the country. Be warned: Amsterdam has the highest number of cycle thefts in Europe. The locals use huge locks and chains to secure their machines, but even these do not manage to foil the thieves all the time. Don't let your cycle out of your sight. Among the best touring areas are:

North Holland

This is the name of a province rather than a general description. It includes Amsterdam which is just as fascinating as the guidebooks claim, but watch out for the tramlines. The province also includes Haarlem, with its old town, and the harbour town of Monnickendam, the fishing community of Volendam and the island of Marken, where the inhabitants pose in local costume. Edam, Hoorn and Enkhuizen are well worth seeing. The tulip fields are at Limmen, and Alkmaar has the famous cheese market. The largest of the Friesian Islands, Texel, has good sandy beaches and little fishing villages.

South Holland

Again, this is the name of a province and it includes Rotterdam (which was rebuilt after the war) and Delft, one of the best-preserved Dutch towns. Try also The Hague (which is elegant with shady boulevards), Leiden (town of canals and museums), Gouda (with its famous old town hall), ancient Dordrecht and the windmills of Kinderdijk.

Zeeland

This is the south-west corner where the roads cross windswept dams and polders, and one always seems to be crossing inlets of the sea. There are many splendid old churches, prosperous farms and orchards. Middelburg, with its old town hall, abbey, Thursday market and national costumes, attracts many tourists while Veere is picturesque with a small harbour.

Gelderland

This eastern area contains the Veluwe National Park with woods, sandhills, heather and high ground. Arnhem has a fine open-air museum. Nijmegen, set in orchard country to the south, has a castle and other notable old buildings.

Limburg

The hills Holland has are found here, in this south-east corner. The ridges reach 1,000ft (305m) and there are heaths and meadowland. The area has been called, with undoubted exaggeration, Dutch Switzerland.

Overijessel

North of Kempen lies the tidy farmland of the north-east polders, an area reclaimed from the sea. The countryside between Emmeloord and Giethoorn is a maze of lakes and canals. Antique cycles can be seen in the De Waag museum of Deventer with a collection from the former H. Burgers' first Dutch cycle factory.

Switzerland

This country, only twice the size of Wales, is so popular with tourists that an effort is needed to escape the crowds, but it has so much to offer scenically that it should be high on the list of any European tour. The tourist brochures do not stress, however, how unpredictable the weather can be, so be ready for periods of cold and rain. There are so many great areas that it is difficult to categorize them, but try these:

Jura
A network of small, quiet roads. The fact that it is often bypassed by visitors makes it a good cycle-touring area. The Jura runs parallel with the French border in north-west Switzerland and forms a high, rolling limestone plateau of up to 3,500ft (1,067m).

Bernese Oberland
This area, south of Berne, is the traditional picture-postcard Switzerland, and the mountains include the Jungfrau and the Eiger. There are lakes and forests and many minor roads which provide exciting cycling.

Valais
Fine mountain scenery in southern Switzerland which includes the peaks of the Matterhorn, Monte Rosa and the Dent Blanche. There are scores of resorts and traffic is heavy. For roughstuff enthusiasts there are plenty of paths around Zermatt.

Grisons
Primarily a winter sports area, this district provides the cyclist with some spectacular summer riding. The canton includes St

Moritz, Klosters, Davos and other famous resorts. The Swiss National Park is in the south-east corner.

Ticino

The scenery ranges from the 9,000ft (2,745m) mountains around the St Gotthard Pass to the huge lakes shared with northern Italy. It has a Mediterranean climate and vegetation, and instead of the usual Swiss-style houses there are villas, palms and terraces lined with cypress trees. Lakeside Locarno and Lugano are holiday centres and Bellinzona has three castles. Away from the main St Gotthard Pass to Como route there are many roads that are quieter and well suited to cyclists.

Italy

A country of great variety ranging from the Alps in the north to the arid highlands of the south. For those anxious to see central and southern Italy, the most rewarding route would be to follow the Appennines south. The Adriatic coast from Rimini to Bari has been disastrously overdeveloped and the ride along the 400 mile coast road is tedious. The west coast has also been spoiled, though not to the same extent. One has to travel to Calabria in the far south to find relatively untouched coastlines. Some cycling areas which can be recommended are:

Aosta and Piemonte

These regions border the French and Swiss Alps, the former being very mountainous and the latter a more varied region. There are many resorts and the area is very popular during the season with fairly heavy road traffic.

The Dolomites

Multicoloured limestone mountains which seem to soar straight up from the meadows. The ski resort of Cortina is well worth a visit, and a route passing through it and continuing to Venice makes a mountainous but more interesting run than does the main road.

Tuscany

This district includes the fine-art cities of Florence, Siena and Pisa. The towns are a paradise for the photographer, but it is necessary to watch out for thieves, a problem that applies equally further south in Rome. It is often best for the budget-conscious cyclist to choose accommodation outside the famous towns and cycle in.

Calabria

This is the toe of Italy, a primitive and sun-baked land with dusty roads and olive trees. The people have been reported to be less friendly than the easy-going Italians that are met further north.

Sicily

The island is extremely hot and arid in summer. It is mountainous with wild, rough roads, and the people are generally much poorer than on the mainland.

Sardinia

A savage landscape with mountains separated by boulder-strewn valleys, but with less traffic than in Sicily.

West Germany

The Germans have a habit of giving exciting-sounding names to certain routes, such as the Romantic Way. These named routes are designed mainly to encourage motor tourism and the cyclist would be ill-advised to follow them. However, you may wish to 'parallel' them, using byroads and crossing the official routes at their highlights. Anyone who visited Germany without making a special effort to see many of the old cities would be missing some of the best sights the country has to offer. Be warned that police can and do stop cyclists who are breaking traffic laws and fine them on the spot. Some good touring areas are:

The Black Forest

This lies east of the Rhine and south-west of Stuttgart, and is renowned for its dark pinewoods, mountains and swift-flowing rivers, but it is a very popular area and all but the smaller roads can be lined with hotels, swimming pools and garages. The mountains mean few roads, so a cunning choice of routes is necessary.

Eifel
In the west of the country, Eifel is a well-loved cycle-touring area of wooded hills, nature reserves and spas flanked by the Rhine Gorge and the Mosel Valley. The Rhine Gorge itself is the stretch between Bonn and Mainz and has the famous brooding ruins of castles, and the terraced vineyards. Lorries are a problem on weekdays.

Alps and Alpine Foreland
Though a small area, this has much beauty, and the images conjured up by the name 'Oberammergau', or by the fairy-tale palaces of Bavaria, probably describe the area better than words can.

The North German Plain
This extends from the north coast down to a line running roughly through the Ruhr. Much of it is fertile farming land, appealing to those who like placid, undramatic scenery. However, there are also marshes and heaths including Lüneburg Heath, an area of heathery moorland between the rivers Weser and Elbe.

Central Uplands
This is a varied but 'typically German' area, consisting in parts of a high, flat plain but mostly of several ranges of hills and low mountains, each range having its own character. Generally, it is a landscape of extensive woods alternating with patchworks of fields where much of the work is still done by hand. Before the hay-harvest, the meadows are thick with wild flowers.

Austria

Three chains of mountains run roughly east–west through the country. The central chain is the highest and provides extremely dramatic scenery for anyone willing to do some really strenuous riding. To the north and south of this range run two chains of limestone alps; the limestone is the cause of the lush meadows and great variety of wild flowers. Within these two chains lie two particularly lovely areas: the Salzkammergut in the north-west, which has Salzburg nearby, and Carinthia in the south-east. Both these areas are famed for their lakes and superb scenery. Roughly one-third of Austria is wooded. Main roads tend to follow the river valleys and are often narrow. The main mountain-pass roads can give enjoyable cycling when not too busy: the Gross Glockner is said to be particularly dramatic. Secondary roads tend to be steep, sharply curved and unmade, being dusty in dry conditions and muddy in wet. Cycling in Vienna is not easy and trams are a useful alternative form of transport. Rainfall tends to be high, and, even in summer, a pair of gloves is useful in the mountains, especially when making long descents when the fingers can become too numb to operate the brakes fully.

Greece

Cycling is superb in this country which provides such a wide variety of scenery. The mountains north of Tripolis and the Taigetos Range are more than 8,000ft (2,440m) high and have some spectacular passes. The three peninsulas extending south into the Mediterranean have some interesting rough roads and grand beaches. In the Peloponnese, the southern mainland of Greece, places of interest include: Corinth, Mycenae, Epidaurus, Olympia, Mistra, Ancient Sparta and Monemvasia.

In western Greece, the country is mountainous with small, poor communities perched high on wild, bare cliffs. Central Greece has the country's largest plain, surrounded by mountains including Mount Olympus at 9,550ft (2,912m). The plain is dull in some areas but attractive in others. Northern Greece has extensive fertile plains with mountains bordering on Yugoslavia. Salonika is a centre for Byzantine relics. South-eastern Greece has the famous attractions of Delphi and Corinth but is one of the more crowded areas. The islands of Rhodes, Corfu and Crete are large enough to repay cycle-touring; to visit many of the small islands it is perhaps better to leave the cycle in safekeeping, take a boat and walk. The people of Greece are exceedingly warm-hearted and hospitable.

Spain

The landscape varies from scorched desert-like plains to snow-topped mountains, and the country has much to offer the adventurous. The Pyrenees provide a 250 mile long range which enables crossings to be made into France to sample the two very different cultures. Small rough roads lead to some of the most attractive areas and gears in the low 30s are needed. The north of the country has a broad strip of good touring territory with a fine coast and mild weather. The areas around Bilbao and San Sebastian are rather busy. The centre of Spain consists of a huge plateau, a sparsely populated and remote region where it is wise to carry emergency supplies of food and water. The east and south of the country have been savaged by commercialism. The main coast road carries heavy traffic and provides little enjoyment for the cyclist. Andalusia, in the south, is said to be the most 'Spanish' region. It has the greatest number of sunshine hours, least rain and mildest winters of anywhere in Europe, and a vivid landscape of snowcapped mountains, olive groves, orange trees, vineyards and flower-decked white houses. Many of the beaches are still unspoiled. The cities of Granada and Seville should be included in a tour of this area. Cycling in the mountains is tough, but the scenery is among the most magnificent in Europe.

Spring and autumn are the best times of the year for cycling. If touring in the summer, do not leave your cycle in the hot sun with the tyres pumped hard as they could explode as the air expands. Punctures are best mended in the evening: in the heat of the day the rubber solution becomes less effective. In anywhere except the northern Basque country, cycling between June and August is very tiring.

Portugal

Fewer people visit Portugal than the more-publicized European playgrounds, yet it is one of the most rewarding countries for cyclists. It has a climate without extremes of heat or cold, and it is generally cooler than Spain. It is good cycling country at any time of the year, the spring being generally warmer than the autumn.

The country can be divided scenically into two halves. The area north of the River Tagus is mountainous, with a narrow coastal plain, though the peaks rarely exceed 5,000ft (1,525m). South of the Tagus, wide stretches of bleak heathland are interspersed with large areas of cultivation. The beaches of the Algarve are in the extreme south. Lisbon is attractive and is sited on the hills above the Tagus, and the coast to the west of the capital has some fine beaches and good scenery. English is rarely understood, though many Portuguese have a second language learned while working abroad, sometimes French or German. A knowledge of Spanish may allow written Portuguese to be understood, but the spoken language is dissimilar. Road surfaces vary greatly but are generally not nearly as good as in more northern parts of Europe. However, the attractiveness of the countryside and the relatively cheap food, wine and accommodation more than make up for this.

For the cyclist seeking a winter break, the Algarve will compare well with anything in Europe. The main road running east–west along the south of the country from Cape St Vincent to the Spanish border is busy, often with high-revving mopeds screaming past. There is a network of minor roads roughly paralleling the main route, and though these wind through some rugged, hilly countryside, the effort is well rewarded by the sight of masses of almond trees in blossom when much of Europe is covered in snow. Cape St Vincent and nearby Sagres are a must for their great views, especially when the winter Atlantic is hurling waves and clouds of spray far into the air.

Yugoslavia

The regions of Yugoslavia vary not only because of wide differences in terrain, but also because the country is really a federation of six republics, each with its separate history and character. About three-quarters of the country is mountainous or plateau, and one-third is forested. The indented coast with its clear waters and many islands is, despite its barrenness, considered by many to be the finest in Europe. The coastal strip is narrow, backed by steep mountains. The valleys within these mountains are also narrow and often run parallel to the coast, making access into the mountains difficult. In the south, the mountains are virtually continuous, culminating in the rugged, wild heights of the south-east. In the east there are the broad agricultural plains of the Danube Valley around Belgrade.

The main coast road is tarmac throughout and very scenic, though it is far from flat and also very busy. The main inland route runs through Ljubljana, Belgrade, Nis, Skopje and so to Greece, but it carries far too much traffic for its two lanes and the number of wrecked vehicles by the side of the road bear witness to the dangers. Main roads in the north-west and those linking cities are likely to have good surfaces. In the south-east, any good road surface should be looked upon as a rare gift from the gods. Yugoslavian drivers can be bad and may force a cyclist off the road when trying to pass where there is just not room to do so. In view of the bad road surfaces, it is inadvisable to expect to average much more than 30 to 35 miles a day unless a great deal of main road riding is envisaged.

Hungary

Hungary is a republic with a fairly liberal regime, well inside the Communist camp. The hill forests are still inhabited by deer and wild boar, and wild geese arrive in their thousands. Domestic geese in the care of a goose-girl are a common sight all over the Hungarian steppe, and gipsy music is a feature of Hungarian life.

The Great Hungarian Plain, to the east of the River Tisza, and the northern part of the Danube Plain are vast and featureless. In the north and west of the country there are mountains, though these are of no great height. Lake Balatron, in the western hills, is the largest lake in Central Europe and is lovely to cycle around. In the south-east is the region of Transylvania, the home of Dracula. Camping other than on recognized sites is strictly illegal, but the law does not seem to be enforced.

Budapest has many cobbled streets, and the roads in towns are generally not good. Also taxi drivers can be a menace in the cities. Food and drink are fairly cheap. In the summer, the climate is unexpectedly hot during the afternoon, often over 80°F. Rainfall is at its highest in May.

Iceland

Only a small part of the island has the normal tourist amenities, and its appeal to cyclists is only to those who are self-reliant and can cope with all conditions. The country resembles the Scottish Highlands rather than Scandinavia but with everything on a far grander scale and with volcanic and thermal activity added.

A disadvantage to touring is that there is often only one road between centres. The south-west peninsula is unrewarding. The mid-western Snaefellsnes peninsula has a great variety of landscape and a choice of routes. The rider should decide which area he wishes to visit and seek advice locally, perhaps using buses to cross uninteresting country. Nevertheless, Iceland, which has a much milder climate than might be imagined, has much to offer the determined traveller that cannot be found elsewhere. The geysers are a popular attraction and can be found in many parts of the island, particularly in the south-west. Small fishing villages which have houses with gaily painted roofs are dotted all around the coast. In mid-June the midnight sun can be seen.

The United States

Americans have recently 'discovered' cycling and have applied the drive and enthusiasm which is so characteristic of that amazing country to getting the very best out of it. Cycling clubs have sprung up in large numbers, and the traditional enthusiastic welcome which Americans show to visitors is even more marked among bikies. The local cycle store will almost certainly be a mine of information about cycling in the area, and will probably have a range of booklets giving details of the best back-road routes. For America is not Europe and there are many roads where a cyclist who has any regard for his safety had better not be. The author recalls riding after dark along Highway US 1 through the islands of the Florida Keys, where there is no other road at all, as one of his worst nightmares! Yet North America has greater rides, more fantastic scenery, and calls for more superlatives generally than anywhere else that a bicycle can go. Perhaps above all countries, this is the one place where the advice should be: Just give it a go.

Many people who visit North America make the mistake of trying to see too much – a fault not restricted to cyclists. It is not possible to tour America by cycle as you would Europe, for the conditions are entirely different. For example, much of New England can be seen comfortably in a tour of two or three weeks, but to cross the country would take at least seven weeks, and while this might be an achievement, it would not be particularly pleasurable as much of the land crossed would be harsh, barren and largely devoid of interest.

Make up your mind whether you want to see the east or the west, for there are many fine tours that could be made lasting three or four weeks in each. Taking the east first, the Appalachian mountain chain which stretches from the Canadian border to Georgia, a distance of 1,500 miles, gives spectacular riding. Although of moderate altitude, these mountains are lush with vegetation. Of course, the full run is too much for one trip, even of a month's duration. Among the highlights are the White Mountains of Vermont, best seen in the spring, and the Blue Ridge in Virginia, for the autumn. This route allows you to visit Washington and, depending on the time available, you can stay in the mountains south of the capital for another 700 miles, or hop on a train and return to New York.

For a West Coast tour one way is to fly to Vancouver or Seattle, cities which straddle the border between the US and Canada. It is best to travel south to take advantage of the prevailing wind. The scenery along the Pacific Coast is truly magnificent, and it is only a day's ride up into the mountains where a stop can be made at Crater Lake in Oregon. For anyone getting as far south as California, perhaps by combining the ride with air travel, there are the giant redwoods in the northern part of that state. Further south, Yosemite National Park should not be missed. The weather along the West Coast is often delightfully cool, helped by the fresh northerly breeze.

Cyclists who have returned from the United States say that the Everglades make an interesting tour, despite the scarcity of roads in this swampland. At the southern end of the national park, Highway 27 from Homestead (on the outskirts of Miami) to Flamingo provides an excellent scenic ride. The Everglades teem with wildlife, including alligators, tropical birds and swamp deer. Hawaii has also been recommended as an excellent place in which to tour.

Other suggested touring areas are:

New England

This comprises Maine, Vermont, New Hampshire, Massachusetts, Connecticut and Rhode Island. It is an area of green rolling hills, rich in history, and good starting places for tours include Boston or Montreal. Youth hostels are more plentiful here than in other parts of America.

South Central States

These are Virginia, West Virginia, North Carolina, South Carolina, Tennessee and Kentucky. Start in Washington DC and visit this region famous for its 'southern hospitality'. One way to tour the area is to take the Chesapeake and Ohio Canal towpath which runs close to the Potomac River. It is a cyclists' and joggers' trail and has camp-grounds.

Pacific North-West

Washington and Oregon are the two states concerned here. A tour can begin in Seattle or in Vancouver. It is an area of high mountains and dense rain-forests, with the grand coastline mentioned earlier. A system of ferries connects the beautiful San Juan islands, a perfect area for cycle-camping.

California

This state, about twice the size of Britain, is one of the most interesting for the cycle-tourist, having every type of terrain within its borders. Especially worth visiting are the San Francisco Bay area, the coast between San Francisco and Los Angeles, and the Sierra Nevada foothills south-east of Sacramento.

Canada

What has been said about the huge size of the United States applies also to Canada – only more so. It is a continent, not a country. Each province has its own attractions: perhaps British Columbia is the most scenic, but Ontario has the Niagara Falls and Toronto, and Quebec has Gaspé, the Laurentian Mountains and Montreal. Alberta has many attractions with its Rocky Mountains, Banff and Lake Louise.

For cyclists who prefer the back roads to highways, the best touring grounds in Canada are southern Ontario (especially the Niagara Peninsula), southern Quebec and the Maritime Provinces (Nova Scotia, New Brunswick and Prince Edward Island). The byways carry little motorized traffic though many are dirt roads. Canadian highways are well surfaced but carry heavy traffic. In northern Ontario and most of the western provinces there are virtually no other roads than these. Cyclists who wish to tour the Rockies, for example, must either use these or roughstuff along the hiking trails. The Rocky Mountains Ridge Road, which runs between Jasper in the north and Banff in the south, is superb and well endowed with youth hostels. It is a busy road in summer and uncyclable in winter.

The best times to visit Canada are between mid-May and mid-October. Snow can be expected anywhere above 3,000ft (915m), but such is the range of summer temperatures that anything from sunstroke to frostbite may have to be guarded against.

GAZETTEER OF CYCLING ROUTES

Introduction

Had time and space been unlimited, this section could have included ten times as many routes, or a hundred times, or even more. There is no end to the number of cycling routes that can be compiled within the British Isles. They have, beyond doubt, the world's finest cycling country, partly because of the wealth – the only word for it – of quiet lanes and tracks, partly because the countryside changes every few miles, and partly because of the villages that line the way. The flowers, trees, animals and birds that fill the countryside, despite the effects of mass-production farming and the spread of the urban landscape, make it a marvellous place for those who love it. Finally, there is the weather. The beauties of Britain exist because of the climate, however much we pour abuse on it. It is the alternating rain, sun, frost and wind which give us the green vistas that are seen from windy hilltops, or the willows overhanging a village pond.

These routes have been compiled with the intention of showing something of England's charm off the beaten track. Anyone riding them may wonder why a well-known beauty spot has been avoided. The answer is probably that it is just too well known, too crowded and too litter-strewn to have been included.

The routes have been set out so that if the cyclist becomes lost at any point, he merely has to follow the local signposts to the next village marked in bold type on the route. While it is not strictly necessary to use them in conjunction with a map, to do so will make the rides far more enjoyable, and will enable them to be varied to suit personal tastes. Almost without exception they can be made longer or shorter at will. (Note that the distance given at the head of each route, and its metric equivalent, are approximate only.) It is not claimed that a route is necessarily the 'best' in an area, merely that it gives the true flavour of the country through which it is passing.

Most of the routes have been ridden by the author, the rest have been supplied by experienced cyclists who know the areas well. Anyone who feels that the author has included so many references to old churches that he must be some sort of nut about the topic is probably correct.

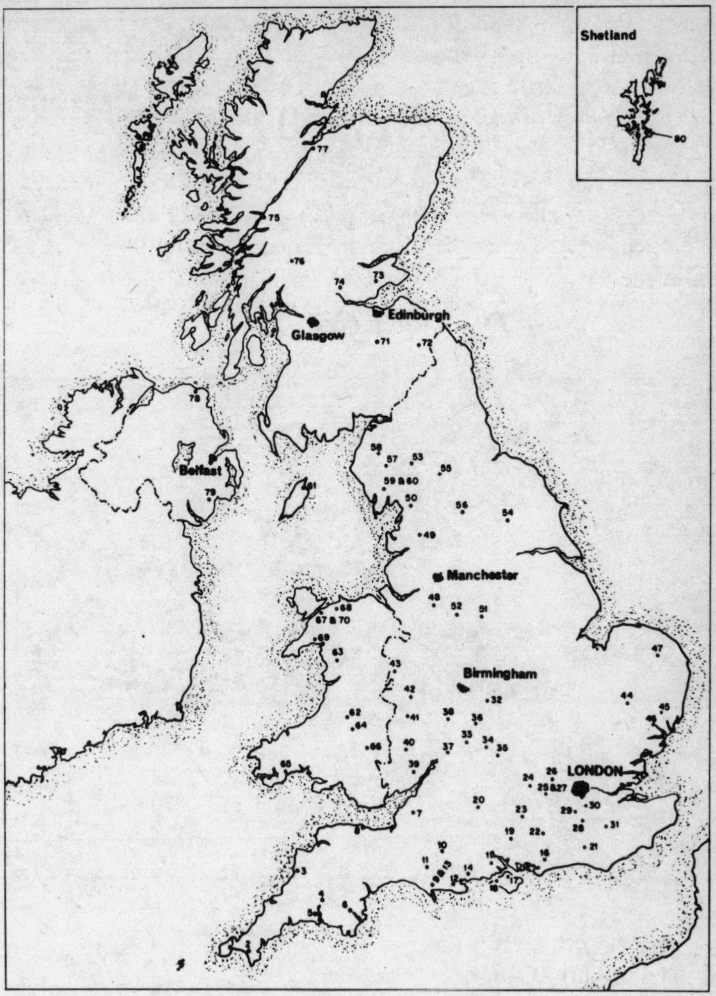

Location of Routes

ENGLAND

The West Country

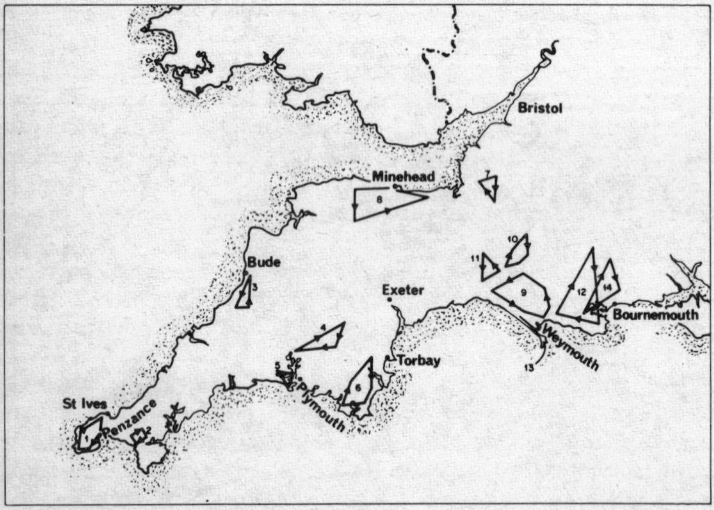

1 AROUND LAND'S END

40 miles (64km) – Cornwall
Starting point: Penzance
OS sheet 203, Bartholomew map 1

The contrast between the 'two Cornwalls' – the picturesque coast and the wilder, sometimes harsh uplands, scarred by stone circles, tumuli and disused lead and tin mines – is particularly evident to cyclists who tour the toe of the peninsula. A whole day can easily be spent on this ride, making detours along cliff paths whenever it seems prudent to do so.

Penzance The main street has the somewhat surprising name of Market Jew Street, and on it stands a statue to Sir Humphrey Davy, who invented the miner's safety lamp and was born in the town. Ride along the coast road west to

Newlyn Although the town is rather overdeveloped, the harbour is well worth a visit, and despite the decline of the Cornish fishing industry, fishermen still mend their nets there and unload their catches. Stay on the coast road and pass the lifeboat station at Penlee Point (open to the public). The island that can now be seen in front, just off the coast, is St Clement's Isle, which is reputed to have been the abode of a hermit. Ride on to

Mousehole This is the sort of village that is thought of as typically Cornish, with twisting narrow streets and blue and white paintwork. The name of the village, by the way, is pronounced Mow'sell. The road turns inland here and runs through the hamlet of

Paul The road climbs steeply from here. At a T-junction go left to

Lamorna This is more of a valley than a village. Its cascading stream, ending up in Lamorna Cove, is a popular spot with both artists and visitors. Take the road down to the cove then retrace up the valley and at the B3315 turn left. Climb the hill and just after a farm is reached on the right there are two pillars of stone about 12ft (3.6m) high. These are known as The Pipers, who are reputed to have made music for the Merry Maidens on a Sunday and so were turned to stone. The Maidens did not escape either: they are the blocks of stone which form a circle to the left of the road, about ½ mile from The Pipers. Continue to

Treen There is a track down to the spectacular headland. If taken, retrace to the village and continue west to

Land's End This spot may be a little disappointing with its rash of car parks and 'last' shops and pubs in England. It is best visited when the south-westerly gales are driving the seas on to the rocks and the tourist aspect of the place can be forgotten. Follow the road through the village of

Sennen the most westerly village in England, to

Sennen Cove This is reached down a steep incline. The water is spectacularly clear here and there is good surfing. Retrace to the main road and follow it until its junction with the B3306, taking this road to the left over moorland to

St Just The old mining town has a rather grey appearance, but there is a road down to the left to

Cape Cornwall This is the only headland in England which is officially called a cape. Retrace and follow the road to

Morvah There is now grand countryside to pass through and, if at all possible, take one of the many tracks to the left to see some of the finest cliff scenery in Cornwall. Continue to

Zennor The church is famous for the carved bench-end of the Zennor Mermaid who is said to have enticed the squire's son away. There is a path down to Zennor Head. Continue along the very attractive road to

St Ives Despite the crowds which pack the little town every summer, this is a fascinating spot. The light, which once attracted so many artists, makes the sea a deep blue, and the harbour with its colourful boats, and the blue and white houses make this a truly traditional Cornish town. Visit the Barbara Hepworth Museum and as many other art exhibitions as possible. To avoid the busy Carbis Bay road, retrace up the hill and take the B3311 running right across the narrow Cornish peninsula to

Penzance

2 ROUNDABOUT HELSTON

13 miles (20km) – Cornwall
Starting point: Helston
OS sheet 203, Bartholomew map 1

Cornwall is not all coves and beaches: inland the scenery soon becomes hard with windswept, barren land. The land may at times seem disfigured by old tin mines and quarries, but this is more typical of the 'real' Cornwall than are the souvenir shops that litter so many of the coastal villages. This route tries to take in something of both faces of this ancient district.

Helston Can there be anyone who has not heard of Helston's Furry Dance? On 8 May each year townsfolk garlanded with flowers and headed by fiddlers dance through the streets and in and out of the houses. Be early if you wish to see this old rite – the first of the dances begins at 7 A.M. Though the town is not uninteresting it is most likely to be used as a centre from which to tour southern Cornwall. For the purpose of this ride, take the B3304 south-west out of the town, crossing the river, and stay on that road for the 3 miles to

Porthleven While this is a quiet little corner of Mount's Bay during the summer, it is a wild place indeed when the autumn gales sweep the coast and even today relics of old shipwrecks are still cast up on the beaches to the east of the town. From the west side of the harbour, take the minor road running just inland from the cliff from which there are some grand views, and stay with it for the 3 miles to

Ashton The rider is now on high ground, but the climb continues, crossing the A394 and passing around the west flank of Tregonning Hill. The ancient cross near the main road, the remains of castles and ancient encampments all demonstrate how important this high ground was in controlling the coast and defending the harbours from raiders. Stay with the road as it runs north-east to

Godolphin Cross and continue on again for another mile to the junction with the B3302 where go right and remain with this road for a steady descent of 3 miles to

Helston

3 BUDE BYWAYS

10 miles (16km) or 20 miles (32km) – Cornwall
Starting point: Bude
OS sheet 190, Bartholomew map 3

This is two routes in one – or to put it another way an easy run for an evening or a hard 20 miles suitable mainly for mountain goats. Either way there are some great views.

Bude Visitors flock to the resort each year, largely for the superb coastal scenery. There is a good beach and surfing. Ride south from the town on the minor road which passes through

Lynstone Soon it picks up the cliff and stays with it for 3 miles to

Widemouth Sands where the road returns to sea level. Those on the shorter of these two rides, having enjoyed the wide seaward views with a minimum of exertion, can turn left here and make the gentle climb to the junction with the A39 where, going left again, they may make the easy return to Bude. For those wishing more scenery, stay with the cliff road and begin the ascent of

Penhalt Cliff Each hill is followed by a steeper one, until, 300ft above the sea, the road plunges down to cross the stream at

Millook Haven Up climbs the road again to almost 400ft at

Bynorth Cliff The gradients ease for a couple of miles, then comes another series of switchbacks until sea level is again reached at

Crackington Haven Up goes the road again over the downs to the junction with the A39 at

Tresparrett Posts The return to Bude along the main road is now easy compared to what has gone before. Anyone wanting still more hills should turn off right (adding 3 miles to the route) at

Wainhouse Corner and take the minor road through

Jacobstow,

Week St Mary and

Marhamchurch to
Bude

4 A TASTE OF DARTMOOR

40 miles (64km) – Devon
Starting point: Yelverton
OS sheets 191 and 202, Bartholomew map 2

There are only a limited number of roads that cross Dartmoor, so this route includes some doubling back. It is a hilly ride but always an interesting one. The first 6 miles consist of a largely continuous ascent to North Hessary Tor, though only a few stretches need to be walked, and the descent on the return journey makes exciting riding.

Yelverton Turn right on leaving the town, following the signs to Princetown. After a couple of miles or so, the country opens out and the land becomes rough moorland with ponies grazing close to the road, and sheep running across it. Though the road is busy in summer, at other times this is a wild and lonely place. The view behind gets better and better the higher you climb, and with low gears the road can be ridden without too much effort. Hut-circles, barrows, cairns and the traces of early man are littered all over the moor. North Hessary Tor, to the left of the road and with a television transmitter aerial on top, is the highest point. Continue to
Princetown The town's most famous feature, the prison, is to the left. The austerity of that place seems to have rubbed off on the rest of the town, though there are plenty of places to have tea, thanks to the large number of coaches which bring tourists to the spot. The town was named after the Prince of Wales (later George IV) as it and the whole of the moor formed part of the estates of the Duchy of Cornwall. The church, claimed to be the highest parish church in England, was built by French prisoners of war. Continue to
Two Bridges Cross the A384 and take the minor road to
Postbridge Here there is an old clapper bridge constructed of a series of loose stone piers supporting large stone slabs over the infant River Dart. Leave the village and then take the first road to the right, signposted to Widecombe in the Moor. This is a delightful road, plunging down between the tors, a road edged with soft green turf, close-cropped by sheep and with the occasional moorland pony. Follow the signs to
Widecombe in the Moor This is one of the most attractive villages on Dartmoor and has nothing of the sombre character of Princetown. Widecombe is, of course, known for the song about Uncle Tom

Cobleigh, which is a pity as the shops sell more souvenirs of that song than anything else. The church, which has much more claim to merit, is the real feature of the place, with its enormous tower which forms a landmark for miles around. Retrace the route for about 1 mile and take the byroad going south which connects back to the A384. Turn right on to this road, a grand route which goes through the heart of the moor, passing

Dartmeet where the east and west branches of the Dart converge. The road continues to

Two Bridges where you turn left and retrace through

Princetown and down the 6 mile fast descent, this time with the views ahead, to

Yelverton

5 KINGSAND AND CAWSAND

15 miles (24km) – Devon and Cornwall
Starting point: Plymouth
OS sheet 201, Bartholomew map 2

This is a short but interesting run for an evening, or longer if you intend to spend some time in the delightful twin villages of Kingsand and Cawsand. A word of caution about the Cremyll ferry: while it will usually accept a small number of bicycles, some difficulty has been found in getting them accepted at the height of the season. If in doubt, make the crossing from Plymouth by the Torpoint ferry, and follow the signs.

Plymouth See the city centre, rebuilt after the wartime bombing, the Barbican, and visit the Hoe where Drake is reputed to have played bowls while the Spanish Armada advanced. From the city centre follow the signs towards the Brittany Car Ferries terminal. Shortly before the terminal is reached there is a sign to the Cremyll ferry, down a rough lane to the right. Take the ferry across the Hamoaze to

Cremyll Climb up from the landing stage to Maker Heights and see spectacular views across Plymouth Sound. Descend to the twin villages of

Kingsand and Cawsand These are typically Cornish villages, with twisting narrow streets and attractive cottages. Yachts which often anchor in Cawsand Bay make an attractive picture. Proceed up the hill to

Rame This is a hamlet with a fishermen's church, and there is a track to Rame Head from which there are more fine views. Retrace to Rame and follow the signs to

Millbrook which stands at the head of a shallow creek. Bear right along the edge of the creek and then turn left at All Saints' Church, taking a winding, hilly road to

St John another largely unspoilt corner. Climb up out of the village to the junction with the A374. If time allows, a detour can be taken to the left for 1 mile to visit Antony House (open), in which case retrace and descend to

Torpoint The little town is not particularly attractive, but it is the landing point for the Torpoint ferry which, despite the new tollbridge, still rattles on its chains across the Hamoaze to

Devonport This once-famous naval harbour is now largely in 'moth-balls', and the rather busy road can be taken back to

Plymouth

6 SOUTH DEVON

55 miles (88km) – Devon
Starting point: Totnes
OS sheet 202, Bartholomew map 2

There are limitless variations to this route: to turn down almost any lane or path is to find some new and delightful aspect. Particularly in the South Hams, south of Kingsbridge, there are sunken lanes between banks of flowers or ferns, and tracks that lead to the sea or to coves. In most cases, however, it is necessary to retrace and many of the byways do not connect up to make a continuous route. The roads chosen for this route have been selected to give the most dramatic coastal scenery and the most charming towns and villages, but the temptation to turn down at least some of the roads that are not mentioned should not be resisted.

Totnes The town is attractive and sits on the west bank of the Dart. There are the ruins of a Norman castle, and the Brutus Stone, in Fore Street, is reputed to be the spot where the town-crier stood. The proclamation of a new sovereign is still made from the stone. Leave the town by crossing the stone bridge in the direction of Paignton. After climbing up the main road for 2 miles, turn right on to a minor road, signposted to Stoke Gabriel. On the right there is a cottage with a plaque in the garden saying that William of Orange called his first Parliament there. Follow the signs to

Galmpton Turn right, passing close to Maypool Youth Hostel, and after 2 miles descend to a ferry landing. If the ferry is on the opposite bank, there is a brass bell on the left of the landing which can be rung to summon it. Cycles are carried for a moderate fee. Cross on the ferry to

Dittisham The village is famous for its thatched cottages and plum orchards. It clings to a hillside in true Devon fashion. The church has interesting pulpit, screen and fonts which are claimed to be remnants of the earlier Saxon church. There is a very steep climb up from the ferry. Follow the Dartmouth signs. (There is a short-cut to Dartmouth by taking a track on the left ½ mile out of the village, but this involves crossing Old Mill Creek and is a muddy and hilly ride.) Continue climbing up from the village, and turn left at a prominent crossroads, making a fast descent to

Dartmouth This is one of Devon's most attractive towns, the yachts alone making the harbour a fascinating place. The castle provides some grand sea and river views, and there is a ferry to Kingswear if time permits. Take the secondary road running south along the river, and rejoin the main coast road at

Stoke Fleming From here on there are sweeping views out to sea on the left. There is a very fast descent to

Blackpool Sands The pines on the cliffs make this a much-photographed spot. Continue to follow the road to

Slapton Sands The road is raised slightly above the beach and gives wonderful views in both directions. During the autumn gales this is a windswept spot, with the seas crashing over the road. In summer it is very busy with visitors. On the right is Slapton Ley, a stretch of water which provides a habitat for many types of wildlife. The road turns inland at

Torcross Follow it up the hill. It is worth stopping to look at the coastal views that unfold here. Continue to

Kingsbridge If time is pressing, 12 miles or so can be cut off the route here by taking the road to Aveton Gifford, but this leaves out some great scenery. Otherwise, turn left in the town on to the A381, through Malborough to

Salcombe Despite the crowds that pack it during summer, this is a town well worth seeing, with one of the finest yachting harbours in the West Country. If time allows, take the very steep hill up to the youth hostel, continue past it, and push the bike up the track and over a couple of stiles to

Bolt Head It is worth the effort for the view up and down the coast and also up the estuary to the town. It is a particularly grand view on a summer evening. Retrace to Salcombe. Follow the A381 back again to

Malborough Go straight on at the crossroads to

Hope This is another 'typical' Devon village with whitewashed thatched cottages, and it is also a good place to have tea. Hope was once notorious as a smuggling cove, but is now better known for its crabs. Take the road out to

Aveton Gifford There is a particularly fine Early English church here. Turn right off the Modbury road, taking a byroad north to

Avonwick where a right turn on to the main road will take the rider back to

Totnes

7 SMILING SOMERSET

16 miles (26km) – Somerset
Starting point: Wells
OS sheet 183, Bartholomew map 7

Somerset is a hilly county, so this route has been chosen to avoid the big climbs while passing around or between the picturesque hills that give the county its character. Anyone who wishes instead to make the many short, steep climbs will have no difficulty in varying the route.

Wells The cathedral quarter of this ancient town, with its mellowed stone buildings, mature lawns and old gateways gives the whole city an air of tranquillity. It is a wonderful place in which to spend a summer afternoon. Leave the town by riding along the A371 eastwards to

Dulcote The hill here – Dulcote Hill – to the south of the main road, gives a wonderful view of the cathedral for anyone prepared to scramble up. Unfortunately, the south side of the hill has been visually spoiled by quarrying. Despite this, take the minor road going south from Dulcote and passing the quarries. The view soon improves as the lane slips between the hills on either side on its way to

North Wootton Go right in the village, bearing left after the church and following the minor road to Redlake Farm where bear left through the hamlet of

Laurel Street and on to the A361 where go right into

West Pennard Pennard Hill, a little to the east, is dramatic, hilly cycling country with steep, short climbs and sudden descents for anyone with the energy. Those mountain goats can disport themselves there, while our route takes us south of West Pennard, through

Coxbridge and on to

Baltonsborough which is easy country with orchards on these south-facing slopes. Follow the signs to

Butleigh A memorial in the church commemorates the Hood family,

of naval distinction, whose home village this was. Now it is a simple ride to take the lane north-west along Wootton Hill to

Glastonbury This busy and rather industrial town may lack the grace of the better-known ecclesiastical centres, but the importance of its abbey has meant that it has long held a place in the development of England. Glastonbury Tor is more than 500ft high and is capped by the fourteenth century tower of St Michael, making it a landmark for miles from the plains around. Take the A39 for the remaining 5 miles back to

Wells

8 EXMOOR AND THE COAST

33 miles (53km) – Somerset
Starting point: Minehead
OS sheet 181, Bartholomew map 7

Minehead stands on the edge of Exmoor, and though the coast suffers from having rather too many caravan sites and holiday camps for many people's taste, this is still some of the most beautiful country in the South-West. The ride is hilly, but it has been kept short to allow plenty of time for walking up hills and looking at views. It could easily be extended into the heart of the moor; a visit to some of the scores of chapels that dot Exmoor would in itself make a 'point' to the ride.

Minehead This little town has more to offer than first appears. Ignoring the souvenir shops, visit the higher part of the town, to the west of the main streets. There is an attractive alley called Church Steps. Work back south through a maze of streets to the main Porlock road and follow it to the right for 3 miles to a right turn to
Selworthy This is one of the most photographed and sketched villages in Somerset, made especially attractive by its thatched cottages and village green. Retrace along the lane to the main Porlock road. (If time permits, divert to the right here to visit the village of Allerford, which is much less well known than Selworthy but equally attractive with a packhorse bridge. Retrace.) Take the main road left, away from Porlock, and in 1 mile take a right turn to
Luccombe The village nestles under Luccombe Hill on which are the signs of ancient settlements. A track leads up. The road from Luccombe climbs and then descends steeply to
Wootton Courtenay Ride through the village, and at the T-junction with the main Dunster road, go right, away from Dunster to
Timberscombe Stay on this road, which is very attractive with hills all around, passing over a right-hand hairpin bend across a bridge until, 1½ miles after the bridge, you reach the hamlet of
Wheddon Cross At this ancient crossroads go left, ignoring the turn to Cutcombe, and climb up the open heights of the Brendon Hills. For mile after mile there are grand views, and signs of ancient settlements such as barrows and cairns. After about 9 miles of this road, you come to the hamlet of
Raleigh's Cross Bear left following the Watchet signs. There is a spectacular run down to
Watchet An attractive harbour here makes this a pleasant spot. Take the coast road to the west, past
Blue Anchor (which sounds more attractive than it really is) to
Carhampton Go right along the main road and turn left at the sign to
Dunster This is another attractive and popular village with the remains of a castle and a market cross. Follow the signs for the last couple of miles back to
Minehead

9 THE HARDY COUNTRY

55 miles (88km) – Dorset
Starting point: Weymouth
OS sheet 194, Bartholomew map 4

The country that Thomas Hardy, poet and novelist, wrote about has changed less than most of England. Dorset is still largely unspoiled despite some disastrous development along the coast. The lanes, rich in flowers during the summer, are a delight for the cyclist. This route links the high downland country with the villages in the valleys and the wild coastline of Chesil Beach. Anyone who wants to extend the tour at the finish could continue south to Portland (see Isle of Portland route).

Weymouth This is Hardy's Budmouth. The town is Georgian with some interesting buildings which have not been entirely ruined by development. Ride along the coast road out to the east to
Preston Turn left off the main road opposite the pub and go on to
Sutton Poyntz There is a duckpond here with some pretty cottages. The mill by the pond is mentioned in *The Trumpet-Major*. If time allows, take the footpath at the end of the village leading up to the downs where a white horse has been carved in the chalk. From the top there are sweeping views across to Portland. Leave Sutton Poyntz by bearing left up a steep hill to a T-junction at the top of the downs. Turn left along Came Down, take the first right, then pass the golf course on the left and enjoy the grand downhill run that lasts halfway to
Dorchester An interesting town with some good teaplaces, a Hardy museum and some quiet, tree-lined walks. Continue north-east on the A35 for nearly 1 mile, then turn right at a sign for
Stinsford Hardy's heart is buried in the churchyard – his ashes are in Westminster Abbey. Continue to a crossroads and go left to
Higher Bockhampton Hardy's birthplace is a picturesque thatched cottage down a track on the right. It is signposted and open to the public as a museum. Continue to the A35, then go right and up Yellowham Hill to
Puddletown A large village with an attractive church. Turn left on to the A354 and then first left again on to the B3142. At a T-junction go right to
Piddletrenthide Go left up a steep hill to the top of Bramble Bottom, and follow the road to
Cerne Abbas This is one of the prettiest villages in the county, but in addition to its cottages it has two major claims to fame. The first is the figure of the Cerne Giant carved in the chalk on Giant Hill. It is an immense carving, and the club he wields is 40yd (36.5m) long. The second feature is the ruins of the abbey. Take a minor road going west, cross the A37 (a Roman road) and continue to
Maiden Newton There is an interesting old mill with arches over the

stream. Continue west along the A356 and after a little more than 1 mile, turn left to

Toller Porcorum This was once a Roman settlement, and its name appears to mean Place of the Pigs. Follow the signs to

Powerstock Nearby are two ancient British village sites and the remains of a royal hunting lodge. The lanes twist and turn through hilly country which seems to have changed little over the centuries. Any of the lanes going west will bring the rider in about 4 miles to

Bridport There is a wide main street where, on market days, stalls are set out. The town was once renowned for the manufacture of hangman's ropes – hence the phrase 'stabbed by a Bridport dagger'. Turn south by the Georgian town hall, where there is a sign to West Bay, but before reaching it, bear left at a sign to

Burton Bradstock The road now runs along Chesil Beach, the graveyard of many ships. The beach between here and Portland is all pebble, with large pebbles at the Portland end which become progressively smaller until they are mere gravel at the western end. Continuing east, the road climbs steeply, still following the coast, and from the summits there are sweeping views up and down the Channel. The swoops and climbs make this both the most demanding and the most rewarding part of the run. There is finally a very steep descent into

Abbotsbury This is another of Dorset's more attractive villages with honey-coloured stone cottages. Just south of the village, St Catherine's Chapel stands at the top of a steep hill – worth the scramble for the views. Follow the sign to

Portesham and make a right turn on to the B3157 (signposted Chickerell). It is worth diverting slightly off the road to visit the village of

Langton Herring which lies to the right of the B3157, rejoining it to pass through

Chickerell and so back to

Weymouth

10 THE BLACKMOOR VALE

22 miles (35km) – Dorset
Starting point: Shaftesbury
OS sheet 183, Bartholomew map 4

The Blackmoor Vale is pure Hardy Country: it is the land of Tess and Angel Clare but despite its literary fame it is little visited and its villages remain backwaters, well off the arterial routes to the coastal resorts. In contrast, Shaftesbury, standing high above the vale, is a windswept spot, bitterly cold in winter. It sits on a great ridge 700ft above sea level, a place of narrow cobbled streets, many so steep that handrails are provided for the safety of pedestrians. To stand on Castle Hill and look out across the vale when a storm is coming up from the west is an experience indeed.

Shaftesbury Leave the town in a south-westerly direction on the road signposted to Marnhull, but be sure to hang on to the brakes until well clear of the town! Down plunges the road for 3 miles to
Stour Row Continue to
Todber and follow the signs to
Marnhull This is Marlott in the Hardy novels, the home of Tess. Nash Court, a little to the north, was given by Henry VIII to Katherine Parr – the wife who survived him. Work north through the lanes, following the signs to
Fifehead Magdalen The lush countryside here is well watered by the River Stour and its tributaries. Take the road out of the village going north, cross the A30 and turn left into
Kington Magna The Norman church is set on the flank of a hill above the village giving a good view from the churchyard. Continue to
Buckhorn Weston Climb out of the village, going due north riding along the ridge of Shave Hill where there are some good views to
Cucklington After the church, turn right to the junction with the B3081 and follow this road to
Gillingham This is the most northerly town in Dorset and 2 miles from Wiltshire and the same distance from the Somerset border. Remain on the B3081 for the 4 miles back to
Shaftesbury

11 THE CERNE GIANT

18 miles (29km) – Dorset
Starting point: Dorchester
OS sheet 194, Bartholomew map 4

The countryside north of Dorchester is an area of gentle hills rising from the valley of the River Frome towards the ridge of high ground running east and west of Cerne Abbas. It is a land remote in history: many of the villages still keep the names by which the Romans knew them, e.g. Toller Porcorum, Toller of the Pigs, but the Romans are relative newcomers to the area. Maiden Castle, the finest prehistoric hill fort in the country, is but a few miles from Dorchester, and life was going on there 4,000 years ago. The hills all around here are littered with the burial mounds of long-forgotten people.

Dorchester The Romans laid out the town's four main streets in the shape of a cross. From the town centre go north on the A37 and after the prison turn off right to
Charminster Continue north for four miles and then turn off left down a minor road signposted to Cerne Abbas. It is a steep, swooping lane, tumbling around the shoulder of Black Hill from Kiddies Bottom and ends in the enchanting village of
Cerne Abbas The figure of the giant is carved on the side of Giant Hill a little to the north of the village. Just how old it is is a matter hotly disputed, and whether he is a fertility symbol, or a god or a warning to neighbouring tribes is something that may be argued over for many years. The giant is not all that Cerne has to offer: the village is full of pretty cottages, many with ornate carving on their beams, and there is the Abbey. Although little of what was once an important ecclesiastical establishment now remains, the gatehouse, with its great bay window and the carved arms of the fifteenth century, are well worth photographing. Leave the town, riding west and cross the A352 staying with this rather hilly lane to
Sydling St Nicholas This pretty spot is typical of the many tucked-away villages the county hides. Continue due south through the village for 3 miles to the junction with the A37. To avoid making the return journey along this busy road, turn left on to it for only ½ mile through the village of
Grimstone turning off right well before the village of Stratton. Take the first left after leaving the A356 and pass through
Bradford Peverell and so along the old Roman road back to
Dorchester

12 DORSET BYWAYS

50 miles (80km) – Dorset
Starting point: Corfe Castle
OS sheets 194 and 195. Bartholomew map 4.

This is a route for lovers of wild, windswept country who do not mind bumping along the occasional bridleway on which the going can be moderately rough. The rewards are sweeping views from hills and clifftops. One note of caution: The route passes through land still used for weapon training, and the roads in this part may not always be open. Signs at the start of the affected area – west of Corfe Castle – clearly state whether these range roads are open, which is usually at

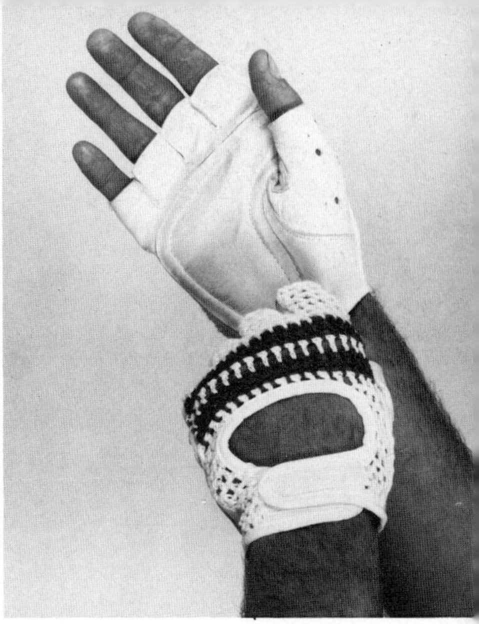

A 'training top' from Peugeot and (*right*) 'track mits', which make riding easier on the hands and give some protection in the event of a fall

Quiet roads can have their problems too . . . these ducks provided an unexpected hazard (*Hamish Smith*)

A quiet track on the South Downs (*Ken Bollingbroke*)

An extract from the 1:50,000 Ordnance Survey map (*Crown copyright reserved*)

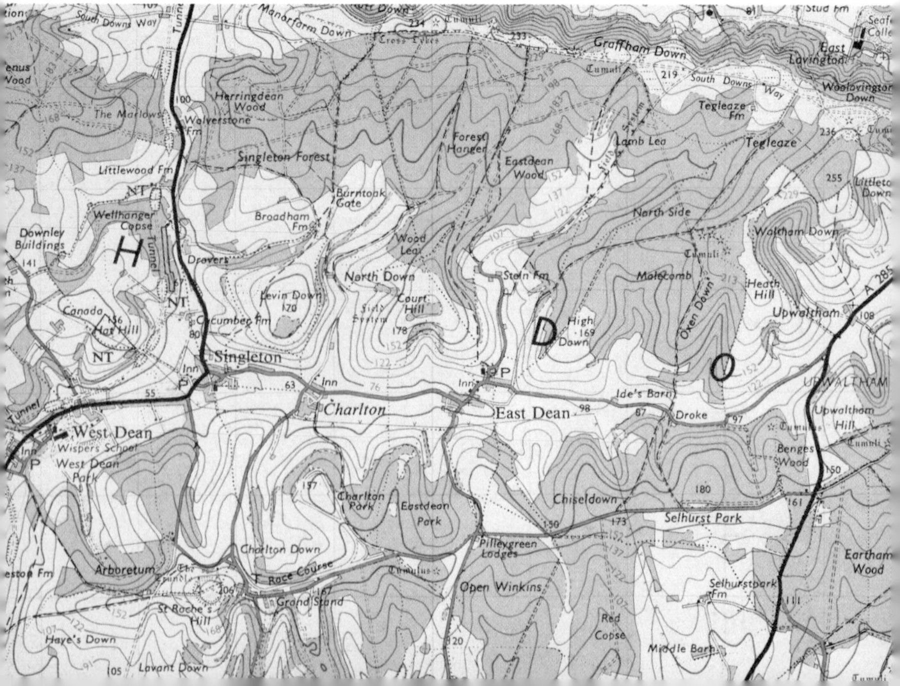

Unsuitable for motors it may be, but this road in Central Wales has some grand views for anyone prepared for a little roughstuff

Youngsters make camp at a rally at Meriden, the centre of England

Evening meal for two cycle-campers

An alternative to camping is to use youth hostels. This one is Tanner's Hatch, in Surrey

(*Above*) This machine is well balanced, though even for a lengthy camping trip it is overloaded. (*Below*) How not to carry camping gear. But at least this machine, seen in Belgium, stood up to the strain!

A support vehicle is a common sight on French rallies

A competitor takes part in a club map-reading competition

Not a bicycle made for three but a tandem with a Rann trailer added to the back for the elder child. The tandem has been adapted to carry the youngest member of the family safely. Mother rode a solo machine behind

This mother doesn't find that a youngster on the back of the cycle slows her down, even when climbing a long hill

A pause for lunch high in the Brecon Beacons of Wales (*Ken Bollingbroke*)

Whether riding alone or with a club, there is always time to pause in the delightful villages of England (*Hamish Smith*)

weekends, but also at other times. Anyone planning to come from some distance could first ring the local police station for information.

Corfe Castle The ruins of the castle dominate the village. From its construction in Norman days to its destruction during the Civil War, it has had a colourful history, and half an hour is well spent wandering around its massive walls. The cottages in the main street that lead to the castle are of stone, and also have stone roofs, an indication of the ferocity of the winter gales that can strike this part of the coast. Riding along the main street in a northerly direction, turn left immediately after the castle. Proceed through the hamlet of

Church Knowle This little road soars and descends over the great Purbeck ridge, ending with a wonderful swoop down Whiteway Hill and so into

East Lulworth a pretty village with a castle, or perhaps more accurately a fortified house as its position would have made it difficult to defend. Retrace a few yards to the entrance to the village and continue to

West Lulworth The famous cove is at the bottom of the hill; though in high summer it is full of cars and trippers it makes an interesting diversion out of season. If you divert to the cove, return to the village and turn west at the signpost to Dagger's Gate. After a mile, Newlands Farm is reached on the left. Take the surfaced track just after the farm, a bridleway which runs due west along the high cliff-land marked on the OS map as The Warren. The byway is bumpy but easily rideable. This is a truly wonderful stretch of country with distant views out to sea. It continues like this for 2 or 3 miles, past White Nothe and Burning Cliff, the last so named because of the oil that seeps through the chalk, occasionally catching fire. Finally a minor road is reached which takes the rider to the A353, and a left turn here brings him to

Osmington The village is pretty with thatched cottages and lies just off the main road. Return to that road and continue west, swooping down a long hill with a white horse cut out of the turf on the right of the road. Brake hard at the village of

Preston and turn right opposite the pub. In ½ mile the rider will reach

Sutton Poyntz Take the right fork at the start of the village and pass the duckpond with its thatched cottages. The watermill near the pond is mentioned in Hardy's *The Trumpet-Major*. Take the narrow lane going left immediately past the pond, then right in a few yards at a T-junction. Soon the road begins to climb steeply, with sweeping views to the south and west, the island of Portland standing out like a long whale in the distance. At the top of the hill a crossroads is reached. Go left, fringing Came Wood, descend a sharp hill and take the first right signposted for the golf club. After the clubhouse, follow the twisting road, which is always interesting, until

Dorchester This is the county town with a museum to the novelist and poet, Thomas Hardy, a regimental museum and a good place for refreshments, even on a Sunday. Leave the town by taking the A35 east, crossing Grey's Bridge. Half a mile after the bridge, make a right turn to

Stinsford Here is the church, with its pretty churchyard where Hardy's heart is buried (his ashes are in Westminster Abbey). Follow the lane east and then north, watching for small signs to Hardy's birthplace at

Higher Bockhampton The cottage which is the writer's birthplace is a pretty thatched structure set in an Old English garden and is open to the public. Continue along the rough track on which the cottage is situated, and into the woods beyond it, following a broad earth track leading north-east, picking up any of the several lanes which then lead to

Puddletown Continue through the village and make a right turn at a signpost to

Tincleton Ride in an easterly direction along the valley of the Frome for 3 miles to

Clouds Hill This was the hideaway and last home of Colonel Lawrence – Lawrence of Arabia. His house is now a museum. There is now an easy descent of 5 miles across heathland to

Wareham from where it is a pleasant ride for the last 4 miles to

Corfe Castle

13 THE ISLE OF PORTLAND

15 miles (24km) – Dorset
Starting point: Weymouth
OS sheet 194, Bartholomew map 4

Portland is not an island in the normal sense of the word, being joined to the mainland by a strip of shingle which is part of Chesil Beach. Anyone expecting this piece of Dorset, jutting out into the Channel, to have the soft character of the rest of the county will be surprised. Portland is stark and desolate with scarcely a tree on it, but its high limestone cliffs give some good views, and when there is a swell running, the sea beats in on them in a white foam. This is an ideal run for an evening, or for an afternoon when there would be plenty of time to visit the lighthouse or merely lie on the clifftops and look at the view.

Weymouth Visit the harbour, which is the best part of a town largely spoiled by too much holiday development. Go over the road bridge across the harbour and follow the signs to
Wyke Regis This is largely a built-up area, though a track can be taken to see the remains of Sandsfoot Castle which overlook the harbour. If visited, retrace to Wyke Regis. Follow the main road on to the strip of shingle connecting Portland to the mainland. In the autumn gales, the sea can break over this road. Portland Harbour is on the left and often holds many naval vessels which are retained in 'mothballs'. As the island is reached, Portland Castle is to the left. It was built by Henry VIII on the site of a Saxon fortification. Make the extremely steep climb (a long, hard push) to
Fortuneswell This is a stark village of sombre stone houses with, nevertheless, grand views across the sea to the west. The graveyard of the church looks out to sea and many seamen have been buried here, some of whom died when their sailing ships were driven on to Chesil Beach, a place feared by sailors as they passed up and down the Channel. Continue along the high ridge of the island to
Easton This is the centre of the island, and around can be seen quarries from which Portland stone has been taken for such buildings as St Paul's Cathedral and University College, London. Continue south along the eastern edge of the island past Church Ope Cove and Freshwater Bay, again with good views across the green turf, to
Southwell The church here was built in memory of those who died when the ship *Avalanche* sank nearby in 1877. One hundred people lost their lives on that stormy night. Take the track down to the coastguard station and lighthouse at
Portland Bill The lighthouse is open to the public and there is a spectacular view from the top. The race can be seen as a mass of turbulent water south of the Bill. Retrace to Southwell and take the road to
Weston and from there back to
Fortuneswell and
Weymouth

14 AROUND POOLE HARBOUR

45 miles (72km) – Dorset
Starting point: Bournemouth
OS sheet 195, Bartholomew maps 4 and 5

The green whaleback hills which appear on the skyline as soon as one cycles south-west from Bournemouth form the Isle of Purbeck, which, as so often is the case with the word 'island', is nothing of the sort. Purbeck is an island only in the sense that it is bounded on the south and east by the sea and on its northern flank by Poole Harbour. Were it not for the existence of Swanage, with its holiday crowds, Purbeck might have been a forgotten corner of England. As it is, the roads there are still far less congested than almost anywhere else along the coastal strip to the east, and the coastal scenery, designated an Area of Outstanding Natural Beauty, can challenge even the best in Devon and Cornwall.

Bournemouth Follow the signs out of this very congested town to the Sandbanks ferry. For the last mile before the ferry, which is about 3 miles from the town centre, there are good views of Poole Harbour and Brownsea Island, where Baden-Powell held the first Scout camp. In the holiday season, there will be a long queue of cars and coaches waiting to board the ferry. As a cyclist, you are a privileged person on small ferries. Ride to the head of the queue, pay the few pence demanded and push your machine on as a foot passenger. You will be far away on the other side when the motorists are still queuing. The ferry arrives at South Haven Point. Follow the road across attractive heathland to

Studland If time permits, walk down to Old Harry Rocks and then retrace. A mile out of Studland, bear left and follow the signs to

Swanage This is a much prettier seaside resort than many along the South Coast. If you have time, visit nearby Peveril Point, and Tilly Whim Caves, the latter about 1 mile from the town. From the centre of Swanage, take the A351, signposted to Wareham, but after 1½ miles turn left through

Langton Matravers and after another mile, left again by a group of small quarries near the summit of the hill where there is a sign to

Worth Matravers This is a most attractive village, happily little known, where you can get tea near the post office; alternatively, there is an old whitewashed pub just north of the village, called the Square and Compasses, which was a favourite haunt of the painter Augustus John. From the centre of the village, take the footpath signposted to Winspit Cove, humping the bike over a stile. (In muddy weather, this section can be omitted as the route eventually returns to Worth, but the scenery along the coast is so spectacular that it should be included if at all possible.) There are several more stiles to be negotiated, but the track is rideable with care. On reaching the cove, pause to watch the sea breaking on the rocks, then push the bike up a path to the right. This is steep and it requires a little ingenuity to get the bike up, but once on top there is a path running along the clifftop with magnificent views of the coast. It is not difficult to ride and, being a few yards in from the cliff edge, is safe if care is taken to avoid any places where there have been landslips due to coastal erosion. The coastguards are quick to post warning notices where there is danger. Follow the path past the coastguard station and turn right on to a stony road going inland. Follow this until it joins a lane, and turn right to return to Worth Matravers. Leave the town by taking the left fork near the Square and Compasses, and after 1 mile turn left on to the B3069. There is a grand view here of Corfe Castle strategically filling a gap in the hills. Many people would rank it as one of the finest views in Dorset. Continue through

Kingston taking great care on the sharp bends on the swoop down to join the main road (A351). Go left to

Corfe Castle The castle is worth visiting (or you can merely walk around the ramparts) and the town is a good place in which to obtain tea. Leave by the A351 signposted to Wareham, and if time allows, after 2 miles turn right and ride the 5 miles over heathland to the village of

Arne This is a little-known spot with some good views of Poole Harbour. Retrace to the A351 and continue to

Wareham Yet another attractive Dorset town. Remain on the main road through

Lytchett Minster to

Poole and

Bournemouth

Southern England

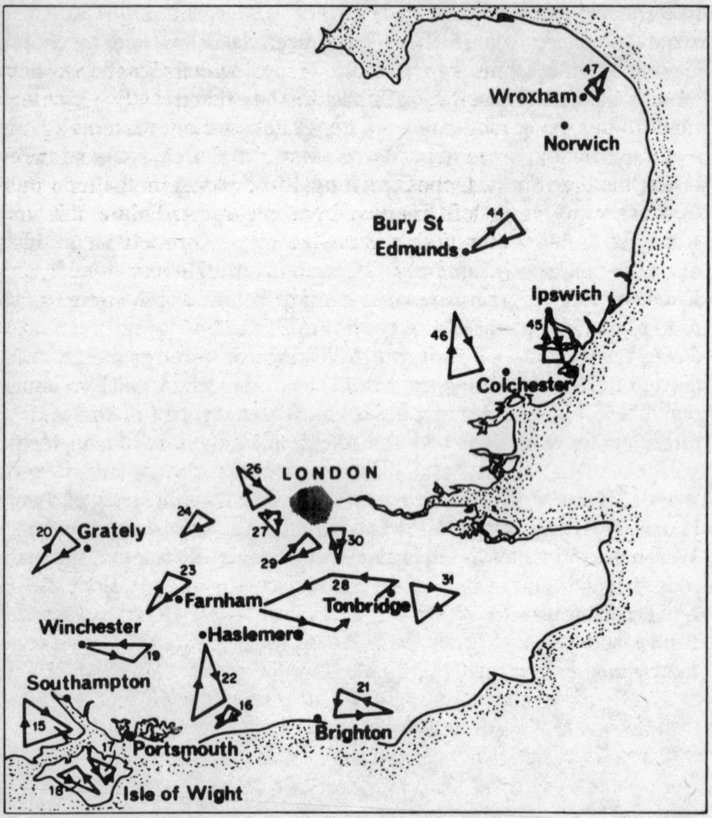

15 SOLENT TOWNS AND THE NEW FOREST

25 miles (40km) – Hampshire
Starting point: Brockenhurst
OS sheet 196, Bartholomew map 5

This ride, which could equally well be started from Lymington or Beaulieu, takes the cyclist around some of the most popular yachting harbours in the south of England, including Bucklers Hard, where Nelson's *Agamemnon* was built, and later some of the Mulberry harbours used during World War II. It is a short ride to allow for the pace of the potterer. The scenery is varied with coastal inlets, attractive towns and bridleways through the forest, which is always best enjoyed at a slow pace. *Note* Much of the New Forest is Crown land with no legal rights of way. Any instructions from foresters should be complied with by cyclists.

Brockenhurst This is more of a large residential village than a town. Leave Brockenhurst station on the A337 by riding towards Lymington, and take the second road on the left after the level-crossing where there is a signpost saying 'church'. Pass the church and continue for a few hundred yards. Opposite a long, low building on the right there is a bridleway going left, marked by a fingerpost. Follow this until it reaches a T-junction with a gravelled road. Turn left on to this and continue along it, ignoring two turn-offs to Royden Manor on the left. On reaching a crossroads, go straight on along the road to

Boldre The incumbent of the church from 1777 to his death in 1804 was William Gilpin, a naturalist, sometimes called the Gilbert White of the New Forest. Opposite the Red Lion Inn, turn left and then immediately right on to Boldre Lane. After a little under 1 mile, at a T-junction, turn left on to the road to Lymington. Go straight over a set of traffic lights, taking the Bournemouth road, and follow the A337 where it turns left and is signposted to the town centre.

Lymington The largest and most attractive town in the region. The abundance of creeks once made it a thriving town for smugglers, but now it is firmly in the hands of the yachtsmen. Ride along the main street and down a slope to a T-junction with Gosport Street, then follow the Isle of Wight ferry signs. On reaching the ferry car park, continue on the road which passes to the left of it, go on for 2½ miles and, just after crossing a cattle grid, take a right fork signposted to Sowley and Bucklers Hard. Continue to follow the signs to

Bucklers Hard The village consists of a broad street of cottages leading down to the river; a picturesque and often-photographed spot, with a maritime museum. Follow the signs to

Beaulieu The abbey and Lord Montagu's motor museum, with its souvenir shops and restaurants, are too well known to require further mention. Leave Beaulieu on the B3054 by riding towards Lymington, and where the road forks with the B3055 to Brockenhurst, take the right fork. After 50yd, turn right into Furzey Lane. After passing the last house on the left, called Forest Heath, turn half left on to a track and enter

Hawkhill Inclosure At the top of the rise, fork left and at the foot of a downslope, turn off to the right. At a crossroads with a wooden tower at the corner, turn right, then leave Hawkhill Inclosure and enter an unnamed inclosure. Turn left at a T-junction which looks rather like a crossroads because of an earth track opposite. On leaving the inclosure, turn left and then take the first right to enter New Copse Inclosure. Go straight ahead at two sets of crossroads and on reaching the motor road, turn right on to it. Turn left at the junction, following the Brockenhurst road over the bridge and, after 1 mile, arrive back at

Brockenhurst

16 CHICHESTER AND ITS HARBOUR

9 miles (14km) – Sussex
OS sheet 197, Bartholomew map 5
Starting point: Chichester

This short ride is unashamedly an excuse to visit the delightful harbour and yachting centre of Bosham. In summer – and this is essentially a ride for warm, sunny days – Bosham swarms with people enjoying themselves in boats; there is a collection of little shops selling craftwork, books and, of course, sailing gear. Tea can easily be obtained there.

Chichester Anyone attending the theatre, perhaps on a Saturday evening, might wish to spend the Sunday morning before returning home trying this ride. A shopper bike packed into a car boot would be quite adequate. Spend a little time in Chichester and then ride out in a north-westerly direction on the B2178 so avoiding the shorter but very busy main road. Stay on this road to

East Ashling then turn left and in ½ mile you are in

West Ashling Continue through the village, pass Bosham station and cross the A259. The road now passes between attractive houses with large gardens, and the number of boat trailers drawn up alongside the roadway gives some indication that the harbour is just ahead. In moments the rider is in

Bosham Ride down the village street to the harbour which is one of the oldest in England. The Danes made many raids on it, and it was from here that King Harold set off for Normandy. There is a legend that King Canute's daughter is buried in the church, having been drowned nearby. Certainly the church should not be missed. It stands just back from the water surrounded by trees, and the gravestones tell of some of the tragedies that befell mariners in previous centuries. There is a large area of grass between the church and the harbour which makes an ideal picnic spot from which one can indulge in

people-watching. When the scene palls, return up the village street to the A259, go right on it and one is soon back in
Chichester

17 THROUGH THE INLAND VILLAGES

27 miles (43km) – Isle of Wight
Starting point: Cowes
OS sheet 196, Bartholomew map 5

The problem for the cyclist on the Isle of Wight, particularly during the summer, is to avoid overcrowded holiday resorts. Both this route and its companion, which follows coastal roads, keep well clear of icecream parlours and shops selling seaside rock; those wishing to find just such attractions will have no difficulty. The inland route is through quiet country with picturesque villages, and it climbs one steep ridge of hills from which there are superb views.

Cowes The run starts from East Cowes; anyone arriving at West Cowes will find that there is a ferry connecting the two halves of the town. Take the minor road to the right of the A3021 and follow it round to
Whippingham Visit the church which was restored to a design by Prince Albert. He and Queen Victoria attended services there when they were at nearby Osborne. Cross the A3021, follow the road around, and then cross the A3054 to
Wootton Common Go left at the crossroads, and in 2 miles reach
Robin Hill Country Park Continue to the A3056, go south along it for ½ mile, then left off the main road to
Merstone On reaching the A3020 turn left on to the main road to
Godshill This village, with its thatched cottages and pretty gardens, is one of the most visited on the island. The fourteenth-century church is interesting. Continue east on the A3020, and after 1 mile reach
Sandford Go left here and cross the A3056 to
Newchurch This is another pretty village with thatched cottages and neat gardens. Continue through the village and, after crossing a stream, ride on for 1 mile to a T-junction below Mersley Down. Go left, then double back right to a viewpoint which gives one of the best views on the island. (It's a bit of an effort to ride up but worth it.) Continue on, then take the next left and in a little under 2 miles go left again to
Havenstreet This was at one time a haven on Wootton Creek, which then extended further inland. There is a steam railway centre here. Follow the lane round to the left for about 3 miles to

Wootton Common Go straight over the crossroads and join the A3054. Turn left and ride along the main road towards Cowes, bearing right on to the A3021. On the right, shortly before the end of the run is

Osborne House The state and private apartments of Queen Victoria are open to the public. Many of the rooms have been retained exactly as they where when Queen Victoria died there in 1901. It is then a short ride back to

East Cowes

18 WEST TO THE NEEDLES

32 miles (51km) – Isle of Wight
Starting point: Yarmouth
OS sheet 196, Bartholomew map 5

Some of the most spectacular scenery on the island is to be found in the extreme western corner, where the Needles, capped by a lighthouse, jut out into the Channel. It is often worth leaving the bike for a while and scrambling down to the sea, particularly at Alum Bay, which is famous for its coloured sands.

Yarmouth Take the A3054 west over the bridge which crosses the River Yar to

Totland In the right weather conditions, there are dramatic sunsets across Totland Bay. Take the B3322 to

Alum Bay The coloured cliffs are at their best after heavy rain when the surfaces are freshly exposed. It has become a fashion to buy or fill paperweights, or simply phials, with the widely differing colours of the sands. Continuing west, you reach the coastguard station and a viewpoint on the landward side of the Needles. Although this corner of the island can become crowded in the season, it is a fascinating spot and should not be missed. Return on the B3322 for ½ mile, and then fork right to

Freshwater Bay The coastal stretch between the Needles and Freshwater Bay includes Tennyson's Down, where the poet frequently walked claiming that 'the air on the Downs is worth sixpence a pint'. Freshwater Bay is not improved by some rather characterless modern building, but down on the seashore the air is clear and there are caves on both sides of the bay to be explored at low tide. North of the bay, there is an area of marshland where the River Yar rises, and this provides a habitat for large numbers of birds and insects. From Freshwater Bay, join the A3055, going east, and in 3 miles turn left to

Brook At nearby Brook House there is a tree planted by Garibaldi, the Italian patriot. There is a nature trail nearby. Turn right on to the B3399 to

Mottistone where there is a Tudor manor house. Go through the picturesque village to

Brighstone A pretty village which has a church with a massive tower where the man who was to become Bishop Samuel Wilberforce, opponent of Darwin, was once rector. Continue to

Shorwell which lies in a valley on the south side of the chalk downs. The village has thatched cottages, and there are several Elizabethan manor houses in the area. Take the B3323 north to

Carisbrooke While the village is charming, the main point of interest is the castle which stands on a wooded hill to the east of the town. Carisbrooke Castle dates back to the twelfth century. In the centre of the fortifications is the Governor's House, once occupied by the Governor of the Isle of Wight and now the castle museum. The castle saw action in the Civil War, and Charles I was a frequent visitor in happier days. Retrace to the village and take the road going north by the post office. At the A3054 go left, and in 1 mile go right and then first left to

Newtown Visit the Old Town Hall, a building which indicates the importance which the village once had. The harbour was used in Roman times, and much later was deep enough to contain a squadron of warships. But over the centuries it silted up and is now a nature reserve. Take the minor road signposted to Shalfleet. On reaching the A3054 go right into

Shalfleet Turn left, taking the byroad to

Wellow and

Yarmouth

19 THE VALLEYS OF MEON AND ITCHEN

38 miles (61km) – Hampshire
Starting point: Winchester
OS sheet 185, Bartholomew maps 8 and 5

Hampshire is not a county which calls for superlatives to describe its scenery, rather it is the charm of its meadows beside small rivers, the warmth of the old red brick houses seen on a summer's evening or its quiet villages well off the main roads. This route passes through just such country and includes perhaps the loveliest of the Hampshire villages, East Meon.

Winchester This is a town that delights in its river, the Itchen, a clear, sparkling brook that splits into a number of channels. There is so much to see in Winchester, particularly the cathedral and its close, the Great Hall and the Round Table and the City Mill. There is an information centre in the main street. Start from near the youth hostel, crossing the old bridge, and ride south-east along a minor road, cross the A33 and St Catherine's Hill will be on your right. It is 2 miles to

Morestead In a little under 2 miles, a crossroads is reached, turn left, passing Longwood House on the right, and in a further 2 miles reach

Lane End Down This is a crossroads, where turn right and remain on this little road for 5 miles to

Warnford Here we join the River Meon. Turn left on to the A32 to

West Meon Although the village is not as attractive as its better-known neighbour, East Meon, it has some interesting corners and cricket buffs may be interested to see the grave of Thomas Lord, the original owner of Lord's Cricket Ground in the churchyard. Take the minor road running east along the river valley signposted to

East Meon The downs rise steeply above the village, and it is on the lower slopes of this rise that the famous Norman church stands. Across the road from the church is the Court House, a Tudor structure, but it is in the simpler buildings that lies the charm of East Meon for it is a village of unselfconscious beauty. Retrace your route for a little more than a mile and turn right up the hill past Bereleigh House for 2 miles to join the A272 where turn left and remain on the road until the signposted turn-off to

Cheriton The village is best known for the Civil War battle that was fought here in 1644, and the actual battlefield is a mile east of the village. It can be reached by a track starting from the end of the village called Northend. Continue for ½ mile from this point and then turn left at Cheriton Mill, following the course of the Itchen to

Tichborne The place is little more than a hamlet with thatched cottages and an old rectory but has an engagingly simple church which has escaped Victorian restoration. Continue along the course of the Itchen, crossing the A31 to

Itchen Stoke and then

Itchen Abbas Stay with the road through

Martyr Worthy and

Abbot's Worthy to rejoin the main road for the last 2 miles to

Winchester

20 AROUND STONEHENGE

24 miles (38km) – Wiltshire
Starting point: Grately
OS sheet 184, Bartholomew map 8

The little station at Grately is well served by trains from London, and is an ideal hopping-off place for a ride around the high Wiltshire plain which can include Stonehenge. Part of this route is over broad grassy paths which can become muddy, but the views make it all worth while.

Grately If descending from the London train, leave the station and cross over the railway bridge (going north-west), then take the first road on the left. At a crossroads, the way ahead appears to be but a field track. Press on along it and it will soon be seen that it is a perfectly adequate trackway and in fact is marked on the Ordnance Survey map as Portway, the Roman road. Its course runs directly beside the railway line for 4 miles with grand views to the right. When a metalled road is reached, turn right on to it and enter the village of
Idmiston Bear left in the village for
Porton Turn right at the crossroads in the village and cross the A38 continuing until the A345 is reached after 2½ miles where turn right on to the main road and continue to
Amesbury In addition to being an attractive town in its own right, there is an information centre here which provides leaflets on Stonehenge. Continue to the traffic roundabout on the A303 and turn left on to it. Stonehenge soon becomes visible in the fork formed by the A303 and the A344. Take the right-hand fork (the A344) for the entrance to
Stonehenge There is an admission charge. After visiting Stonehenge, retrace along the A303, past the point where you emerged from Amesbury and make a long climb up while the view opens out to the left. Turn off the main road, to the right at a signpost to
Cholderton Follow this road back to
Grately

21 A TASTE OF THE SOUTH DOWNS

28 miles (45km) – Sussex
Starting point: Lewes
OS sheets 198 and 199, Bartholomew map 6

The windy uplands along which the South Downs Way runs are normally seen as the province of the walker, but that long distance footpath is in fact a bridleway on which the cyclist can also disport himself. This route gives just a taste of its delights but also shows something of the lovely villages which nestle under the range of hills.

Lewes One of Sussex's more interesting towns, full of odd corners with the South Downs rising all around it. The grey and romantic ruin of the Norman castle make an excellent photograph. Leave the town by pedalling north on the A26. After a mile, go right on to the B2192 and after another mile go right again at the signpost to Glynde. The famous opera house of Glyndebourne is on the left in a fairy-tale setting. Wagner, heard in an English country house surrounded by parkland, is a musical experience that defies comparison. Continue to the village of

Glynde The countryside here is rolling and gentle which gives no real trouble to even the least energetic rider. This is the home of the South Down sheep, first bred near this village by John Ellman in the late eighteenth century, and indeed he was also a social reformer who turned Glynde into a model village. Pass over the level-crossing and then bear right where you will soon reach the A27. Cross directly over it, on to a rough but surfaced byway climbing steeply between some cottages. Now begins a delightful climb, a little over a mile long, but it is no penance to push the cycle up it as this gives more time to admire the view to the west which unfolds steadily. At the summit, the surfaced road ends and there are wooden gates to left and right marked with the acorn emblem which identifies the South Downs Way. Take the gate on the left along a track which can be ridden without too much trouble in dry weather. From a height of almost 600ft, the bridleway climbs past Firle Beacon and then descends to the valley (prepare for some bumpy riding) to finish in the centre of

Alfriston The church of St Andrews here is known as the Cathedral of the Downs, but the village is better known generally for the two half-timbered pubs which face each other across the main street, and for the old grocer's shop where the goods are displayed much as they were at the turn of the century. Alfriston is a peaceful place, much frequented by walkers, but life was not always so serene as this was a well-known smuggling centre and many a dark deed was done as casks were rowed up the Cuckmere River from the nearby sea. Go north on to the B2108, cross the A27 and after 3 miles take a lane on the left to

Chalvington, then

Ripe and

Laughton The rider is now on the B2124; turn left and follow this road through

Ringmer and so back to

Lewes

22 THE SOUTH DOWNS

50 miles (80km) – West Sussex
Starting point: Haslemere (just inside Surrey)
OS sheets 186 and 197, Bartholomew maps 5 and 8

A hilly run with some magnificent panoramic views, equal to anything else in southern England. It is a fairly tough 50 miles, and a whole day may be needed. Have some low gears, or be prepared for plenty of walking, but the effort will be well rewarded. Chichester, the most southerly point on the run, could easily be used as an alternative starting point. The route crosses the South Downs, giving wonderful views of them from both sides, and explores many of the delightful villages that nestle in Belloc's 'great hills of the South Country'. It is a route that is probably at its best in the early summer, when the cloudscapes are seen to advantage and when the thickly wooded areas around Haslemere are just coming into full leaf.

Haslemere Leave the town by going east on the B2131, and after ½ mile turn right, up Haste Hill, at the signpost to Black Down. From the top there is a series of delightful downhill swoops along lanes which pass through thickly wooded country with tantalizing views away to the left. Turn right at the T-junction to

Lodsworth The village has some attractive half-timbered houses, and a seat under the chestnut tree on the village green makes a good picnic spot. The church is worth a visit, with its unusual mixture of old and very modern. At the A272, just south of the village, turn left and then immediately right, to

Selham A delightful tiny church includes some Victorian windows which bear the arms of the Plantagenets, and some of the medieval dukes and kings – the whim of a rector who believed that his wife, and therefore his children, were descended from such lineage. Continue on along the lanes to the junction with the A285, then turn right for

Duncton Go through the village and climb Duncton Hill. At the summit there is a viewpoint with extensive views to the north-west. Descend the hill, and in 2 miles take the single-track lane on the right, signposted to East Dean. From the lane there are open views of wooded downland; it is a most picturesque area with fine cloudscapes and plenty of attractive picnic spots.

East Dean The village has a duckpond with willow tree. Turn left and go along the lanes for 4 miles to the A285 where a right turn will bring you to

Chichester The cathedral is one of the main features of this historic town, its spire seeming to pop up everywhere. The city is a combination of medieval, Georgian and modern architecture, and Roman work can still be seen in the medieval walls. The four main streets follow the pattern of the roads that existed in the time of the Romans. An example of good modern architecture is the Festival Theatre.

(For anyone who wants to cut the route short and is prepared to leave out Chichester, this can be achieved by riding west from East Dean, through Singleton and West Dean to the B2141 north-west of Chichester and rejoining the route there.)

Leaving Chichester, take the A286 going north, and after Mid Lavant bear left on to the B2141 to

Chilgrove There are wide views again here. Continue on, and a mile before South Harting, at the top of a hill marked 1 in 8, take a right turn into a lane. The lane plunges down, making it a spectacular descent through a series of twists and turns (tandem riders beware!) to a crossroads, at which point a right turn leads to

Elsted Here there is a Saxon church, described in a pamphlet within the building as 'having no special claim to fame, just being one of many small churches which enrich the English countryside'. It is a delightfully simple building and well worth a visit. Carry on to the A272, cross it, and you are in

Iping There is an attractive bridge over a small river, which is in fact the River Rother. Turn right at the sign for Woolbeding and follow the lanes to

Fernhurst This has brought you to a main road (the A286) which can be followed by turning left up a very steep hill for the last few miles back to

Haslemere The main point of interest is the museum, which by its attractive exhibitions could be a model for other similar institutions. Joseph Whymper, the Victorian water-colour artist, lived here – he was the father of Whymper the mountaineer. In a cottage on nearby Shottermill Common, George Eliot wrote much of *Middlemarch*, and Tennyson had a house not far away at Lurgashall. Music lovers will be familiar with the Haslemere Festival of Music held each year.

23 DOWNLAND VILLAGES

18 miles (29km) – Surrey and Hampshire
Starting point: Farnham
OS sheet 186, Bartholomew map 9

Farnham is within easy rail reach of London and is an excellent little town in its own right in which to spend half a day. This ride links some of the pretty villages which lie to its west, and combined with some hours spent in Farnham would make a grand day out for anyone wanting to get away from the big city.

Farnham The mellowed red brick of the town with its Georgian houses and shops gives it rather a sleepy air, despite the heavy traffic which enters it. Farnham has always been a meeting place for travellers as it stands at the 'crossroads' between the west of England and Canterbury. The present day traveller will want to see the castle, one of the best examples of twelfth-century domestic castles in the country. It is approached by climbing the hill called Castle Street, the charming architecture of this street forming a pleasant introduction to the old fortress. The market, which is held on Fridays, was originally held in this street but now largely takes place in a square just off it. Ride out of the town by travelling south-west along the main street and in ½ mile take a right turn signposted to Crondal. At first the road is rather disappointing with uninteresting houses, but that soon changes. Do not take the next Crondal turn, but bear left at the sign to

Long Sutton You are now in Hampshire, and every bit of this part of the county is studded with brick and timber cottages, mostly restored by those with the income and enthusiasm to keep them up. The swoop down that the cyclist will have just made to reach this village is one of the delights of east Hampshire and the village itself maintains the interest. Try not to miss the little church, built in the thirteenth century and still largely unchanged. Turn right in the village, just after the church, skirting the east side of a military airfield and follow the lane to

Odiham Those who love quiet corners will linger here for it is a delightful little town, the sort of place one feels has been happily missed by the motorist. There is a Tudor vicarage and many other buildings of great age. If time permits, the village of North Warnborough is only a mile away to the north-west. Just outside it is the remains of the castle from where King John left to seal the Magna Carta. If this diversion is taken, return to Odiham. Retrace along the road by which you entered the town for about ¼ mile, then turn left and shortly after right, on a lane which passes Rake Farm, and watching for signposts, follow its twists and turns to

Crondal Seek out the church: the avenue of limes leading up to its door make it well worth the visit. In the vestry is a chest, believed to date from 1400, made of oak, iron bindings and leather. Follow the land south-east from the village, so avoiding the main road, and the rider will soon be back in

Farnham

24 A THAMES VALLEY DIVERSION

22 miles (35km) – Oxfordshire and Buckinghamshire
Starting point: Henley on Thames
OS sheet 175, Bartholomew map 9

The area north of Henley, among the lower slopes of the Chiltern Hills, provides attractive wooded scenery; it is particularly splendid in the autumn when the beech leaves are golden, or in the spring. This ride has been planned for anyone looking for a pleasant summer evening run, or a lazy afternoon. It includes a surprising variety of scenery from shady woods to the high pastures near ancient Grim's Ditch, and from almost forgotten bridleways to main roads.

Henley Leave the town by taking the main road (the A4155) southwards. Pass the approach to the railway station, which will be on the left, and ½ mile further on turn right at a fingerpost to Harpsden. Continue to

Harpsden Court There is an ivy-clad ornate stone gateway, which is worth pausing at and possibly photographing, and also a church. Continue along a pleasant lane to

Sonning Common There is a duckpond here, conveniently opposite the Butcher's Arms, making it a good place for a picnic. Cross the main road and follow the minor roads towards Stoke Row. At the Unicorn pub, take the narrow Colmore Lane which runs by the side of the inn. There are interesting flint and brick barns and cottages along here. Soon, the lane becomes a track and twists through the woods. The route can be muddy after rain but is always rideable and very pretty. After 1 mile, a tarmac road is reached at a T-junction. Turn left, and after another ½ mile, go right at a spot marked on the Ordnance Survey map as Witheridge Hill and continue towards Nettlebed. The lane soon becomes a track banked by high hedges which in summer are a mass of wild flowers. The track is stony, but at least this means that it does not become muddy except after very heavy rain! A T-junction is soon reached, and a sign proclaims that the lane you have just navigated is 'English Lane – no through motor road'. At the T-junction, a path leads straight ahead to Grim's Ditch. If you wish to visit this old earthwork, lock the bike and later retrace. Take the right arm of the junction and continue into

Nuffield The parish church is worth a visit, and a sign there says 'Water tap on church wall', a thoughtful message for a hot day. You are now on a high, windy hill. Continue through the village to the junction with the A423, then turn right and almost immediately left. Strictly, this is a diversion as the route will in any case return to the

A423, but there is such a delightful dog-leg of lanes that it is well worth making that left turn to Huntercome End, then turning right at the T-junction where there is a sign to

Nettlebed The highlight of this village of attractive Georgian and Victorian houses is the large kiln, for Nettlebed was the centre of the brickmaking industry for the area from at least 1365. Products from the kiln (open, admission free) include the bricks for Wallingford Castle and tiles that can be seen in the walls and roofs on many local houses. Take the A423 towards Henley, but to avoid the rather monotonous ride, turn right after 2 miles at the sign to

Broadplat There are more attractive old houses here. Follow the signposted lane back to

Henley on Thames

25 THE THAMES VALLEY

35 miles (56km) – Berkshire and Buckinghamshire
Starting point: Windsor
OS sheet 175, Bartholomew map 9

In the towns of Windsor and Eton alone there is enough to occupy anyone for many a happy hour. Add in some delightful scenery and the River Thames and all the ingredients are there for a wonderful cycle-touring area.

Windsor Visit the castle, go to the Guildhall and walk the narrow streets of the town. Leaving the town from the castle gate, turn right downhill, then left down River Street, following the Eton signs. Dismount at the pedestrian thoroughfare of Thames Street (on the left) and push the bike along it and across the river; there are good views on both sides of the bridge. Once across it, you are in

Eton The street straight ahead is lined with antique shops. Pedal along it to the buildings of Eton College (open to the public at certain times) on both sides of the road. In the centre of the town turn left at the traffic lights on to the road signposted to

Dorney Ride through the village and turn left at a signpost to Dorney Reach. Pass the Tudor manor house of Dorney Court and visit the tucked-away Dorney Church, which is thirteenth century and has an unusual seventeenth-century gallery. Peacocks from the neighbouring Court often wander around the churchyard. Continue north along the road, go over the motorway and cross the A4. At a T-junction, go left and at the next T-junction, where the B476 is reached, turn right on to that road. (If desired, divert left for 1 mile to Taplow for refreshments and then retrace.) Pass the Canadian Memorial Hospital on your left, and shortly after turn left at a sign for Bourne End and Marlow. Pass (or visit) Cliveden, a National Trust house (open). Next comes an interesting 1 in 8 descent where the road runs under a canopy of trees (care is needed on the S-bends). There are good views to the left. Take a left turn into

Bourne End Ride along the A4155 towards Marlow. After 1½ miles, turn left on to a minor road to

Little Marlow This is a village usually missed by the motorist, for it is not on the road to anywhere, yet it is a most attractive spot with pretty gardens and large, shady trees. Leave the village by the Queen's Head pub, taking a wide public footpath alongside a high brick wall (the only way out of the village apart from retracing). Cross the first narrow lane and go right at a T-junction where the path meets a surfaced lane. Push through a small wooden gate on the left, after a few hundred yards, giving access to a dual carriageway which leads straight into

Marlow This gracious town, with a large ornamental bridge over the Thames and pathways along the river, is a good place for refreshments, having plenty of teashops. Leave the town by crossing the bridge and ride through

Bisham Turn right on to the dual carriageway of the A404 to

Burchett's Green Continue to the T-junction and turn right on to the A4 for a few hundred yards, then take the first left, which is called Bottle Lane and is signposted to Shottesbrooke. The lane is delightfully quiet after the past 2 miles of busy roads. Ride over a railway bridge, and ½ mile after that there is a flint and brick cottage on the right looking like a chapel. At the side of the cottage there is a pathway through an avenue of limes. Go through, and after ½ mile of track a small manor house appears on the right with a surprisingly large church next to it. The church was built in 1337, and one memorial to a naval captain tells of his battles with pirates in the South China Sea. This is an idyllic spot with glimpses into the manor house garden from the churchyard. On leaving the church, continue along what is now a well-surfaced track, past a small lake on the left, and rejoin the road. Here, follow the B3024 through

Paley Street and so back to

Windsor

26 THAMES DELIGHT

30 miles (47km) Buckinghamshire and Berkshire

Starting point: Marlow

OS sheet 175, Bartholomew map 9

This is a perfect ride for a summer's day; it may lack dramatic countryside but instead it has a charm associated with cottages, old pubs, stately parkland and the ever-near River Thames with its colourful display of boats and boating people. The route has been planned so that the prevailing westerly wind is likely to be behind the cyclist on the straight, exposed stretch of the Drift Road along which cattle were once herded to the London markets. To have the wind in your face on that 3-mile stretch is purgatory!

Marlow This is a town which seems to 'belong' naturally to the Thames; along its banks are quiet grassy walkways where pleasure craft moor and which make pleasant picnic spots. Shops in the town sell boating gear and walking sticks and there is a peaceful feeling about its streets despite the traffic that throngs there in summer. It is also a good place for finding teashops open, even on a Sunday. Leave the town by riding south over the ornamental bridge and follow the signs to

Bisham then stay beside the river to

Hurley There is a grand old half-timbered pub here called the Old Bell. Ride through the village and turn right on to the A423 and after 1½ miles turn left off the main road at the hamlet of Rosehill following the sign to

Warren Row Proceed on through pleasant wooded countryside to

Knowl Hill and turn right down the A4 to

Hare Hatch The busy road is left behind here and the cyclist is soon again on a quiet lane as he turns left, following a sign to

Waltham St Lawrence This is a truly delightful village with a huge tree outside the village pub which is the perfect place for a pint with the cycle left alongside the seat under the tree. The village church is beside the pub, well worth a visit in itself, and there are some interesting little lanes and cottages behind the church. Continue south through the village, cross the B3024 and the road will swing gently left, crossing the M4. The cyclist is now on the Drift Road, one of the old ways along which cattle were herded to London. The wide grass verges which still remain remind us of the grazing that took place during those slow journeys. The road is almost dead straight for 3 miles, at which point turn left at a sign to

Fifield Ride on, crossing the A308, rejoining the Thames at

Monkey Island The road recrosses the M4 and the cyclist is then in

Bray Again, this is a very pretty spot and worth the odd half hour spent exploring. Continue north on the B3028. Avoid being drawn into the centre of Maidenhead by going right on to the A4 and then left on to the A4094 alongside the Thames. Continue to

Cookham The main road continues back to Marlow, but a much better route is to turn left in Cookham at the sign to Cookham Dean and pass to the south of

Winter Hill For anyone with time and energy to spare, there is a road up the hill which gives grand views to the north. If this is taken, retrace and then continue on the minor road going west which passes under the A404, so returning to

Marlow

27 ROYAL WINDSOR

10 miles (16km) Berkshire
Starting point: Windsor
OS sheet 175, Bartholomew map 9

Even a 'shopper' bike could make this trip which could be a good introduction to anyone new to the sport of cycle-touring for, while it is short on miles it is long on interest. Basically, it is a ride through Windsor Great Park, happily traffic-free, with some good distant views. The ride takes in the meadows at Runnymede and the Kennedy Memorial. There are plenty of teaplaces nearby.

Windsor The town is dominated by its grey castle with its ceremonial guardsmen in scarlet tunics and busbies. It is well worth visiting, or if time does not allow, at least wander around the narrow twisting streets and enjoy the quaint shops. Starting from the castle, ride south (away from Eton) and at the large traffic roundabout at the edge of town take the A332 (the Bracknell road) for ½ mile to

Queen Anne's Gate This is the entrance to Windsor Great Park and is easily recognized by the prominent car park on the opposite side of the road. You are now mercifully free of traffic noise as you cycle along Queen Anne's Way for 1½ miles, turning left at a collection of buildings known as the Village and passing the base of a hill on the summit of which is an equestrian statue to King George III. It is worth dismounting and clambering up to the statue for the view along The Long Walk which ends with the castle in the background. Continue the pleasant ride through the parkland until

Bishopsgate is reached. There is a tempting pub just outside the gate. Here, we leave the park and continue through

Englefield Green on to the A328 following this road north to its junction with the A308 on the banks of the Thames. We can now turn right remaining alongside the river. The Kennedy Memorial soon appears on the right and is well signposted. It is best to leave the cycle safely locked at the entrance and wander around on foot. On

the opposite side of the road, the river is fringed with meadows which are open to the public. These are the meadows of
Runnymede so famous for the sealing of the Magna Carta by King John. Magna Carta Island is visible here but the land is private. After spending some time in this delightful spot, retrace along the A308. The road crosses The Long Walk near the castle and so gives us a second view, this time from the opposite direction. The rider is now back at the roundabout by which he left the town. Continue back, following the signs, into
Windsor

28 THE NORTH DOWNS

100 miles (160km) – Surrey (with a short excursion into Hampshire)
Starting point: Godalming
OS sheets 186 and 187, Bartholomew map 9

A really long route, in fact exactly 100 miles. It starts by the national headquarters of the Cyclists' Touring Club, and was planned by members of the West Surrey District Association as the course for a Veterans' Ride, an event which is held on a regional basis in various parts of the country every three years. Though it winds around the North Downs, there are surprisingly few steep hills. Entrants for the Veterans' Ride are all more than fifty years of age, and many are in their late seventies. The time allowed is twelve hours, and most complete the course in that time. The route is based on a figure of eight shape, with Tilford as its centre point, so it could easily be split into two halves and ridden on separate occasions. Also, it is possible to cut out the last 10 miles or so by following the Godalming signs from Cranleigh, instead of taking the longer, more picturesque route detailed here. It is a route which includes the very best of Surrey: almost every village has an interesting church, and there are buildings of architectural interest, from cottages to manors, all along it.

Godalming Starting with the CTC headquarters on your left side, ride away from the town and immediately take a left turn up King's Road which leads through a built-up area and across a railway line. Soon the country opens out into a pleasant secondary road; follow the signs to
Compton The church, which has Norman and Saxon features, is justly famous and originally had two anchorite cells, one of which survives. The village was the home of the Victorian painter G. F. Watts. Ride through to the A3, turn left on to the main road, and after a little under 1 mile turn right to

Puttenham A charming and peaceful village. There is a tablet in the church to a climber who died in the Pyrenees in 1912. Five of his friends went out from England to search for him, found the body, brought it back and buried him in the churchyard. Turn left on leaving the village at a sign to

Cut Mill There is an attractive lake lined with silver birches on a crossroads shortly after the hamlet of Cut Mill. Go straight over towards Elstead, but before reaching that village, turn right at the T-junction towards Tilford, and make a left turn, again following the Tilford signs. The countryside around here is well wooded and, with the small lakes and streams that dot the area, is a wonderful place for bird-watchers. Do not descend into Tilford, but make a right and then an immediate left turn into Sheephatch Lane, and follow the signs to

Millbridge Cross the A287 and keep the stream on your left – the stream is, in fact, the infant River Wey. Avoid going into Dockenfield by making a left turn, and then another left turn at a convent. The road passes through a farmyard and reaches the A325 at Sleaford. Cross the road and follow the sign to

Kingsley A mile out of the village, take a left turn signposted to

Oakhanger and follow the signs to

Selborne This is a pilgrimage spot for any naturalist, for it was the home of the naturalist the Reverend Gilbert White, who wrote the *Natural History and Antiquities of Selborne*, during the eighteenth century. His home is preserved as a museum, and the building is shared with the Oates Memorial Library – a tribute to Captain Oates of Antarctic fame. The parish church has a modern stained-glass window depicting the birds that White mentioned in his book. Despite the large numbers of visitors, this Hampshire village is unspoiled – and it is also a good place to stop for refreshments. Retrace along the village street, and take the B3006 south-east and turn off at the second left towards

Blackmoor There are some steep hills on this road, but this is amply made up for by the beauty of the wooded lanes. From Blackmoor, cross the A325 at Whitehill and follow the signs towards Liphook. However, do not enter the town, but 1 mile before it, take a left turn into Tunbridge Lane and pass through

Headley It is reputed that St Paul's Cathedral can be seen from the church tower. Continue on through

Arford All this part of the route is exceptionally attractive, and takes you to

Frensham Ponds a beauty spot popular with anglers and dinghy sailors. Nearby are three hills known as the Devil's Jumps. The church in the village of Frensham houses a huge copper cauldron. There are doubts about what it was used for, but there are tales of witches and fairies. It is an easy ride to

Tilford There are two medieval stone bridges over branches of the River Wey, and a village green. J. M. Barrie is said to have written *Peter Pan* and *Dear Brutus* in a house nearby. This is approximately the halfway point in the run. From Tilford, go north and pick up the signs for

Elstead Ride along the B3001, which is a rather busy road, to Milford, where there is a complex of main roads (but also a café). Cross the main roads at the traffic lights and take the Godalming road, then almost immediately turn right at a sign to Milford station, cross the railway line and follow the signs to

Hambledon This is an attractive village with some delightful gardens, and views across to Sussex. Avoid going on to the A283 by making a left turn in the middle of the village and take the byroad towards Chiddingfold. Chiddingfold is most attractive, but the route in fact turns left immediately before the village. However, many people will wish to divert slightly to see it, and the famous Crown Inn with its old woodwork. If you do so, retrace a few hundred yards and pick up the signs towards

Dunsfold Another attractive village. There is a holy well here with a carving of the Madonna. Cross the A281 and ride to

Cranleigh A sizeable town where tea can easily be obtained. Ride through the town and bear left at the old memorial, following the signs to Ewhurst. Just before that village is reached, turn right to

Ewhurst Green and continue on, following the signs through
Walliswood Continue east to the A29 and turn left on to it and carry on through
Ockley Turn right off the main road, pass Ockley Church and take the first right into
Weare Street This may justly be claimed to be the most attractive road in Surrey – 2 miles or so of byroad twisting downhill alongside a stream, heavily wooded, and in summer a mass of wild flowers. It is not always easy to find, but is to the west of the railway line. Recross the A29 and follow the lanes to
Ellen's Green Continue on to
Rudgwick Turn right at the A281 to
Bucks Green Take the main road towards Guildford, but make a right turn after 1 mile to return to
Cranleigh There is a tempting signpost here to Godalming, but if the full 100 miles are to be completed, ignore it and take the B2128 towards Wonersh, bear left north of Rowly and turn right on to the A281. In ½ mile, turn off the road on to a bridleway, and follow this round through
Thorncombe Street and
Bramley Though this section can be omitted, it does give a chance to ride off the road, and the countryside is always attractive. From Bramley take any of the several lanes going west, and return to
Godalming

29 TO THE SILENT POOL

13 miles (20km) – Surrey
Starting point: Guildford
OS sheets 186 and 187, Bartholomew map 9

Guildford is one of the most attractive towns in Surrey and is well served by rail from London and the many suburbs that lie along the line to the south of the metropolis. This short ride has been planned so that anyone living south of the capital can slip away with the bike by train and in half an hour or so be in beautiful countryside with gentle wooded hills.

Guildford Even as one stands in the main, cobbled street of this old county town, the green wooded hill known as the Hog's Back can be seen in the distance above the buildings. The attractions of the town, however, do not extend to the area around the railway station: it is easiest to push the bike from the station through the maze of one-way streets and shopping malls to the centre of the town which is the true heart of Guildford. The alms houses are justly famous as one of the most photographed buildings in the county; along the street is the old grammar school, while tucked away on the east side of the street is the ruined castle – a good spot in which to eat sandwiches. Leave the town by riding south on the A281 and after a mile turn left into a surburban road called Pilgrim's Way (in fact part of the long-distance footpath of that name). As the road climbs, the views to the south open out, and on a clear day it is possible to see the distant ridge of the South Downs. The chapel of St Martha, used by the pilgrims on their way to Canterbury, is a short distance off to the south. If visited, return to the minor road and continue east to the junction with the A248 just before

Albury This, surprisingly, is a village of chimneys; they pop up everywhere on cottages and larger houses, often of red brick, designed in ingenious spirals. Continue on the A248 to the junction with the busy A25 where go left to

Silent Pool The pool is just off the A25 to the north, where the road becomes a dual-carriageway, and there is a fingerpost showing the track leading to the pool. There are several versions of the legend of this quiet pond but all have in common the theme that a beautiful peasant girl was bathing in its clear waters when King John (always a likely villain) who was riding by saw her and urged his horse towards the maiden. To escape his clutches, she moved into the deeper water and was drowned. Return to the A25 and turn left on to it (in the direction of Dorking). After ½ mile, at a crossroads just north of the village of Shere, turn left and begin the long climb up to

Combe Bottom Without doubt, this is a stiff climb and most cyclists get off long before the top. It gets steeper the further up it you get, ending with a left-hand hairpin where the gradient is 1 in 7. A few hundred yards after the hairpin, take the left turn, signposted to East Clandon. From here you reap the reward of the long climb for there is now a grand descent, mile after mile of downhill swoops with views from the Kent border in the east to the Hampshire downs in the west and with Guildford sitting like a toy town to your left. At the junction with the A246 turn left for the easy 4 miles back to

Guildford

30 OVER THE SURREY HILLS

22 miles (35km) – Surrey
Starting point: Woking
OS sheets 186 and 187, Bartholomew map 9

Woking may not be picturesque but it does have a fast rail service to Waterloo with trains every few minutes. This is an ideal route for anyone wanting to get out of the capital for a day, or even half a day. It is a fairly hilly ride but the views make up for that.

Woking Leave the station by the exit into the car park – not the exit to the town centre. Turn right and join the main road in the direction of Guildford. A mile after leaving the station, make a left turn at a traffic roundabout and continue to

Old Woking The little church is set back in a lane amid some pretty cottages and is worth a visit. Continue on, past a golf centre, pass the Maybury Arms and take the next road on the right, signposted to Ripley. The ride now leaves the houses behind and climbs over Pyrford Common. At the summit is a grand view towards the North Downs, and the medieval church of St Nicholas is on the right in a few yards. Descend the steep curving hill and at the bottom, beside a small river and a canal, is the ruined Newark Priory. Stay with this road for the short ride into

Ripley This is a spot which has a place in the history of cycling for near the close of the last century the Anchor Inn in the high street was the mecca of many cycling clubs who rode out on the old Portsmouth road. Cross the village street and continue south-east; the road soon passes over the A3. The ride is now through pleasant pastoral countryside. A mile from Ripley, turn right into Hungry Lane. Continue to

East Clandon The church here is justly famous. Cross the A246 at the edge of the village and begin the long climb up Clandon Downs. This rather tough hill is frequently used by racing cyclists on evening training rides, and the sight of gaily coloured racing vests is a frequent occurrence. As the road climbs, the views open out until at the summit the view ranges from Kent in the east to the distant hills of the Hampshire Downs in the west. Continue to a T-junction where go right and immediately begin the descent of

Combe Bottom There is a right-hand hairpin at the start of this famous descent and then a delicious race down for a mile to the junction with the A25. Go straight over the main road to visit

Shere This is one of Surrey's prettiest villages and a good spot for refreshments. The little Tilling Bourne runs through the centre. Retrace to the A25 and turn left on to it. This is a rather busy road but as it climbs steadily wide views open out to the south with, on a clear day, the bulk of the South Downs just showing on the horizon. At the summit is

Newlands Corner It is usually possible to get refreshments at this popular beauty spot. The road now swoops down to

West Clandon Clandon Park (open during the summer) is on the left. Continue the ride through

Send and follow the signs into the centre of
Woking

31 ORCHARDS AND HOPFIELDS

45 miles (72km) – Kent
Starting point: Tonbridge
OS sheet 188, Bartholomew map 10

Cyclists will find that this part of Kent contains some of the county's most attractive villages – quiet places away from main roads and often having an air of spaciousness. The orchards and hopfields, though covering a smaller acreage than in earlier years, still give Kent its particular charm, with the inevitable oast-houses popping up from the landscape. Though these are no longer used for their original purpose of drying hops, they have passed into the hands of people who have converted them to private homes, and very well they look. One of the delights of this ride is that it involves an unusually high proportion of twisting lanes; often there is a choice of routes to the next village, but by observing the small signposts you should have no great difficulty in following the main route.

Tonbridge The suburban development that has occurred north and south of the town has left the centre like a thin 'waist' with the ruins of the castle and the water-meadows along the Medway providing some interesting spots. Leave the town by riding in a northerly direction and follow the A26 for about 2 miles, turning right on to a minor road to
Golden Green This is a tiny village with a corrugated-iron chapel that has acquired a railway clock. The tower that can be seen to the north is part of a nineteenth-century eccentricity called Hadlow Castle. Continue to
East Peckham At the junction here with the B2015 go left, and then take the right fork for
Yalding The village is on a tributary of the Medway and has an old stone bridge crossing it. This is one of the many Kentish villages which has a harmony in the architecture, though the houses are certainly not uniform in design, ranging from Georgian brick and plaster to simple weatherboarding. All around here are hop gardens, bean fields and cherry orchards. If the right week in spring can be struck, the whole area is ablaze with blossom. Follow the road south-east through the hamlets of
Hunton and
Chainhurst to

Marden The road to here has been enlivened by splashes of colour from cottage gardens, and though Marden has a small industrial estate, it, too, is an attractive place where gardens abound. Take the road east along the line of the railway to

Staplehurst It was here in 1865 that Charles Dickens was in a train derailment, but it does not seem to have turned him against Kent, and he continued to write extensively about the county. Leave the town by the Sutton Valence road, but after 2 miles turn right near New Barn Farm to

Headcorn This is another village of attractive old houses, two of particular note being next-door to each other on the south side of the street: Shakespeare House and Chequers. Retrace a short distance and pick up the sign to

Frittenden The sharp-pointed steeple here can be seen for miles around. Follow the minor road south-west, and cross the A262 to

Cranbrook Here there is a windmill which is still kept in working order and is the second tallest in the county. There is a long high street with half-timbered houses of varying styles and periods. Altogether, this is a delightful spot. Continue northwards along the B2085 and A262 to

Goudhurst Pause at the duckpond with its chestnut trees, and look at the tile-hung cottages. The church is well worth a visit, but it has had its share of troubles – it was struck by lightning in 1637 and rebuilt, then struck by Hitler's bombs in 1940 when much of the glass was lost. Go north along the B2079 for 1½ miles, then turn left to

Horsmonden This is a village which has the surprising tradition of being a gun-making centre at the time of Charles I. One of the local inns is called The Gun, and there are relics of gun-making in the church. Continue to

Brenchley another attractive village with some fine tile-hung cottages. Take the B2160 and B2161 north through

Five Oak Green then go left along the B2017 to

Tonbridge

The Midlands

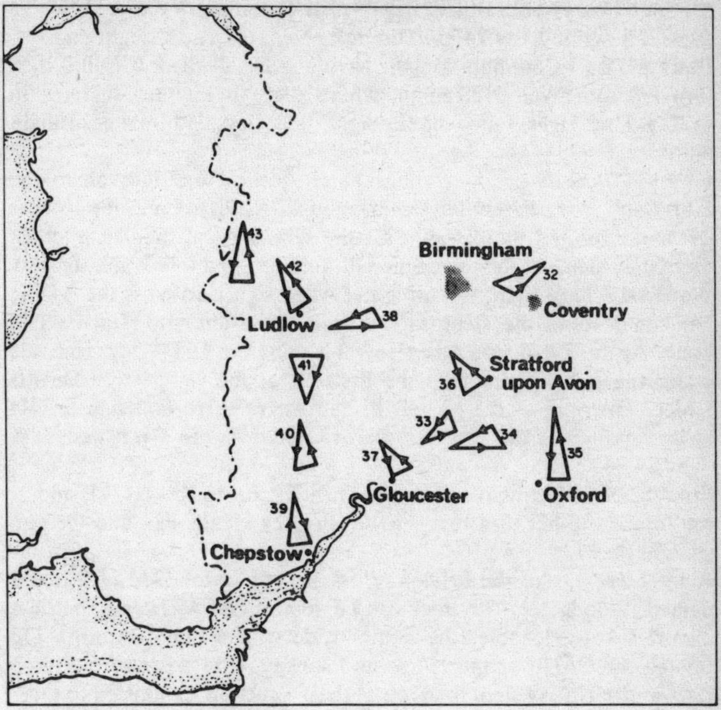

32 FOREST OF ARDEN

25 miles (40km) – Warwickshire
Starting point: Meriden
OS sheets 139 and 140, Bartholomew map 19

This route starts at the Cyclists' War Memorial, which was erected in 1921 at the reputed centre of England – reputed because there are several other claimants. The run is sometimes used by cyclists attending the annual service as a pleasant afternoon ride, and it was devised by members of the Birmingham and Midland District Association of the CTC. It consists almost entirely of lanes and the occasional bridlepath, and there are no hills of any real size. The countryside is so delightfully rural that it is easy to forget that Meriden is only 12 miles from the centre of Birmingham. *Note* The B4114 is still shown on some maps by its old designation of A47.

Meriden Leave the Cyclists' Memorial and, riding towards Coventry, climb Meriden Hill. At the top of the hill, ignore the left turn and continue to a large traffic island. Bear left and cross the A45, where there is a signpost to Corley. Turn left again, then go straight on to

Hawkes End Continue straight on along Bridle Brook Lane, then turn left into Wall Hill Road, where there is another signpost to Corley. Fork right, following the signs to Corley, and then go straight on to

Corley There is an interesting church here. Turn right on to the B4098 and immediately left (signposted to Astley). Continue to bear left and cross the motorway. Pass the service area, then turn left at the Astley sign. At the top of the hill, fork left and follow the signs to

Woodend Turn right, following the Arley sign, and cross the B4102. Do not descend the steep hill, but go sharp left into Tippers Hill Lane. At the T-junction turn right, following the Old Arley sign, ride under the railway and take the first left at the signpost to Devitts Green. Go right at the top of the hill where there is a sign to Old Arley, and left at the sign to Ballards Green. At the T-junction, turn right to

Church End (attractive church). Turn left on to the B4114, and at the top of the hill turn right at the Birchley Heath sign and then go straight on to

Ridge Lane Take the bridleway on the left at the side of a house named 'Woodgate'. The track can be very muddy after rain, but it is almost always rideable (the author rode it in a thunderstorm). On joining the B4116 at the Horse and Jockey, turn left and then first right at the Hurley sign, then left at the T-junction signposted to Over Whitacre. Go straight on at the top of the hill and take the next right, again signposted to Over Whitacre, to the B4116. Go left, then right into Sandy Lane and left on to the B4114 to pass

Over Whitacre Church (worth a visit). Go straight on where the B4114 goes sharp left at the Fillongley sign. At the top of the hill after Daw Mill Colliery go right (there is no signpost). At the next junction go left, then right at the sign to Shawbury and right again at the signpost to Shustoke. Fork left at the Maxstoke sign and then make a right turn, again following a Maxstroke sign. At the bottom of the hill take the right turn which is signposted to Coleshill, and then turn left at the Meriden sign, and continue to

Maxstoke Church Go right, again signposted to Meriden, and pass under the motorway alongside

Packington Park bearing right at the sign to Meriden to cross the A45 into Birmingham Road which leads into Meriden. Alongside this last stretch of road is Forest Hall, home of the Woodmen of Arden, an ancient society of archers who can often be seen practising at weekends.

33 THE GARDEN OF EVESHAM

18 miles (29km) – Hereford and Worcester
Starting point: Evesham
OS sheet 150, Bartholomew maps 13 and 18

For centuries, the Garden of Evesham has been a place of fertility, an area of market gardens and orchards. Despite the import of fruit from the Continent, there is still apple, pear and plum blossom a-plenty to be found in this delightful valley, although blossom time can vary by several weeks from year to year.

Evesham An attractive town, though its two main streets may be choked with traffic on summer weekends. One of its more unusual claims to fame lies in the proximity of the two churches in the centre, All Saints and St Lawrence, which share the same churchyard. Leave the town on the A44 riding east, then turn left by the church at Bengeworth on to the B4035, then left again on to the B4510 to
Offenham Cross Continue, and after a mile the River Avon will be reached. Cross to the northern bank at the lock and take the minor road through a caravan camp to
Harvington Here is Harvington Hall, one of several houses in the district where priests were hidden during the persecutions of the sixteenth century. Indeed, Queen Elizabeth was warned that Worcestershire was 'much warped towards Popery'. The priests' hiding places can still be seen. Continue to
Church Lench turning left by the church to
Sheriff's Lench (These are two of a cluster of charming little villages, all bearing the name of Lench). Continue to
Badger's Hill and follow the road to
Fladbury Cross Continue over the B4084 to
Fladbury Here is Craycombe House, the home of Francis Brett Young, the novelist, now a country club. Proceed to
Charlton and then on to the junction with the A44 where go left for the last mile back to
Evesham

34 PICK OF THE COTSWOLDS

40 miles (64km) – Gloucestershire and Oxfordshire
Starting point: Burford
OS sheet 163, Bartholomew map 14

Most of the better-known towns and villages in this part of the Cotswolds are included in this run. It is easy, pleasant cycling, and the hills are gentle. The villages, almost without exception, are built of the warm-toned Cotswold stone, and the rivers Windrush and Evenlode are among the most beautiful streams in the South Midlands.

Burford A busy little town with a main street where every second shop seems to sell antiques. There are two roads travelling west out of the town, one taking the north bank of the river and the other the south. While the road on the south side of the river is the quieter, that on the north (cross the river and take the first left) passes through

Taynton This is a village not to be missed. The church is set beside the manor house and the whole village gives the impression of neat grass and paths and the beautiful roofs of the stone houses. Pedal west along the road through the meadows to

Great Barrington There is a deer-park here together with an eighteenth-century mansion. From the road there are views across the valley and to Great Barrington House. Continue to

Windrush The little village sits on the hillside above the river of the same name. There is a mounting-block by the churchyard gate for the use of the gentry of long ago. In another mile comes

Sherbourne another gem of Cotswold architecture. Half a mile out of the village is a crossroads. Turn right (signposted to Bourton-on-the-Water) and commence a climb over a small stream which is Sherbourne Brook. Follow the signs to

Bourton-on-the-Water This is perhaps the most-visited small town in the Cotswolds, largely owing to the attractive bridges strung over the Windrush as it passes along the main street. It has been called the Venice of the Cotswolds, though such titles are largely a nonsense. When the crowds are absent it is a very pretty spot and a good place for a picnic. Proceed to the A429, turn right and then turn off left at the sign to

Lower Slaughter A stream again flows down the centre of the village, with more bridges, though not as self-consciously as at Bourton. Follow the signs to

Upper Slaughter Unlike its twin, Upper Slaughter is built on a hillside above the stream. The manor house here is thought by some to be one of the most beautiful domestic buildings in the Cotswolds. Then follow the signs to

Temple Guiting Of all the villages on this route, this is perhaps the one not to be missed. Its charm lies in the simplicity of the cottages and the sense of proportion. It is a village for the artist, yet it is so tucked away that the crowds completely miss it. If time permits, a diversion can be made to Guiting Power. If so, retrace to Temple Guiting. Bear to the right on leaving the village and pick up the B4077 to

Upper Swell Another picturesque spot. Take the lane to the right for 1 mile to

Lower Swell The hills around these villages give some wonderful views of stone cottages nestling in the landscape. Take the main road for the last mile into

Stow on the Wold However many coaches arrive here, it never seems to rob the town of its charm. 'Stow on the Wold where the wind blows cold' says the old couplet, and certainly the wind does blow through its streets in winter but there are plenty of teashops, and in summer the busy streets are packed with visitors. See the old stocks, which are in the market place, and the Old Cross. Avoid returning to Burford by the main road, and instead go east on the Chipping Norton road. Turn right on to the B4450 and follow it to

Bledington There are some attractive old houses here and a village green (good for a picnic). Follow the road round to the right to

Idbury Here, in the manor house, *The Countryman* magazine was at one time published; it now has its home at Burford. Follow the signs to

Fifield Avoid rejoining the main road just yet and take the minor road south, eventually rejoining the A424 1 mile before

Burford

35 AROUND THE CHERWELL VALLEY

50 miles (80km) – Oxfordshire
Starting point: Oxford
OS sheets 164 and 151 (just), Bartholomew map 14

Oxford is a city of bicycles. Undergraduates still use them to get from their lodgings to lectures, and motorists are more used to cyclists than is the case in other cities of comparable size. The best way for you to enjoy this city of 'dreaming spires' is to ignore the over-detailed guidebooks and simply ride around, turning down any avenue that looks inviting. A complex one-way system prevents the motorist from enjoying the town fully, but as a cyclist you can always dismount and push your machine against the traffic flow. Out of term-time you can lock your machine at the college gates and enter on foot: you will rarely be turned away. The rest of the ride, by contrast with the busy city, is through peaceful villages that flank the River Cherwell, which enters the Thames near Oxford.

Oxford After spending some time in the city, leave by the Banbury road and follow the signs to

Kidlington This is merely an uninteresting suburb. Remain on the A423 for 3 miles, and then make a right turn at a staggered crossroads on to the B4027 where there is a sign to Tackley. After about ½ mile, go left, again at a Tackley sign, and follow a pretty lane to

Tackley Continue in a northerly direction through the villages of

Rousham

Steeple Aston and

Middle Aston All these villages are delightful, with cottages of honey-coloured stone, and the connecting lanes are rich in flowers during the summer. Continue to

North Aston then cross the Cherwell and the Oxford Canal, and travel through

Somerton

Fritwell and

Souldern to

Aynho The cottages owned by a local lord of the manor have apricot trees growing alongside their walls, a gift from the patron who felt they would keep his villagers healthy. This is a pretty spot, despite the main road running through it, and the cycling artist Patterson did a particularly fine drawing of it. Take the road signposted to Clifton and Deddington, that is down a short steep hill off the main road.

Clifton There is an interesting watermill on the Cherwell, where the road crosses the river, and a pleasant little pub. Continue to

Deddington This was a market town during the Middle Ages, though it is now little more than a large village. The rings where horses and cattle were tethered can still be seen in a street called The Bull Ring, and there is also a Goose Green where the birds were sold. The church is enormous for such a small place and has a massive tower. There is a story that the earlier tower fell down, and the locals sold the bells and used the money to buy beer, becoming incapable as a result of their festivities. The place has since been known as Dirty, Drunken Deddington, but this is something of a slander on the village, and in any case it is probably too good a story to be true. At the traffic lights in the village, take the B4031 going west, signposted to

Hempton Ignore the first turn on the left (signposted to Duns Tew), and take the second turn on the left 1 mile out of Hempton. This is at a crossroads, and the road you want is signposted to

Nether Worton There is an attractive manor house here, and the road runs alongside the high wall fringing the parkland, turning sharp left and running south to

Sandford St Martin This is one of the most attractive villages in the area, though little known and very quiet. It has a cricket green which can be good for a lengthy halt. Follow the signs to

Glympton Here there is the tiny River Glyme with a waterfall in the middle of the village. Follow the signs to

Woodstock Blenheim Palace (grounds and house open) is in this delightful if over-popular town. Continue in the direction of Oxford, and ½ mile out of Woodstock is a large traffic roundabout. To avoid taking the main road, follow the signs to

Bladon Sir Winston Churchill is buried here in a simple grave in the churchyard (well signposted). A mile out of the village, take a left turn signposted to

Cassington Return along the A40 for the last few miles to

Oxford

36 THE SHAKESPEARE COUNTRY

35 miles (56km) – Warwickshire
Starting point: Stratford-upon-Avon
OS sheet 151, Bartholomew map 19

Stratford is much more than Shakespeare's birthplace. Despite the tourists and the icecream shops, the town is an interesting one with plenty of fine old half-timbered houses, delightful gardens and, of course, the River Avon. The meadows opposite the Memorial Theatre, with their willows, provide a good spot for a picnic, and the church where Shakespeare is buried, with its spire rising above the trees, can be seen just downstream. There is a pathway for 1 mile or so along the Avon west of the town to the junction with the River Stour.

Stratford-upon-Avon From the centre of the town take the A46 going north-east, which is signposted to Warwick, and after 2 miles take a minor road to the right signposted to

Hampton Lucy The minor road crosses the River Avon here, and on the right is Charlecote Park (National Trust) where deer can be seen along the river's edge. Shakespeare is reputed to have poached deer in this park, though some historians say that there were no deer there in Elizabethan times. Continue to the T-junction with the B4088 and turn right through

Charlecote Continue over the crossroads and past the old airfield at Wellesbourne Mountford, following the signs to

Loxley Go left after the church to the A422, turn left along it for a few hundred yards, then turn right at a signpost to

Alderminster The cycling is easy all along the route here, with no real hills, and pleasant, pastoral countryside. The river in the village is the Stour. Go left along the A34 for about 2 miles to

Newbold on Stour At the end of the village, just by the church, turn right to the hamlet of

Armscote and right again to

Ilmington Ahead lies a series of steep hills forming the outliers of the Cotswolds. Take the road signposted to Chipping Norton, climbing a very steep hill to the summit of Ilmington Downs. Swoop down the hills on the other side to

Chipping Campden This is one of the gems of the South Midlands, but also one of the busiest places in summer. The two main architectural features are the large church, built from the proceeds of sheep farming and often called a 'wool church', and the much-photographed alms houses. They, like almost all the houses in the town, are built of the honey-coloured Cotswold Stone which mellows to a soft grey with age. Leave Chipping Campden by the B4081 going north, and after a couple of miles sweep down under a railway bridge with good views away to the left, and reach the village of

Mickleton At the end of the village, turn right at a signpost for Lower Quinton and skirt to the east of a sharp hill called Meon Hill – the scene of a famous and unsolved murder in the 1940s, and reputed to be connected with witchcraft. At a T-junction, go right and then first left to

Preston on Stour This is an attractive village with a deer-park nearby. Turn left at the A34 and follow the main road for the last 3 miles or so back to

Stratford-upon-Avon

37 ROUND BREDON HILL

38 miles (61km) – Gloucestershire, Hereford and Worcester
Starting point: Cheltenham
OS sheet 163, Bartholomew map 13

To the west of the Cotswold escarpment lies Bredon Hill, which stands above the orchards of the Vale of Evesham and is bordered on three sides by the River Avon. There is considerable contrast for the cyclist taking this route as it ranges from the windswept slopes of Cleeve Hill to the villages which nestle at the foot of the slopes of Bredon Hill. After the first few miles, it is not particularly hilly.

Cheltenham The trees, parks and squares of this Regency town make it a pleasant place in which to stroll or cycle. See the Promenade, just south of the High Street, with its double avenue of chestnut trees, and the Imperial Gardens next to the Town Hall. Leave the town on the A46 going north-east and signposted to Stratford-upon-Avon. Once clear of the town, the road begins to climb. Continue up the side of Cleeve Hill (most people walk up!). There is a youth hostel up the track to the right. In good weather, the summit of Cleeve Hill makes a marvellous picnic spot, but even from the road there is one of the best views of the Vale of Evesham, with the Malvern Hills standing out clearly, Bredon Hill to the north, and far to the west the blue ridge of the Welsh hills. From the summit there is a very fast descent to

Winchcombe This is very much a 'Cotswold town' with warm stone houses, a fine church and historic inns surrounded by wooded hills. See the forty grotesque gargoyles on the outside of the church. Go left in the centre of the town and, ignoring the B4078, take the minor road through the hamlet of Gretton, pass under the railway bridge and continue on to

Alderton This is a pretty little spot in lush country with wooded hills all around. Continue to

Beckford (manor house and the ruins of a priory) and then to

Ashton under Hill There is a track from the village to the summit of Bredon Hill which is well worth taking for the views from the top right across the Midland Plain. Retrace to the village and follow the road round the hill to

Elmley Castle

Little Comberton and

Great Comberton All these villages are attractive, the latter being on a meander of the River Avon. Continue to

Eckington and follow the B4080 south to

Bredon and then take the B4079 back to

Cheltenham

38 AROUND THE WYRE FOREST

22 miles (35km) – Hereford and Worcester
Starting point: Bewdley
OS sheet 138, Bartholomew map 18

Straddling the boundary of Hereford and Worcester with Shropshire is the Wyre Forest – miles of remote forest land, yet not far from the grime of the Black Country. In a sense the forest should no longer be there: one would have expected it to have been cut down by the charcoal burners for fuel as the nearby iron industries grew, yet it has survived unlike so many other forested areas in the district. The route has many short, steep hills; in fact some of the lanes might best be described from the cyclist's point of view as exciting, though considerable care is needed. It is essentially a route for those feeling energetic.

Bewdley The town is Georgian and on the banks of the River Severn, which adds to its charm. It is well worth spending some time exploring its streets. Leave by the B4194 going north-west and climb up through the forest to
Buttonoak Continue on the same road, and after about 2 miles turn left at a signpost to Sturt Common. Follow this road to
Far Forest There is a very steep descent on this road with a sharp left turn over a stream, and great care is needed. Turn left along the A4117 for just over ½ mile, then turn right at a signpost for Heightington. Go straight on at the A456 and follow the road to
Bliss Gate and
Heightington Carry on along the Stourport road to the bottom of Hurtle Hill, and then turn right where there is a signpost to Abberley. Follow this twisting lane which plunges and climbs like a roller-coaster to the village of
Abberley The twin peaks of Abberley Hill were used by Henry IV and Owen Glendower to observe each other before they decided not to go into battle. Turn left at the Manor Arms Inn and take the first right by a barn. Climb a very steep hill which takes a right fork just before some houses. Descend to the A443 and turn right for the B4202. Follow that road for about 3 miles and turn right for
Rock Go through the village, where there is an interesting Norman church, and turn left by the pub to return to
Bliss Gate Again, this is a switchback road. Continue to follow the lane north to the A456, where a right turn will bring you back to
Bewdley

The Welsh Border

(see map on page 93)

39 THE FOREST OF DEAN AND THE SOUTHERN WYE VALLEY

40 miles (64km) – Gwent and Gloucestershire
Starting point: Chepstow
OS sheet 162, Bartholomew map 13

The proximity of the M4 means that many cyclists put their machines on the tops of their cars and head for Chepstow. For those cycling over the Severn Bridge from England, there is a cyclepath – and some great views. Chepstow is the gateway to South Wales and also to the Forest of Dean and the Wye Valley. Although very popular in the tourist season, this region has a network of minor roads and so does not get as congested as, say, the Lake District or Snowdonia where, owing to the mountains, there are relatively few roads.

Chepstow A town of steep, narrow, winding streets with plenty of small shops to poke into. The castle is well worth visiting. Cross the river on to the east bank and turn off the A48 on to the B4228. Follow this road north through pretty countryside to

St Briavels Here, the small castle that King John built as a hunting lodge is now a youth hostel. It is tucked away, by the church, and has a grass-covered moat. Continue on the B4228 through the hamlet of

Trow Green to

Sling Follow the signs to

Parkend Take the B4234 going north right through the centre of the forest. Well-marked trails and viewpoints are all around, and it is worth leaving the cycle for a while and going on foot. There are vast stretches of forest glades with giant trees and much wildlife. The forest covers 22,000 acres, and the boundaries that were fixed in 1668 are very much the same today. This is one of the few remaining royal forests in England. Stay on the B4234 to

Upper Lydbrook and

Lower Lydbrook At the T-junction, go left along the River Wye, which is very picturesque, to

English Bicknor (Welsh Bicknor, where there is a youth hostel, is across the river. It is reached by taking a footpath through the grounds of a factory and crossing a footbridge over the Wye.) Two miles west of English Bicknor is

Symonds Yat This famous beauty spot is a spectacular bend in the River Wye which can be observed from the cliffs high above. To reach it, go right in English Bicknor and right again on to the B4432. After visiting the Yat, retrace down this road, and at

Berry Hill go right on to the A4136 to

Monmouth The town's main feature is the Monow Gate, a striking archway which is part of the old fortifications. Monmouth's most famous sons are Charles Stewart Rolls, joint-founder of Rolls-Royce and also an aviation pioneer, and King Henry V. The town gives them equal prominence with a statue each. Leave by recrossing the river on to the east bank and taking the A466 road, signposted to Chepstow, along the banks of the Wye. Although this is a busy road, it is extremely beautiful – well wooded with rich green hills. It provides a truly magnificent ride showing the Wye Valley at its best, and there are plenty of old pubs and tea-places along the banks. Tintern Abbey is on the left-hand side three-quarters of the way to Chepstow. But try to avoid the road on holiday weekends. Remain on the road to

Chepstow

40 WYE VALLEY MEANDER

19 miles (30km) – Hereford and Worcester
Starting point: Ross-on-Wye
OS sheet 162, Bartholomew map 13

This is essentially a pastoral ride with few hills, a route which stays close to the River Wye as it winds through some of the most pleasant countryside in southern England. The highlight of the ride is the view from Symond's Yat, that most photographed of views which is every bit as beautiful as it is reputed to be.

Ross-on-Wye Pause to look at the plague cross in the churchyard of St Mary's, then leave the town by pedalling south on the B4228 to

Walford After ½ mile, the river reappears on the right and the road clings to its bank following it in a broad meander to a point just south of Welsh Bicknor. The actual village – or rather the church for there is very little of the village – is on the other bank, and anyone wanting to cross will find that there is a footbridge at the spot. It was near Welsh Bicknor that King Henry V spent much of his childhood. However, that hamlet is not strictly on our route, so stay on the B4228 as the road bears away from the river. The old earthwork, Offa's Dyke, is to your right between the road and the river. Continue to

English Bicknor Stay on the same road, right through the village, and after a mile take a minor road on the right (there is only one so no confusion should arise) which takes you to the junction with the B4432 where go right to

Symond's Yat The footpaths through the woods here to the view-points are well signposted. The road now plunges downhill into another meander of the Wye, crossing it near the junction with the B4229. Continue on that road to

Goodrich There is a footpath to the ruins of the castle which is well worth visiting. To avoid taking the busy A40 back, stay on the B4229, crossing the river at

Kerne Bridge and retrace your earlier road for a mile back to

Walford Go left just after the church, by Walford Court, and stay on this minor road all the way back to
Ross-on-Wye

41 HALF-TIMBERING AROUND HEREFORD

56 miles (90km) – Hereford and Worcester
Starting point: Hereford
OS sheets 137 and 149, Bartholomew map 18

England may appear pastoral, a land of fertile farms and peaceful villages, but once it was a land of conflict, as shown by the number of castles built in this part of the country to impose order. But today the rivers Wye, Lugg and Teme meander through a gentle landscape where orchards and hopfields line the banks and small pubs sell locally made cider. On a cycle-tour in this area, above all take your time.

Hereford The city is on the River Wye. Visit the cathedral with its chained library. Leave by riding along the A438, signposted to Brecon, and turn right on to the A4110 at Three Elms Road. Turn left at the Three Elms Inn, continue to the A4103, cross it and go straight on to
Tillington There is a rich mixture of timber-framed and later brick houses, and there are grand views to the Black Mountain and Hay Bluff. The church is interesting. Pedal on to
Weobley It is worth dismounting and walking around the village as it is one of the finest timber-framed villages in England. The church stands at one end of the village and the castle at the other, with the market place and shops in between. Leave Weobley by riding in a north-easterly direction and, after 1¼ miles, take the first left to
Dilwyn Again, it is worth dismounting to look at the half-timbering. The church has a quatrefoil panel of stained glass, from the fourteenth century. At the T-junction in Dilwyn, turn left on to the A4112, then immediately right and right again opposite the church, and pass Dilwyn post office. Keeping right, arrive at the B4457. Turn right at The Firs and right again on to the A4110. After passing over a stream, turn left to
Ivington Turn left in the village by the church and follow the road through to
Leominster This is the county's second largest town and features a ducking-stool, last used in 1809. Look above the shop windows for fine examples of carved timbering. Visit the Market Hall and the folk museum in Etnam Street. Take the B4361 to
Luston and

Richards Castle To the left, up the hill, is one of the earliest Norman castles in England, built in 1050. Continue on the B4361 to

Ludlow For details of the town see the route Shropshire – the Long Mynd and Wenlock Edge. Leave the town in a southerly direction, following the river along Temeside. Follow the road under a railway bridge, go straight on at the crossroads, signposted to Little Hereford, and through Middleton to the A456. Turn right across the River Teme, then left to

Laysters Pole Go straight on across the A4112. (Divert slightly if you wish to see Laysters Pole Church, late fourteenth century with fine roof and a footpath to Wordsworth's Stone.) Take the first right and after 2 miles turn left to

Pudleston Go left at the T-junction and first right to the A44, then turn left and first right at

Steen's Bridge Turn left at the crossroads, and after climbing a steep hill below Risbury Camp fork right to the A417. Risbury Camp is an important Iron Age hill fort covering about 28 acres. At the A417, turn right and immediately left, and follow the lanes south to

Marden and

Sutton St Michael and **Sutton St Nicholas** (More good examples of timber-framed villages.) Turn right at the crossroads to

Shelwick Green Go straight across the A4103 on to the A465 and into

Hereford

42 THE LONG MYND AND WENLOCK EDGE

42 miles (67km) – Shropshire
Starting point: Ludlow
OS sheet 137, Bartholomew map 18

The Welsh Border country has attracted generations of cyclists from the industrial areas of Birmingham and the Black Country. This is an ancient area, and the names of the features give some indication of the awe in which such wild regions were held long ago: Devil's Mouth, Wild Moor and Black Knoll are just a few. Wenlock Edge is the subject of A. E. Housman's famous poem, *On Wenlock Edge*; it is a long, narrow hill dropping away steeply to the north-west, a pleasant place rising from the pastures of lowland England. In contrast, the Long Mynd is a wild spot and has a place much further back in history.

Ludlow The town was planned by the Romans and still has the same grid lay-out for its main streets. Its dominant feature is the castle

which stands above the River Teme. It is worth locking the cycle and visiting it, and also the superb black and white Feathers Hotel and the Reader's House. From the castle gate, turn right down Dinham, bearing right, and just before Dinham Bridge turn right by a signpost to the swimming baths. Follow this road to the A49, turn left, and in 200yd turn right at a signpost to Bridgnorth. Ride under the railway bridge and turn left along Fishmore Road to
Lower Hayton and
Peaton Turn left at the signpost to Diddlebury. At the T-junction, go right to
Broncroft and then left to
Beambridge Go straight over the crossroads and climb the steep hill up the side of Wenlock Edge, freewheeling down the other side to
Rushbury The hill you have just ridden down is Roman Bank, and the Roman soldiers are reputed to have drawn their water from nearby Eaton Brook. Pass the church and fork right to the B4371. Go left on to the B4371 and then first right to
Cardington There are some fine old stone houses. Go left at the Royal Oak, then left at the T-junction and first right, signposted to Caer Caradoc Hill. From Willstone follow the rough track uphill. On reaching the tarmac, bear left at the T-junction and left again on to the B4371. Turn right and ride straight on at the traffic lights to the centre of
Church Stretton This is the Shepwardine of the Mary Webb novels. You are now at the foot of the Long Mynd. Go uphill from the crossroads, signposted to the Burway. At the top of the long hard climb up the Mynd, fork left at a sign to the glider field. At the junction with the glider field, turn left down the bridleway which follows a stream called Minton Batch. Continue down beside the stream until you reach the tarmac, then go left and keep right to
Marshbrook Turn left over the level-crossing and right on to the A49. After 200yd, turn left and climb the hill to
Acton Scott There is a working farm museum here. Continue on to
Ticklerton and
Westhope Follow the lane along the stream marked on the map as Seifton Batch to the B4368. Turn right and left. At the T-junction, go right through
Culmington to
Ludlow

43 NEWTOWN AND THE UPPER SEVERN

38 miles (61km) – Shropshire and Powys
Starting point: Bishop's Castle
OS sheets 136 and 137, Bartholomew maps 18 and 22

The hills through which the upper part of the River Severn flows provide quiet cycling country, untouched by motorways or other busy roads. The small towns and villages of the area are placid places where the architecture is largely English but the language often heard is Welsh. The cyclist is at home here – generations of landladies have provided bed and breakfast for him, and signs offering the ubiquitous 'B and B' appear frequently on cottage gates.

Bishop's Castle The castle was held by the Bishops of Hereford during the reign of King Offa, though the fortifications have long since disappeared. Ride along the B4385 out of the town, going north, and follow the road around the flank of Aston Hill. After 6 miles, the road crosses the A489. Offa's Dyke crosses at this point and there are traces of the old earthwork both to the north and south of the road junction. Continue over to

Montgomery The Welsh call the town Trefaldwyn, but its red brick and half-timbering make it seem rather English even though it lies across the border. Leave by the B4385. Remain on that road, cross a railway then the Severn, and turn right on to the A483. After 1 mile, turn left at the sign to

Berriew Six roads meet here, for Berriew is on one of the great drovers' routes where sheep and cattle were herded between the hill pastures and the winter grazing near the river. Pedalling along these old roads sometimes gives a sense of timelessness to the rides. Follow the B4390 north-west along the banks of the River Rhiw, a tributary of the Severn, through

Manafon to

New Mills Turn left here, crossing the river on to the B4389 to

Tregynon Half a mile out of the village, follow the road round to the left to

Bettws Cedewain Go right opposite the church and push the machine up a very steep hill to the hamlet of

Highgate (For those who object to steep hills, there is the alternative of following the B4389 out of Bettws and after 2 miles turning right on to the B4568.) From Highgate, the road twists and switchbacks down to

Newtown The town still has some converted warehouses from when it was the centre of the flannel industry for the area. Robert Owen, the social reformer, was born here in 1771. Ride along the A489 out of the town, and in 3 miles reach the village of

Kerry Continue for another 4 miles along the A489 to the hamlet of

Sarn There is a choice of routes at this point. Either take the main road to

Church Stoke continuing on to
Bishop's Castle or alternatively, take the minor road to the right, just before Sarn Church, which climbs steeply into the hills and runs by a slightly shorter route along a grand ridge straight as an arrow to Bishop's Castle

East Anglia

(see map on page 93)

44 AROUND BURY ST EDMUNDS

45 miles (72km) – Suffolk
Starting point: Bury St Edmunds
OS sheet 155, Bartholomew map 21

A glance at the map shows all roads radiating from Bury. They mark the line of the old pilgrim ways, trodden by those who came to worship at the shrine of the martyred king, Edmund, for this is one of England's most historic towns. This route takes the rider through quiet countryside with scarcely a real hill at all. Anyone with a passion for old churches needs to allow a very long time to complete the route, for there are many temptations to linger.

Bury St Edmunds Plenty of time needs to be allowed to see the town and cathedral. One of the town's finest features is the great Abbey Gateway, and on passing through it you will find delightful gardens that make a splendid picnic spot. Nearby is the creeper-covered Angel Hotel, a Dickensian spot and the scene of many Pickwickian adventures. Leave by the A143, travelling north-easterly, and turn right just after riding under the bypass. Follow the road through the hamlet of Battlies Green, keeping right at the fork and taking the second on the right to
Beyton Green Continue on past the Bear Inn to
Drinkstone and
Drinkstone Green There is a windmill which is well worth visiting here, and also a craft centre. Fork left past the inn and go through the hamlet of Hightown Green to
Brettenham This is another of Suffolk's extremely attractive villages. Pass the park and turn left by a picturesque moated farmhouse to
Hitcham Turn right on to the B1115 and continue to
Bildeston Another pretty village and it is well worth while pausing to walk around it. The church is some way out of the village along a

lane to the right. There is also the ruin of a chapel to the north, close to Chapel Farm. Continue on the B1115. Down a track to the right is Nedging Mill. If visited, retrace and stay on the B1115 until it joins the A1141, then continue on to

Hadleigh This is a town associated with the painter John Constable, whose painting of Hadleigh Castle is one of his better-known works. The church is particularly interesting, and, with the Deanery Tower and the Guildhall, makes a splendid picture. Leave the town by the A1141, retracing the route, but keep left at Cherry Hill to

Monks Eleigh There are some very pretty cottages here and another fine church. Proceed, following the signs, to

Preston Turn right after passing the inn and left after crossing a stream to

Thorpe Morieux This is just a tiny village with a 600-year-old church. A maze of quiet lanes allows the rider to go north-west through the hamlets of

Thorpe Green
Great Green
Bradfield St Clare and
Little Welnetham to
Bury St Edmunds

45 THE SHOTLEY PENINSULA

25 miles (40km) – Suffolk
Starting point: Ipswich
OS sheets 155 and 169, Bartholomew map 21

This little corner of England has long traditions with the sea through the yachting harbour of Pin Mill, the ships that were built at Ipswich to form the 'Wooden Wall' and the merchantmen that used to come up the Orwell and the Stour, the rivers which border the peninsula. Part of this route is over tracks and pathways, but all are easily rideable.

Ipswich The town makes a good touring centre from which to see the lesser-known rivers of this part of East Anglia, such as the Deben and the Alde. It is an interesting old town with many quaint and tucked-away corners. Leave by taking the A137 south along the estuary of the Orwell and turn off left on to the B1456 to

Freston There is a beautifully situated fourteenth-century church here. Remain on the B1456 to

Woolverstone Turn left just after the post office into Mannings Lane and then right on to a track marked 'footpath to Pin Mill'. There are some good views along here. Continue through the grounds of Woolverstone Park. At the church turn right on to a drive, and at entrance gates go left on to the B1456, turning left after 1 mile into a lane opposite Walnut Tree Farm. Bear left and right around a wood, keeping straight on along a field track where the made-up road turns left, and go down towards the river. There are some splendid views of the Orwell and Pin Mill along here. Continue to

Pin Mill This is a sailing centre, with some good pubs on the water's edge. The village is also attractive in its own right. Leave by a lane to

Chelmondiston There are useful shops here. Go left on to the B1456 and 1 mile further on turn left into Wades Lane. Continue to Charity Farm and turn right on to a track to

Shotley Church This is known as the Sailors' Church and is on a small hill overlooking the Orwell. Continue past the church to the hamlet of

Shotley Street and then go left for

Shotley Gate There are good views of the shipping entering and leaving Harwich Harbour. Retrace along the B1456 for 1½ miles and then go left by a watertower to

Erwarton Continue along the twisting, undulating road through the hamlets of

Harkstead and

Lower Holbrook to

Holbrook Here there is the Royal Hospital School, originally for the sons of seamen. Go left on to the B1080, then right to the junction with the A137, where you turn right and follow into

Ipswich

46 WHERE CONSTABLE PAINTED

30 miles (48km) – Suffolk and Essex
Starting point: Hadleigh
OS sheets 155 and 168, Bartholomew map 21

The attractions of this ride are equally divided between the really lovely countryside through which it passes and the many fascinating villages. For a corner of England that is generally considered to be flat, this is a rather hilly route: it is a ride to be taken at a leisurely pace. During summer weekends the area tends to be rather crowded.

Hadleigh The centre still retains much of the gracious air of earlier years when it was a centre for the woollen industry and the merchants poured their wealth into the buildings. The long main street has many interesting old inns and gabled houses, many with ornamental plasterwork. Visit the Deanery Tower, the Guildhall and the church. There are pleasant walks beside the River Brett. Leave the town by Duke Street, cross the river and stay on this road to

Lower Layham At the church, turn left to see the picturesque watermill. Retrace and after passing an inn go left and then immediately right. At the top of the hill, go right and continue to Shelley Priory Farm. Bear left, then go right at the next junction to

Polstead This is a very lovely village and it has associations with Maria Marten (of the Red Barn). Cross the River Box, south of the village, then immediately go right to the hamlets of

Mill Street and

Stoke Tyo Cross the B1068 and follow the lane to

Nayland There are many fine buildings here, and the church contains a Constable altarpiece. Leave by the Colchester road, taking the first left after crossing the Stour – one of Constable's favourite rivers. At a T-junction, go left and then straight on to

Boxted Work east through the lanes to

Langham Fork right, then left down Gun Hill, where there are some grand views over Dedham Vale. Cross the A12 and bear left into

Dedham This is another beautiful spot with a magnificent church and good picnic areas by the river. Carry straight on past the church, then take the first left, and go left again at Stour House to the A137, turning left into

Lawford Turn left with the A137 down the hill to Manningtree station, cross the Stour, go left at Cattawade on to the B1070 and straight on at the next junction to

East Bergholt Turn left at the crossroads to

Flatford This is the scene of many of Constable's most famous paintings including, of course, 'Flatford Mill'. The village is very busy at holiday times. Following the one-way system, return to

East Bergholt Having seen Flatford, some time can now be spent in East Bergholt, for this is where Constable was born. The area between here and Dedham was where the painter spent his boyhood. He wrote later: 'I associate my careless boyhood with all that lies on the banks of the Stour. Those scenes made me a painter.' Go left at the church, then left again just past the Red Lion to the A12. Cross it to the B1068, taking this road to

Higham Turn right and follow the valley of the Brett to

Shelley This is a pretty, secluded hamlet. Carry on beside the river through

Lower Layham to

Hadleigh

47 VILLAGES OF THE BROADS

28 miles (45km) – Norfolk
Starting point: Wroxham
OS sheet 134, Bartholomew map 26

The Broads are more than just a place of hired motor cruisers, they are an area where the wildlife has a habitat unique in Britain, where herons are a common sight and where water-fowl fly across the sky at sunset like a scene from a Peter Scott painting. If the waterways are crowded during summer, the lanes are not. The villages have the delightful tradition of erecting gaily painted signs giving the name of the village and a carving depicting some aspect of its history. The absence of hills makes the riding easy, but beware of headwinds.

Wroxham The little town, which bustles with people taking on provisions for their boats, stands on the River Bure, and the view from the bridge with the boats jostling to set their occupants ashore, or move off, is colourful. Take the A1151 north, and after about 1 mile turn right at a crossroads and continue on the A1062, turning off right at the sign to

Horning This is a picturesque spot on a bend in the river, a prosperous little place with some attractive pubs. Retrace along the village street and cross the A1062, where there is a sign to

Neatishead Continue to the A1151 and turn right to

Stalham A small but busy market town, where there is a sale every Tuesday morning. Stalham Hall is ½ mile along the road to Stalham Green. It is not open but worth a look from the road. If visited, return to the village and take the B1151 north-east to

Sea Palling As the name suggests, this village is on the coast, or, more accurately, ½ mile inland as is the custom with many Norfolk villages for the coast in winter can be wild and desolate with great seas breaking in against the shore. The village sign has a carving of a lifeboat being rowed out into a huge sea. Follow the road south-east along the coast to

Horsey Just south of the village the road touches the edge of Horsey Mere, and the sails of the holiday boats pop up over the low hedges. Take the Martham road, where there is a restored smock mill (open), to the village of

Martham Stay on the B1152 to its junction with the A149, turn right on to the main road and cross the River Thurne to

Potter Heigham This is a favourite boating centre, with some useful stores. Unfortunately, in recent years, it has allowed rather too many hot-dog shops to spoil what used to be a charming spot. The feature of the village is its narrow stone bridge, and a small crowd is often to be seen by it watching for the pleasure craft which inch through the tiny archway, in the expectation that one which is bigger than the opening will try to get through. They do not usually have to wait long. Take the road signposted to

Ludham and return to

Horning in the opposite direction from which it was first visited. Enter the village by turning off the A1062 at the sign to Horning Church. This is 1 mile from the main village and is worth seeing as it stands on its own very attractively on the banks of the Bure. A path goes down to the water. Continue along the byroad into the main village, which is known locally as Lower Street, and return from there, along the route originally taken, to

Wroxham

Peaks and Pennines

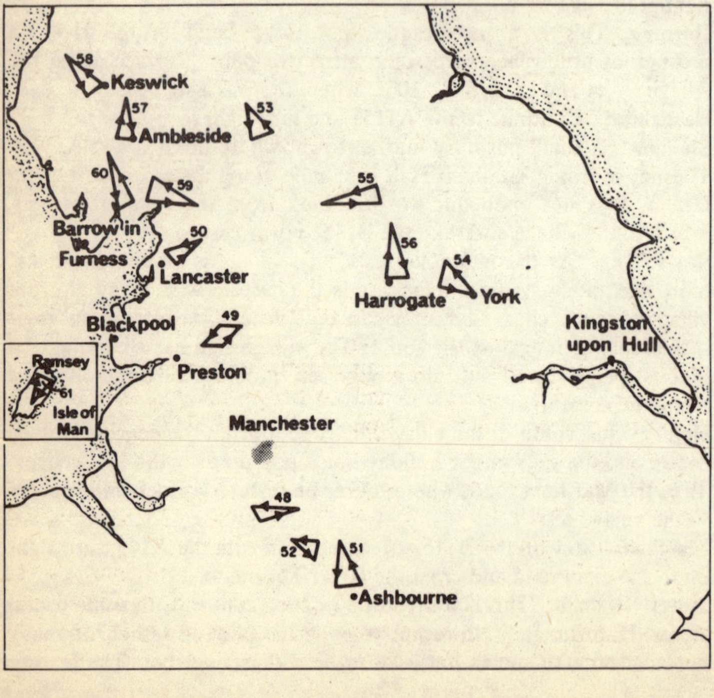

48 THE LEGEND OF THE WIZARD

17 miles (27km) – Cheshire
Starting point: Alderley Edge
OS sheets 109 and 118, Bartholomew map 28 or 29

The corner of Cheshire which lies just south of Manchester is well served by British Rail as it carries large numbers of commuters into the city from this pleasant belt of countryside: indeed, this area is more reminiscent of the soft plains of southern England, though the forbidding hills of the Peak District do reach just into our ride, giving a strange contrast in so short a journey. By putting the cycle on the train to Alderley, even a half day can be long enough for a trip far out of the city.

Alderley Edge Ride south on the A34, climbing rapidly, and after ½ mile turn left on to the B5087, signposted to Macclesfield. In ½ mile, the edge which gives its name to the town appears on the left. This short, steep wooded bank, now in the hands of the National Trust, is steeped in legends and no doubt was the scene of some strange happenings. The best-known tale concerns the wizard who reputedly lived here, guarding the entrance to an underworld in which a band of knights lie sleeping. When England is in danger, it is said, they will awake and take up arms again. Lock the cycle and wander around the paths of this strange old place. The views through the trees alone make it worth while. Remount and continue along the B5087, passing a pub appropriately called The Wizard, then take any of several lanes off to the left signposted to

Prestbury The town is attractive if a little pretentious. Cross the railway line and follow the signs to

Bollington For the first time on the ride we feel the chill of the northern hills for the high country which forms the Pennines hangs above us. Take the road running north-east signposted to Pott Shrigley. This is a steep climb and the hedges and fences of lowland Cheshire now give way to the stone walls of the high sheep country. In a mile the cyclist is in

Pott Shrigley Now comes the reward for the long climb as you descend in a westerly direction amid sweeping views, crossing the Macclesfield Canal and reaching

Adlington Cross the A523, riding due west along a minor road to the junction with the B5358 where go right and turn off the road at the first lane on the left. After a mile, the A538 is reached. Turn right on to it and then almost immediately left for

Kirkleyditch and so continue the descent to
Alderley Edge

49 PENDLE HILL AND THE WITCHES' COUNTRY

35 miles (56km) – Lancashire
Starting point: Clitheroe
OS sheet 103, Bartholomew map 31

The Lancashire witch hunts of 350 years ago, and the number of women who were hanged as a result of them, has given this area a reputation as a hotbed of witches, and even today it is possible to find people who believe in the evil eye. Clitheroe is surrounded by wild, bleak hills; it is sombre country and it is not difficult, when the clouds gather on Pendle Hill, to feel that something supernatural might happen at any time. This route is in a figure of eight, not because of any connection the figure may have with the dark powers, but so that it can be ridden in two parts if desired.

Clitheroe This is a sombre town, rather grey, and in winter the wind is funnelled down between the moors and through the valley where the town stands. Leave it by riding east and following the signs towards Padiham. At a crossroads after 1 mile go straight on and, leaving Pendleton Hall on the left, climb steeply up Pendleton Moor. The moorland now opens out and there are good views. The summit is called Nick of Pendle, a reminder that the devil inhabited these parts, and there is a fast descent (hang on to the brakes!) to the village of
Sabden Cross Sabden Brook and bear left up a steep hill. At the top there is a small crossroads; go left to avoid losing height and after about 2 miles go left again, down a steep hill, signposted to Newchurch. On the right near the bottom of the hill is Sabden Hall, where one inhabitant died 'after an old hag's curse'. Continue to
Newchurch Bear left out of the village and ride (or push) up the very hilly road for 1 mile to
Barley The wild summit of Pendle Hill rises to the left. Cycle along the road around the flank of the hill, watching for a sign-post to
Downham Go left after the church, crossing the line of the Roman road to
Chatburn In addition to the Romans, packhorses used this route in long-gone centuries as it was possible to cross the Ribble and pass between the great fells. Ride north, following the Slaidburn signs. After the Forest of Pendle you are now entering the Forest of

Bowland – a much larger area with higher hills but a more open landscape where there is little fear of meeting boggarts, wizards, fairies or other assorted creatures. Pedal along the road north among the fells, descending to

Slaidburn This is an attractive village, and descending from the fells is the best way to appreciate it. The trees and pleasant stone buildings are a relief after the wild country. Cross the river and turn left to

Newton Follow the Clitheroe signs and climb over the fells for a final descent into

Waddington From here, it is but a short ride back to

Clitheroe

50 CATON MOOR, IN THE FOREST OF BOWLAND

30 miles (48km) – Lancashire
Starting point: Carnforth
OS sheet 97, Bartholomew map 34

The area of gritstone moorland east of Lancaster is designated as an Area of Outstanding Natural Beauty. The route goes over wild, high moorland with grand views. It is strenuous for the cyclist and 'off the beaten track', though the road surfaces are good for such a wild place.

Carnforth There is a convenient railway station here, and also a large railway museum. From the town centre, bear left past the station to

Warton The prominent hill to the left is Warton Crag, which has an Iron Age fort on top; there is also a nature trail. Cross the railway line, the A6 and the M6 to

Borwick Turn right and follow the lane over the railway and the River Keer before climbing up Capernwray Hill. The road twists to the summit, then you swoop down in a fast left-hand curve to

Sunny Bank Turn left and then immediately right to

Gressingham Ride along the road through the village and cross the River Lune at

Loyn Bridge This is an interesting old bridge with passing places and it is guarded by a motte and bailey. Follow the road round to

Hornby The castle here is not open. At the end of the village street, do not follow the main road round to the right but continue straight ahead to

Butt Yeats Watch for the remains of an old cross at the crossroads.

Caton Moor now looms ahead. Climb steeply, and do not turn left to Wray but go straight on along the wild moorland road, past a farm called Thornbush, keeping the summit of the moor to the right and the river (the Roeburn) in the valley to the left. There are some fine waterfalls after heavy rain. The road meets the river at the farm of Lower Salter. Beyond the farmhouse, as the road bends, pass through a gate on the right, descend, then climb to

Haylotts Farm The fells are now all around, and this is 'roof of the moors' country. It is in such wild places as this that the cyclist feels the true freedom of the sport, the real joy of high places. Pass through the farm gate, turn sharp right and follow the unmade track which drops to cross a gill before climbing towards

Winder This is merely another farm. Pass through a gate and turn left. Ride along the tarmac road as it climbs and then skirts the southern edge of Caton Moor. The scenery along here is magnificent, with great windy skies. Follow the road down to the village of

Brookhouse Turn left into

Caton Go left on to the A683, turn right within ½ mile, at the signpost to Halton, and cross the River Lune at the beautiful Crook o' Lune. There is a picnic site here, though the cyclist who loves wild country may have already eaten on some high hillside. Ride along the road as it bears left to

Halton At the junction with a major road, go straight uphill, cross the M6 and turn right at Four Lane Ends. After 1½ miles, turn left to

Bolton-le-Sands Turn right along the A6, and so return to

Carnforth

51 A TASTE OF THE DERBYSHIRE DALES

25 miles (40 km) – Derbyshire
Starting point: Ashbourne
OS sheet 119, Bartholomew map 29

This route has been kept very short to allow for the cycle to be left and for the rider to proceed on foot along some of the dales. It is often possible to get right through them with a bike, putting it on the shoulders where necessary, such as when crossing the stepping stones at the southern end of Dovedale, but many people may prefer to leave the machine locked up and walk for a while in the peace of these beautiful and quiet retreats.

Ashbourne This market town is best known as the place where an unusual game of football takes place every Shrove Tuesday. The whole town becomes the 'pitch' and the object is to get the ball from one end of the town to the other by, apparently, any means. Any number seem to play. Leave the town by the A515 going north, and stay on this road to the attractive village of

Fenny Bentley Climb on up the main road for another mile and then turn right to

Tissington This village is famous for the well-dressing ceremonies which take place in May. The wells are garlanded with complex wreaths of flowers, possibly the relic of a pagan ceremony to ensure a pure water supply for the rest of the year. Keep to the right and after another mile, drop down to a ford. It is rather deep and there is a footbridge on the left. Turn left, and in another mile go left again at the signpost to

Parwich Just after the church, turn left to

Alsop en le Dale Continue to the A515, go left on to it and then take the first right, down a very steep hill (use lots of brake), to

Milldale You are now in the heart of the Derbyshire Dales country, and this is a good place to leave the cycle for a while, or else be prepared to push it at times along the paths. To the north are Wolfscote Dale and Beresford Dale, and to the south is the better-known Dovedale, though this tends to be rather crowded in holiday times. There are too many delights in these dales to describe in detail, but watch out for the caves which occur frequently in this limestone area, and there are waterfalls, crags and stepping stones. The area is rich in wildlife. Roughstuff enthusiasts might like to ride on the path along the east side of the river through Dovedale to the stepping stones, rejoining the route near Thorpe. It is not a difficult route but does involve negotiating some steep rocky paths. Otherwise, from the bridge at Milldale follow the signs to

Alstonfield and

Hopedale to

Ilam There is a youth hostel here converted from a castle-like hall. The village is attractive and situated in the Manifold Valley, a place beloved of fishermen, with the Isaac Walton Hotel there to cater for them. Pedal on eastwards to

Thorpe The steep rounded hill to the north of the village is Thorpe Cloud. It is well worth scrambling up its grassy slopes for the view of Dovedale. Keep to the left through the village and climb to the road junction at The Dog and Partridge. Turn right and then after 1 mile fork right down the hill to

Mapleton Go straight through the village and follow the road to

Ashbourne

52 BUXTON AND THE GOYT VALLEY

35 miles (56km) – Derbyshire
Starting point: Buxton
OS sheet 119, Bartholomew map 29

Although the reputation of Buxton has spread far and wide, the Goyt Valley is not nearly as well known as it deserves to be. The little River Goyt flows among high rugged hills, and the tiny valley is a rift in the moorland where the snow lingers late. The author rode the route one Easter when enormous icicles were still clinging to the banks overhanging the river.

Buxton This is known as the Capital of the High Peak and is a stately town of dignified architecture. See the Crescent and the Pavilion Gardens. Leave the town by taking the A5002 going north-west from the Devonshire Hospital. Although the town itself is situated at 1,000ft (305m), the road goes up steeply to the summit of Long Hill, 400ft (122m) above the town. There are some good views all the way up (if you have the breath left to enjoy them!). Turn left on to a lane, where there is a small shrine on the right. The road then drops steeply to

Errwood Dam The pine forests around the dams here and the wildness of the hills make this a grand place. There are picnic spots close to the water – or choose your own wild one. Cross the dam and follow the road alongside the lake. The road climbs steeply as it leaves the lake. The pointed hill to the right is Shining Tor. About 2 miles from the lake, go right and then left to cross the A537 and almost at once go over a staggered crossroads at the junction with the A54. Continue over wild moorland which is

Axe Edge Moor Descend Axe Edge, and at the junction with the A53, go straight over along a lane which drops steeply (this is exciting riding). Fork right after 1½ miles, keeping High Edge on the left, cross a cattle grid and continue on a gated road to the B5053. Turn right on to this road, at once crossing the tiny River Dove, and then climb to

Longnor Follow the signposts to

Sheen and then

Hartington This village of stone cottages has one of the country's first youth hostels, which is still extremely popular as it is an ideal place from which to explore the southern half of the Peak District by cycle. Leave the village by a lane running north from the duckpond to the hamlet of

Pilsbury The road goes sharply up a hill. Remain on it to the junction with the A515. Go left and then turn right at a sign to

Chelmorton The church claims to be the highest in England. Turn left near the church, go right, then right again, and left on to the A6 to return, past

Lover's Leap to

Buxton

53 THE EDEN VALLEY

31 miles (50km) – Cumbria
Starting point: Appleby
OS sheets 91 and 90 (just), Bartholomew maps 34 and 38

This area lies between the Pennines and the mountains of the Lake District. Appleby was the ancient county town of Westmorland and is now in Cumbria, so to maintain its old county name it has decided to call itself Appleby in Westmorland.

Appleby Each year, during the second week in June, Appleby New Fair is held here, which, despite its name, is one of the oldest in the country. It is colourful and noisy and has a certain notoriety, with some pubs remaining closed for the duration of the fair. Take the A66 Penrith road north-west to

Temple Sowerby This pretty spot is sometimes called the Queen of Westmorland villages and is renowned for its attractive houses. The village takes its name from the Knights Templars who at one time owned the manor. Turn right by the church and follow the lane until it joins the B6412, turning right on to it to

Culgaith and on to cross the A686 into the village of

Langwathby All along this part of the route the road has been keeping close to the River Eden with plenty of good picnic spots. Go north to

Little Salkeld and after leaving the village, take a left turn to

Long Meg Long Meg and her Daughters comprise an ancient stone circle with Long Meg, the largest stone, being aloof from the others and of a different type of stone with unknown ciphers. Return to the crossroads and go straight across to

Hunsonby Go straight across the A686, turning right in ½ mile to

Skirwith South of the village is Skirwith Abbey. Go left to

Kirkland To the right of the road are the Hanging Walls of Mark Anthony, the rather grand name for the grassy mounds which are part of an ancient cultivation system. You are now well in the foothills of the Pennines, with Kirkland Fell and Wildboar Scar to the north-east. There are tracks up into the fells which can be taken if time permits. Descend by the steep hill to the village of

Blencarn With the great, threatening fells still on the left, traverse along the foothills through

Milburn and

Knock to

Dufton The route has been an easy one beneath those great bluffs, but from Town Head in this village commences one of the most famous roughstuff crossings of the Pennines – the High Cup Nick route to Teesdale. However, this route takes the easier, southerly road back to

Appleby

54 HOWARDIAN HILLS AND VALE OF YORK

56 miles (90km) – Yorkshire
Starting point: York
OS sheets 100 and 105, Bartholomew maps 32 and 33

A not too strenuous ride through some of the loveliest countryside just north of York. The route can be cut short if desired.

York A tourists' Mecca in its own right which could easily keep you occupied for a week. York is the home of the CTC's annual national rally and a good centre from which to tour 'the county of broad acres', the Texas of England. Leave the city northwards along the busy A19, passing St Peter's School (founded in 627 A.D. and boasting Guy Fawkes among its pupils). Go straight on at the traffic lights at Clifton Green, then after a further 2 miles turn right into the peaceful village of

Skelton There is a fine thirteenth-century church here. The route is now along the winding lane to

Moorlands Nature Reserve Here, in early summer, the woods are ablaze with rhododendrons. Go straight on at the crossroads beyond the reserve on to a small road signposted 'local traffic'. The road becomes an unsurfaced track for a while, but emerges on to a metalled surface, where you go left into

Huby Proceed straight on, and beyond the pine woods north of Huby, a left turn at the T-junction, followed by a first right, brings you after a mile or so to

Crayke The houses are gathered on the southern slopes of the first of the Howardian Hills. The village green is a mass of daffodils in spring. A left turn in the village, past the church, brings you to a viewpoint westwards where the Pennines are clearly visible on a bright day. Continue northwards to

Oulston and

Newburgh Priory (open to the public on Wednesday and Sunday afternoons) where a fine topiary hedge guards a mainly seventeenth- and eighteenth-century building which is said to contain the headless body of Oliver Cromwell. Unfortunately, a curse on the tomb prevents anyone from checking the legend! From the hall, a short mile brings the cyclist past the lake to

Coxwold The fifteenth-century church, with its octagonal tower, was once under the ministry of author Laurence Sterne, famous for *Tristram Shandy* and *A Sentimental Journey Through France and Italy*. Sterne is remembered with a small museum in Shandy Hall, at the top end of the main street. Beyond Shandy Hall turn right then immediately left and go downhill to

Kilburn This is locally known as the 'home of the mouseman', where solid oak furniture of the late Robert Thompson always carries as its trademark the symbol of the church mouse, representing 'industry in quiet places'. The workshops are sometimes open to the public and a visit is very worth while. Beyond the village, continue northwards towards the striking

White Horse This was carved out of the hillside in the nineteenth century by the village schoolmaster. Above the horse, gliders from the Yorkshire Gliding Club are framed against the sky. (Beyond lies Sutton Bank at the top of two 1 in 4 hills and a 1 in 5! There is a national park information centre to reward the cyclist with enough energy to battle that high above the flat lands of the Vale of York.) This route, however, avoids climbing White Horse Bank by keeping right at the foot of the hill towards

Oldstead where you go left to

Byland Abbey The present site is several miles from the home village of Old Byland, up on the moors. Still skirting the foothills of the North York Moors, continue to

Wass where a right turn brings you through

Ampleforth (home of a modern abbey and famous boys' public school) to

Oswaldkirk A left turn on to the B1363 gives a pleasant short-cut back to York through the villages of Brandsby, Stillington and Sutton-on-the-Forest. For the longer ride, continue up the hill out of Oswaldkirk to meet the B1257, where you go right and then left to

Nunnington The hall here has been restored by the National Trust. From the hall take the road uphill, in a southerly direction, through the long avenue of trees to the viewpoint at the top. A downhill sweep brings you to the B1257. Go left here to

Hovingham whose hall is the former home of the Duchess of Kent. Continue on the B1257 to

Slingsby (its ruined castle on the left was never inhabited), and turn right at the crossroads for

Castle Howard At the crest of the hill there extends before you a road dead straight as far as the eye can see, with archways and an obelisk to break the view. It is possible to see near the southern perimeter of the grounds a small pyramid containing a bust of the black sheep of the family, symbolically looking away from the house! At the crossroads beyond the house, turn right for

Bulmer then go on to

Sheriff Hutton whose castle is now a stark ruin. Fork left south of the village to

West Lilling and continue to

Flaxton Go right across the pretty Strensall Common to

Strensall Keep straight on now through the villages of

Old Earswick and

Huntington to return to

York

55 WENSLEYDALE

31 miles (50km) – Yorkshire
Starting point: Aysgarth
OS sheet 98, Bartholomew map 35

Wensleydale is a place of views, distant vistas with flaming gorse and heather-clad hills, close-up views such as Aysgarth Falls, or the sparkling white snow on the 'tops' in late spring. There is always something hereabouts to delight the eye. From the point of navigation, this is the easiest of rides, a simple circle around the high fells. For the adventurous there are many variations using the most marginal of roads and trackways, but as always with rides in wild country, the weather must never be ignored: in snow the ride could become impossible and at any time of year the number of steep climbs makes it a very hard 31 miles.

Aysgarth To avoid more main road riding than absolutely necessary, leave the village by the minor road running south-west parallel to the A684 but higher up on the flank of the moor and stay with it to
Thornton Rust Remain with the road as it plunges down to the A684 at
Worton Go left along the main road to
Bainbridge which is the site of a Roman fort. Continue along the valley to
Hawes Here the real climbing begins as our route turns left along the minor road through the hamlet of
Gayle climbing steadily and sometimes very steeply up the side of the fells with great views opening out all the time. The summit is reached a little below 2,000ft on what is an old Roman road. Now comes the reward for the climb as the road swoops down the fell and enters
Langstrothdale If feeling in need of refreshments or provisions, continue to the village of
Buckden which lies on the B6160, otherwise 2 miles can be saved by crossing the river at Kirk Gill and joining the B6160 north of the village. The road now switchbacks north-easterly with spectacular scenery in all directions finally running through
Bishopdale Turn left at the sign to
Thoralby and make a final steep climb over the fell to
Aysgarth

56 NORTH OF NIDDERDALE

32 miles (51km) – Yorkshire
Starting point: Harrogate
OS sheets 99 and 105, Bartholomew map 32

A day ride which combines ancient and modern, the towns of Ripon and Harrogate, with the splendours of Fountains Abbey and the attractions of several pretty Yorkshire villages.

Harrogate Famous as a spa town and a conference centre. Harrogate is also well known to cyclists as the birthplace of the Cyclists' Touring Club in 1878. A commemorative plaque stands in the gardens opposite the exhibition hall in the centre of the town. Leave Harrogate on the A61 going northwards, turning off after 3 miles into

Ripley This attractive little village, now bypassed by the busy traffic, has medieval stocks and a village cross in its small, cobbled square. Nearby stands Ripley Castle and the village church, where it is said that bullet marks can still be seen on the walls, dating from the Civil War. Also noteworthy is the overlarge village institute, boasting the inscription, 'Hotel de Ville'. At the roundabout at the north end of the village, turn left on to the B6165 towards Pateley Bridge, but then take the first right and go uphill towards Fountains Abbey. Go straight on at the crossroads then first right, and keep left until you sweep downhill to

Fountains Abbey This is the most imposing of all Yorkshire's ruined abbeys, nestling in the valley of the infant River Skell. Continue on the B6265, where a right turn brings you shortly into

Ripon This busy market town is well known for its racecourse and its cathedral, whose squat towers are nevertheless visible from some distance. A curfew horn is still sounded in the market square each evening, and high above the wakeman's house a motto proclaims 'Except ye Lord keepeth ye City, ye Wakeman waketh in vain'. Also worth a visit is the twelfth-century lepers' chapel, close by the Ure Bridge on the A61, north of the town centre. From the cathedral, go downhill to the roundabout and straight on for 3 miles to

Bishop Monkton It is well worth making a diversion here by turning left at the crossroads into the village, then right after the Methodist chapel through the ford (footbridge alternative) to follow the stream back to the church. Here, turn left at the T-junction and continue, keeping left, to reach the ornamental bridge over the lake of Copgrove Hall. Take the next right, then go right at the T-junction, straight over the crossroads and continue downhill to the A6055, where a right turn brings you into

Knaresborough A short uphill ride through the main street brings you to the castle ruins, dominating the town and the cliff above the River Nidd. Close by is, reputedly, the oldest chemist's shop in England. A ride down to the riverside is rewarded with striking views of the rocky gorge and the tall graceful railway bridge which carries the trains from Harrogate to York. You should also cross the river to see Mother Shipton's Cave and the famous 'dropping well' where a bizarre collection of objects has been petrified by the salts in the water. From the river bridge at the west end of Knaresborough, a short ride along the A59 brings you back through

Starbeck to
Harrogate

The Lake District and the Isle of Man

(see map on page 93)

57 AROUND HELVELLYN

35 miles (56km) – Cumbria
Starting point: Ambleside
OS sheet 90, Bartholomew map 34

In the summer season the roads used in this route are very busy, as they connect some of the best-known features in this part of Lakeland. If the sun is shining and the holiday traffic is too thick, try one of the other rides in this book, but remember to come back out of season, perhaps when the wind and rain are whipping the cloud across the peaks, for this route is not one to be missed as it includes some of the great views of the Lakeland crags. Although there are plenty of interesting small towns on the route, the chief feature is the continuous spread of mountain scenery which arises throughout the ride.

Ambleside This is a popular area from which to tour the Lakes. It stands on the northerly tip of Windermere; visit the lake before starting on the ride. It is at its most beautiful when there is just a touch of mist on the water. Retrace to the town and ride north on the A591 to

Rydal Dora's Field was planted here by Wordsworth and given to his daughter, Dora. It is a mass of daffodils in spring, and is now held by the National Trust. The field can be reached by locking the bike and walking through the churchyard. Rydal Water, which is probably the smallest of the Lakes, is to the left of the road just after the village. Loughrigg Fell is also to the left, and a couple of miles ahead comes

Grasmere This is the place which is most readily associated with Wordsworth, for it was here that he walked and was inspired to write so many of his poems by the scene around him. But it was also a spot frequented by other writers of the age: Ruskin, Southey, Coleridge all knew and wrote of it. Ride on up the main road for 4 miles, taking a left turn on to a minor road at the beginning of

Thirlmere The road runs along the west side of this lake. Across the lake, just over the main road, rise Helvellyn Screes, and then the

great mass of the mountain above them. From the road along the west side, the lake forms a grand foreground to a magnificent picture. Striding Edge is the ridge near Helvellyn's summit. Continue on the west side of the lake. There is a nature trail here if time permits. Bear right at the head of the lake, cross the A591 and then bear left alongside St John's beck. The road, the B5322, winds between steep fells to

Threlkeld Go right on to the A66 and take the third turn on the right (after 2½ miles), past a farm called Wallthwaite. Continue on this minor road east to join the A5091. Go right on to this road and follow it to the shores of

Ullswater There are wonderful views across the lake to the jumble of fells on the other side. Follow the road to

Glenridding and on to

Patterdale The great mass of the Helvellyn Range dominates Ullswater. There is a path from Patterdale up to Striding Edge, though it would be a foolhardy roughstuffer who took his bike along the actual edge. Anyone who walks up can see, in fine weather, twenty mountains, seven lakes and the hills of Scotland. Ride on along the A592 and start the long climb up through the

Kirkstone Pass It is well worth getting off and walking, for the scenery is so fine. How long the ascent takes should not be important.

At the summit, take the minor road bearing away to the right. You now descend steeply for the 3 miles or so to
Ambleside

58 DERWENTWATER AND THE HONISTER PASS

25 miles (40km) – Cumbria
Starting point: Keswick
OS sheet 90, Bartholomew map 34

There are many people who would claim that the countryside between Keswick, Borrowdale and Buttermere is the loveliest in the Lake District. It is extremely popular during summer – perhaps the best time to see these dramatic fells and beautiful lakes is in autumn or spring when the changes of light add to the charm. The traffic during high season can spoil the main roads for the cyclist.

Keswick To the north of the town lies the great bulk of Skiddaw, while on its doorstep to the south is the beautiful Derwentwater. Leave the town by going south along its shore on the B5289. There are wonderful views across the lake to the Derwent Fells. Near the end of it are the Barrow Falls, where the water comes down 120ft (37m) in two spectacular leaps, and a little further on is the Lodore Cascade. The first is the more spectacular of the two. Continue on past the lake to the hamlet of
Grange Stop a while at the bridge, which is a much-photographed spot. Remain on the B5289, which follows the course of the Derwent, and pass the Bowder Stone, a relic of the Ice Age. The huge boulder appears to balance on a narrow edge. Follow the road through the hamlet of
Rosthwaite to
Borrowdale This is another very popular spot in summer, and those cyclists who like roughstuff might try the lane to the left which gives access to the highest group of peaks in England: Scafell Pike, Scafell and Great Gable. But be warned, the higher parts of the Lake District are only for the experienced and the well equipped, and the weather can change with amazing suddenness. From Borrowdale, continue on the B5289 and start the climb up the
Honister Pass Among early cycling pass-stormers it was very much the thing to have 'done' the Honister, and it is still something of a status symbol today. There are no great problems with it, if you are prepared for some walking: in winter, however, it is another matter. The scenery throughout is superb, and you finally descend past the shores of Buttermere to the village of

Buttermere The little town has a wonderful position, being on two lakes: Buttermere and Crummock Water. If time allows, continue along the road following the shore of Crummock Water, then return and visit the little church. Take the minor road to the right out of the village and climb steeply up into the fells. This is a delightful, airy road, which is followed to
Braithwaite and so back to
Keswick

59 SILVERDALE AND THE SALT-MARSH COUNTRY

20 miles (32km) – Cumbria and Lancashire
Starting point: Arnside
OS sheet 97, Bartholomew map 34

Arnside has the advantage of possessing a railway station which brings travellers from the northern towns, and much further afield, right into an area of great beauty. This short run has been included for any cyclist who comes to the area by train for the day. A shopping bike or a folding cycle could complete the run, and there are many footpaths that make interesting walks. Although hilly, the countryside does not have the same huge crags that are found across the estuary to the north-west.

Arnside The town is on an estuary where seabirds frequent the salt-marshes, and where the tides rush in and out with, it is said, the speed of a galloping horse. Leave by the B5282, passing under the railway bridge, and take the road along the coast. There are good views over the estuary to the left. Continue for 2 miles to
Dalham Tower and turn right through the drive gates. There are deer and herons to be observed here. Bear left to
Beetham Turn right, going uphill through wooded country to
Slack Head This is one of the many places where you could happily leave the bike for a while and walk on the footpaths. Continue to
Thrang End Go up a very steep hill, bearing left to
Yealand Storrs and left again to
Yealand Redmayne Again, it is worth leaving the cycle here and taking the footpaths on the right to Cringlebarrow Woods. Continue to
Yealand Conyers There is a pub here that sells real ale. Turn right in the village, ride up a very steep hill, passing the drive to Leighton Hall, and then go downhill to
Warton By the Black Bull, take a steep climb to the right. Warton Crag, with its Iron Age fort, and a nature trail are now on the right.

Visit if time allows. Continue along the lane, dropping down and passing over a level-crossing. Turn left and left again to
Jenny Brown's Point Continue north to
Silverdale This village is in the heart of an Area of Outstanding Natural Beauty. There is much wildlife in the sands to the west, while the woods and hills all around have a very large bird population. Go north out of the village, turning left at a signpost to Arnside. There is another nature trail here. Follow the lane to
The Cove There are interesting limestone outcrops. Return to the road and continue round Arnside Knott, where there is a nature trail on the hill, and follow the road back to
Arnside

60 LIMESTONE HILLS OF SOUTHERN LAKELAND

30 miles (48km) – Cumbria
Starting point: Arnside
OS sheet 97, Bartholomew map 34

In the rush of visitors to the central fells of Lakeland, this area is often overlooked. For the cyclist, it is a place of narrow lanes and sharp corners, of steep short climbs and exhilarating descents. The scale of the countryside is smaller than that of the great fells, but it has a charm of its own. It is an excellent route when holiday traffic packs the better-known spots.

Arnside This little town is situated at the top of Morecambe Bay on the estuary of the River Kent and is easily reached by train. Leave by the B5282, passing under the railway bridge, and in a little over 2 miles cross the bridge over the River Bela. Turn immediately left and follow the lane, turning right and then left to
College Green Turn right and join the A6, turning left on to it to
Levens Bridge Levens Hall is to be found here – one of the most beautiful houses in the Lake District, with an outstanding garden and examples of topiary. It is open to the public and there are public footpaths through the park between avenues of oaks and beeches. Go left at the traffic lights to the village of
Levens and follow the road on to
Brigsteer About 2 miles after this, bear left for
Crosthwaite This is in the Lythe Valley, where damsons were once the staple crop – one farm is still called Damson Dene. The countryside is now hilly and quite magnificent. It is simple at this point to continue to Bowness, on Lake Windermere, returning through Winster to

make a longer ride. Otherwise, pass the church and the inn and go on to

Dodds Howe Turn left and left again on to the A5074 and then, after ½ mile, take the second minor road on the right, running south. Continue on this road and climb through Park Wood. Pass Witherslack Hall, climb steeply and turn left to

Millside (If the preceding lane has been missed, remaining on the A5074 will still bring you to Millside.) Pass the millstream, where there is a pretty garden. A track on the left leads to a bridleway through woods below Whitbarrow Scar on to the A590 – a lovely diversion for the cyclist who likes woodland tracks. Otherwise, follow the lane to the A590. Turn left on to this road and return to

Levens Bridge A short but overgrown roughstuff section leads from the lane by the AA box to Mabbin Hall. Go right on to the A6 and fork left through

Heversham and drop down through

Milnthorpe Go right on to the B5282, then left over Bela Bridge into Dalham Tower grounds and pass through the deer-park. Follow the signs towards Storth, but turn left at the crossroads, then turn right and follow the road over the level-crossing back to

Arnside

61 OVER THE MOUNTAIN

35 miles (56km) – Isle of Man
Starting point: Ramsey
OS sheet 95, Bartholomew map 31

The Isle of Man is flat at its northern and southern extremities but mountainous in the centre. The motor-cycle TT race is not the only event held there: each year there is also a week of cycle racing which has achieved international recognition. The speeds reached may be somewhat slower, but the enthusiasm and effort put into the amateur events are no less, and the laurels heaped upon the winners are just as highly valued. Road surfaces on the TT course are superb.

Ramsey This is the traditional landing place for royal visits to the island. The town is under the shadow of the mountain, and is protected from the prevailing south-westerly wind by the mountain's huge bulk, making it one of the most sheltered spots on the island. Leave the town by following the A18 south, on the TT course around the hairpin and up the mountain. The Albert Tower marks the spot where Prince Albert stood after climbing up to get a good view of Ramsey. Two miles out of Ramsey comes the

Guthrie Memorial There are some grand views from here, and they get better still as you climb up to
East Mountain Gate The summit appearing on the right is Snaefell. There is a track up to the top. Stay on the same road, past
Bungalow a famous TT vantage point where there is a motor-cycle museum, and
Windy Corner to
Creg-ny-Baa The descent around these bends is exhilarating, but hang on to the brakes! To avoid going into Douglas, turn right just after the village of
Hillberry and go through
Strang and then on to the A1 (the TT course again), following it to
St John's The hill to the south-west of the town, marked on the map as Slieau Whallian, is known locally as Witches' Hill: the power of witchcraft has a very strong hold on the island, or so many people believe. Take the road out to the north (the A4), still on the TT course, from which there are good views across the sea to the left. Descend into
Kirk Michael A mile to the south a path leads down to a waterfall at Spoyt Vane. If visited, retrace to Kirk Michael and remain on the A3 to
Ballaugh There is an attractive byroad leading away to the right, into the mountains, from Ballaugh Bridge, which would make a pleasant diversion if time allowed. Otherwise, continue on the A3 along what the TT riders call the Sulby Straight, go through
Sulby and remain on the road to
Ramsey

WALES

South and Central Wales

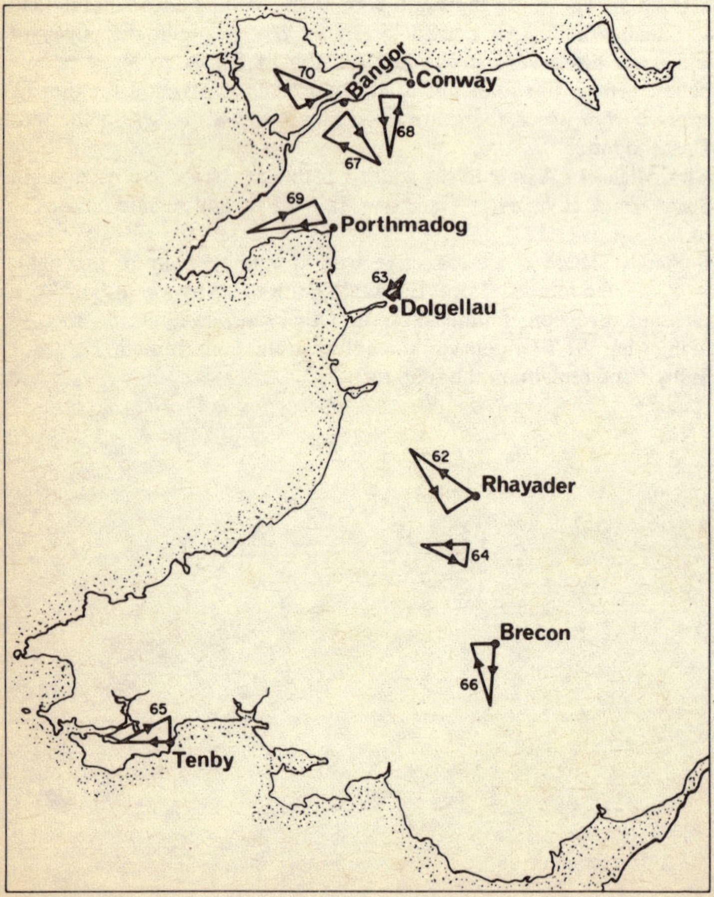

62 THE ROOF OF WALES

75 miles (120km) – Powys and Dyfed
Starting point: Rhayader
OS sheets 147 and 146 (just), Bartholomew map 17

Of all the routes in this book, this is the toughest. It is a ride for the dedicated, a mountain way, plunging and climbing constantly though always on surfaced roads. It is not a particularly long ride, but it can be extended by starting and finishing at Staunton on Wye instead of Rhayader, thus making a run of 125 miles. The shorter route is dealt with here as there are still enough hills to satisfy even a mountain goat.

The scenery, even in rain and mist, can be called truly spectacular, and the roads are largely traffic-free even in the summer. In winter, many stretches are likely to be impassable, and at all times great care is needed as sharp bends on steep descents are frequent.

Rhayader On the wall of the Cwm Arms is a CTC plaque, emphasizing the generations of cyclists who have toured in this part of Wales. Leave the town by the B4518 and cross the River Wye, then take the first right, signposted 'mountain road', and climb up the valley. There are 4 miles of climbing, then a fast descent on a good surface, but great care is needed on the bends. Where the river, the Afon Elan, enters the Craig Goch Reservoir, remain on the north side of the river on the road signposted to Cwmystwyth. Start another 4 mile climb, and look to the left. The large hill is Clawddu Bach. Along its ridge runs an ancient road, across which drovers once herded sheep to market. It would make a wonderful roughstuff route for another occasion, and can be used for a return to Rhayader by anyone with a stout enough heart, in both senses of the expression. Meanwhile, continue on the mountain road between great craggy hills to
Cwmystwyth For those wanting to get in a few extra miles, take the Devil's Bridge road, visit that scenic spot, then turn south to rejoin the route east of Pontrhydygroes. Otherwise, take the road to the left out of Cwmystwyth, staying on the north bank of the river (Afon Ystwyth), and turn left on to the B4574 to
Pontrhydygroes There is a very fast descent into the village. The B4343 then ascends to the hamlet of
Ysbyty Ystwyth The road is a little easier here for a short while, merely undulating gently for 4 miles to
Pontrhydfendigaid A short excursion can be made here, if desired, to see St Mary's Abbey by taking the road to the left at the end of the village. If so, retrace to the B4343 and follow it to

Tregaron There is a convenient café at the crossroads. Take the mountain road to the east, and climb steeply for 6 miles. There are frequent forest areas on the right, and on the left is Y Drum (1,668ft; 509m). The road continues to dip and rise. Cross the border from Dyfed to Powys, and after a very steep descent, you will reach a telephone box at a junction. Take the road to the left, towards Abergwesyn, which climbs steeply. The really steep hills are now ahead. The road twists and turns for 3 miles or so, then turns right and plunges down a 1 in 5 descent with a sharp left-hand bend at the bottom. Hang on to the brakes all the way down. In another 2 or 3 miles, the road plunges down the

Devil's Staircase This is a series of 'steps', followed by zigzags with gradients as steep as anything to be found in Wales. The road crosses and recrosses the Afon Irfon which it then follows to

Abergwesyn Turn left on to the road signposted to Beulah – another long climb between forest-clad hills. There is a welcome descent into

Beulah Take the B4358 out of the village to the north-east, signposted to Newbridge on Wye. Although the most rugged part of the ride is over, this road is still extremely hilly and a real test for anyone who has come this far. Stay on it to

Newbridge on Wye The main road can now be taken to complete the ride, and though it is busy in summer, it is still scenically very attractive following the valley of the Wye. Though hardly flat, it is easy compared to what has gone before. Stay with it to

Rhayader

63 UNDER CADER IDRIS

10 miles (16km) – Gwynedd
Starting point: Dolgellau
OS sheet 124, Bartholomew map 22

One needs a love of austere beauty to enjoy the sombre grey architecture of Dolgellau, but George Borrow described it as one of the most beautiful of spots, having the most beautiful women. The green of the surrounding hills, soft in heavy wet mist, or partly obscured by rain driven horizontally before the wind, makes a background that blends naturally with the Welsh granite. Each year, crowds of holidaymakers flock to the area, and this short ride gives a taste of the hills near the town.

Dolgellau From the north bank of the river, take the A494 east for a few hundred yards and then turn off left (the Llanfachreth road). Continue for a mile while the little road parallels the A494 but keeps well above it. Now prepare for some steep climbing, for it may be a case of frequently hopping off to push for the next mile as the road runs under the east shoulder of a steep hill called Foel Offrwm, which is reputed to mean The Hill of Sacrifice. There are the remains of a hill fort on the summit, now a collection of large boulders. Continue, with good views all around, and the huge mass of Cader Idris never far away, to

Llanfachreth Continue west, but now hang on to the brakes for a spectacular series of descents to a small river which is reached after 1½ miles. Now follow the road south-west under the famous Precipice Walk, rejoining the A494 just south of Llanelltyd and follow this easy valley road for the last mile back to

Dolgellau

64 THE UPPER WYE

20 miles (32km) – Powys
Starting point: Builth Wells
OS sheet 147, Bartholomew map 17

Although a short route, this is a hilly run, the road always going either up or down with no flat bits in between. Much of its charm lies in the contrast over such a small area. At first, the ride passes through the lanes in countryside which bears the characteristics of the Wye Valley, then it changes dramatically as the route goes over wild, open moorland.

Builth Wells A busy little town on the banks of the Wye, and the site of the Royal Welsh Show. The wells mentioned in the name are about 1 mile from the town. Ride west from the centre of the town and turn left up Hospital Road. The large houses soon give way to open views on the right, and the narrow road ducks and dives between, in summer, high banks of honeysuckle and dog-roses. For the next 5 miles there are glimpses across the Upper Wye Valley on the right, and steep wooded hills on the left. The river to the right of the road is the Irfon, which joins the Wye at Builth. At the crossroads with the B4519 turn left, and pass a warning sign saying that the lane ahead is used as an army firing range. The road is only closed when firing is actually taking place. Proceed up the long, steep climb. The views now open out, and there is a viewpoint at the summit which is a marvellous place for a picnic if the wind is not blowing a full gale. Continue along the high moorland to

Drover's Arms Despite its name, this is not a pub but the remains of an old building, once a hostelry, where the sheep drovers halted on their way to market. It is a lonely, windswept spot. Turn left along a rather rough road, apparently surfaced by the army and made of concrete. There are grand moorland views along this stretch, though sheep wander all over the road, as there is neither hedge nor fence, and care needs to be taken to avoid hitting them. At the B4520, turn left to the public house at

Cwm Owen A quarter of a mile past the pub, there is a narrow lane on the left which can be taken as an alternative route back to Builth. It is rather more hilly than the B4520 but follows a pretty little river called the Duhonw. For those who prefer the slightly easier B4520, continue on and descend the steep hill which is marked as a 1 in 4 gradient. This is followed by a descent of 1 in 6 with a sharp right-hand bend over the river, where there is a waterfall. It makes a good picnic spot. Remain on the same road to return to

Builth Wells

65 WEST FROM TENBY

35 miles (56km) – Dyfed
Starting point: Tenby
OS sheet 158, Bartholomew map 11

The little peninsula to the west of Tenby is a favoured spot, with a much lower rainfall than many parts of Wales, a mild winter and a sea which varies in colour from the deepest blue to delicate shades of green. The sands of Tenby soon give way to rocky points where the seas break in a white foam, adding to the colour of this delightful corner. It is at its best in the autumn when the crowds have gone and the weather is still warm.

Tenby From Castle Hill there is a grand view stretching from St Govan's Head in the west to Worms Head in the east. Boat trips can be taken to Caldey Island. Leave the town by going west on the B4318 to

Gumfreston Visit the church, which was built in about 1300. It has an unusual tower which is divided into five sections. The situation of the church, in a wooded 'glen', is very attractive. Continue along the B4318 and in 1½ miles turn left for

St Florence This little village is in a valley that has particular charm. Continue through it and make a very steep climb to a crossroads, turning right on to the

Ridgeway The route, as the name suggests, runs along a high spur giving grand views both to the north and south. Continue along it to

Lamphey There are many attractive old cottages here, but also rather too much modern building. Visit the Bishop's Palace (open) which is a ruin. Go left on to the B4584 to

Freshwater East There is good bathing here, though the area is very busy during the summer. Turn right in the village, going south-west along a narrow lane which follows the coast. The Pembrokeshire Coast Path runs along the cliffs to the left, and it is worth leaving the cycle and scrambling along the pathways in the area. Continue to

Stackpole Follow the lane to the junction with the B4319, where you go left to

Castlemartin The road continues west and brushes the coast at a headland called Little Furzenip. Stay with the road to the junction with the B4320. There are many signs of earlier habitations along this coast, in particular barrows and burial chambers. Go right on to the B4320 to

Pembroke This is a good place for refreshments and there is a ruined castle to visit. Leave the town on the A4075. If traffic is heavy, you can make a right turn at a crossroads 1 mile out of the town and follow the lane through Stephen's Green to Milton. Otherwise, stay on the main road, which merges into the A477 to

Milton There is a network of lanes to the north around the Cresswell and Carew rivers, any of which provides good cycling. If taken, retrace to Milton. Continue on the A477, and after 1 mile turn right on to the B4318 for the return to

Tenby

66 THE BRECON BEACONS

38 miles (61km) – Powys
Starting point: Brecon
OS sheet 160, Bartholomew maps 12 and 17

The Brecon Beacons are a national park, and this route, which is half roughstuff and half on good roads, takes in some of the very best scenery. At the worst spots, the track consists of loose scree and climbs steeply among the peaks, but the views can only be called magnificent. The end of the ride consists of several miles of uninterrupted downhill pleasure on a first-class surface, again with grand views.

Brecon The town, on the River Usk, is a touring centre with a cathedral and the remains of a castle. Sarah Siddons was born in a pub here in 1775. Leave by crossing the bridge over the Usk, travelling west, and in a few hundred yards take a left turn which is signposted to St David's Hospital. The road climbs and plunges up into the hills until, after about 3 miles, a T-junction is reached. Turn right; after 1½ miles the road ceases to be surfaced and soon becomes a track. Continue on, climbing steadily and pushing where necessary. The views behind become more and more magnificent as you climb.

The ridge forming the actual Beacons is to the right, and the track climbs on, always well marked, passing over a saddle on this ridge. It is worth stopping here and taking in the panorama behind, as from this point the view changes. The descent is now made on the track, which is rideable with care to

Neuadd Reservoirs The views here are of steep, tumbling hills, often covered with pines, ringing the lakes. Take the track to the right which leads to the dam wall and rejoin the surfaced road just below the lower lake. The lane twists along the valley of the Taf Fechan and at one point crosses a waterfall. This part of the route is particularly scenic. Continue to the very large lake which is the

Taf Fechan Reservoir Ride alongside the lake for the next 2 miles and bear right at the sign to Trefachan, passing a prominent quarry on the right. Join the A470 at

Cefn-coed-y-cymmer (shortened on signposts to Cefn-Coed) Turn right to avoid going into Merthyr Tydfil, and continue on the main road for the whole 17 miles of the return journey. The road is not particularly busy and the scenery is always dramatic with three lakes alongside it. At the summit of a hill, pass the adventure centre on the right, and the road then swoops downhill for mile after mile, past Llwyn-y-Celyn Youth Hostel back to

Brecon

North Wales

67 AROUND SNOWDON
45 miles (72km) – Gwynedd
Starting point: Bangor
OS sheet 115, Bartholomew map 27

This is one of the great cycling routes of North Wales, climbing from the coast right through the Snowdon Range. The road winds past sombre lakes, always with a magnificent backdrop of mountains, sometimes seen in the sun, sometimes with cloud and a soft mist whirling past them, and at other times with the rain being driven horizontally before the wind. The gradients are not severe as the roads go through the passes and follow the course of the tumbling Welsh rivers. The route uses good roads at all times. It is a ride to take all day over, not because it is hard but because it would be unthinkable not to stop regularly and simply gaze at some of the finest scenery in Britain.

Bangor A busy and rather crowded little town at the northern end of the Menai Strait, but from its higher parts the Snowdon Range can already be seen. From the railway station, ride along the A4087 eastward to the junction with the A5 and follow the road around with Penrhyn Castle on the left. For those who object to the main road, there is a byroad going south off the A4087 ½ mile east of the railway station, but it is not as attractive as the main road, which follows the River Ogwen to
Bethesda This is a slate-quarrying town, and the grey stone gives it a rather grim appearance, but the Nant Ffrancon Pass is just ahead. Begin the climb up the pass, and the scenery soon becomes magnificent. The River Ogwen is in the valley on the right, and the sharply pointed mountain, forward and to the right, is Y Garn. Continue to the mountain rescue centre at Ogwen Cottage on the western tip of Llyn Ogwen; Idwal Cottage Youth Hostel is up the track on the right. There are some spectacular waterfalls where the river leaves the lake. If time permits, lock the cycle and walk up the track beside the mountain rescue post to Llyn Idwal, a lonely lake. You are now entering Cwm Idwal, the finest of all the Welsh cwms – a vast amphitheatre of cliff and ridge. The Idwal Slabs, on which generations of climbers have learned their craft, are here, and in the dark cliffs to the left there are clefts and crags with the romantic names of the Nameless Cwm, Devil's Kitchen and the Cherry-Tree Wall. Retrace

to the road at Llyn Ogwen and retrieve the bike. Continue on the A5, passing along the shore of the lake. The large whale-backed mountain on the right is Tryfan. The road descends, with the pretty River Llugwy on the right, to

Capel Curig An interesting little town, much given to selling climbing gear and the products of Welsh craft industries. Swing right on to the A4086 and pass two lakes on the left, connected by a narrow channel. The large mountain away to the left is Moel Siabod. The road points directly towards Snowdon and, weather permitting, it can be seen as the highest point in a broken skyline of peaks. Continue to the hotel at

Pen-y-Gwryd The hotel is a sacred spot for climbers. It was here that some of the planning was done for the first successful Everest expedition, and the signatures of many of the members of that party are preserved on the ceiling of one of the bars. There are also many other mementoes of famous climbers on view. If the weather is bad, the route can be shortened here by turning right along the Llanberis Pass. Otherwise, you should take the left fork where the road becomes the A498, signposted to Beddgelert. After 1 mile there is a grand viewpoint by a milestone, looking up a valley to Snowdon. The road descends, still through dramatic scenery, with rivers and lakes on both sides; the bare slopes give way to conifers and grass replaces heather. Bryn Gwynant Youth Hostel is attractively placed above Llyn Gwynant. Continue to

Beddgelert An attractive large village near the scenic Aberglaslyn Pass, surrounded by mountains. The name is reputed to mean the Grave of Gelert, the faithful hound of Prince Llewelyn, which was slain after it had saved his infant son from a wolf. Unfortunately, the well-known tale is untrue, and the name actually means the Grave of Kelert, an early saint, but this does not stop large numbers of people from visiting the supposed grave of the dog. Turn right on to the A4085 and ride with the river on the left and mountains all around for about 6 miles to

Snowdon Ranger Youth Hostel The hostel is on the shore of Llyn Cwellyn, and was formerly the home of a well-known guide to the Snowdon range. For anyone with the time (and a stout pair of boots) there is a footpath from the hostel to the summit of Snowdon, though it is more than 4 miles of hard walking. Continue the descent along the road towards Caernarvon, leaving the mountains behind and reaching the lowlands. Reach the village of

Croesywaun If a shorter but hilly route is preferred, take the byroad on the right leading north-east for the return; if you want a rather longer but less strenuous road, continue into

Caernarvon Its great castle is surrounded on three sides by water and is one of Britain's most important ancient fortifications. It is now an easy 9 mile run back along the A487. Just before Bangor, the Menai Bridge is reached on the left, and so the route ends in
Bangor

68 CONWAY VALLEY AND THE SWALLOW FALLS

40 miles (64km) – Gwynedd
Starting point: Conway
OS sheets 115 and 116, Bartholomew map 27

The Conway Valley cleaves its way into Snowdonia providing a fertile strip between the ranges of hills and mountains. This run goes out along the west side of the river into the wooded and beautiful hills around Betwys-y-coed, and then back along the east bank of the river or, alternatively, over the high moors to the east.

Conway The town is a walled fortress roughly in the shape of a Welsh harp, and the castle is the dominant feature with massive walls (even by the standards of castles). Leave the square by the castle and turn left through an archway below the south wall of the fortress. This leads to

Gyffin Hill from which there is a good view. Ride around the east flank of the hill, turn right on to the B5106 and then go immediately left and follow the signs to

Roewen This is a place of quaint cottages and small streams, and is one of the most attractive villages in the district. Retrace to the first turning right. The winding road crosses two stone bridges and connects to the B5106. Turn right on to this road and follow it south past an aluminium works at

Dolgarrog Continue on to the junction where the Llanrwst road comes in on the left. Gwydir Castle, which is more of a fortified house than a castle, is here and it stands in fine grounds with gardens and peacocks. Do not take the Llanrwst road, but continue south on the B5106 with the river on the left and wooded, steep hills to the right until

Betwys-y-coed This is one of the showplace villages of North Wales, and although car parks are provided for all the coaches that arrive, they still seem to spill on to the narrow streets of the village. There are many craft shops and places for tea. The name means Chapel in the Wood, and its main attraction is the clear river which tumbles down over a series of cataracts that are known as the Swallow Falls. A mile to the south of the village is the Fairy Glen, a rocky glade with overhanging trees and a still pool below. The river is beautiful all along here, and a little further south it hurtles through a rocky channel, again overhung with woods. Retrace to the village and cross

Waterloo Bridge As the name suggests, this was built in 1815, and its designer was Telford. Turn left over the bridge and follow the road through very scenic country to

Llanrwst The hills here are not of Snowdonian proportions but are still attractive. The town is the birthplace of Inigo Jones, the Jacobean architect. A quick return can be made by following the main road along the east bank of the Conway, but a far better route is to return by way of the Abergele road, climbing up a winding hill for 3 miles and turning left at the Colwyn Bay signs. There are magnificent views of mountain, moorland and sea all the way to

Conway

69 THE LLEYN PENINSULA

40 miles (64km) – Gwynedd
Starting point: Porthmadog
OS sheets 123 and 124, Bartholomew map 27

West of Porthmadog, the motor traffic is largely left behind and there is a network of lanes in this narrow neck of land in which the sea is never more than a mile or so away and where the mountains of Snowdonia form a backdrop. The weather, too, is kinder than in the mountains, and when there is rain and mist over the peaks, Lleyn is often bathed in sunshine.

Porthmadog A popular holiday resort which boasts associations with Shelley, who stayed there, and T. E. Lawrence, who was born near there. Nearby is Portmeirion, the Italian-style model village. Leave Porthmadog by the A497, following it to

Criccieth (Alternatively, a diversion can be made leaving the main road at the hamlet of Pentrefelin to visit the church of Ynys Cynhaern, where David Owen, the harpist and composer, is buried. In this case, the road is rejoined near Criccieth.) Criccieth is dominated by its castle; there are two beaches here though they are rather stony. The main road leads on to

Llanystumdwy Near here, David Lloyd George spent his childhood, and there is a museum in the village. The narrow bridge over the river needs to be taken with care, and during the summer season traffic lights control the traffic flow. Continue along the main road, past the holiday camp, to the small town of

Pwllheli The harbour is something of a sun-trap, and yachts shelter there, making it an attractive spot. A mile out of the town take a right turn on to the A497, signposted to Nefyn. Anyone wishing to make this short run rather longer can continue through Abersoch and a maze of lanes to the end of the peninsula. The narrow roads are fringed with wild flowers in the summer, and during the winter the stormy seas are impressive. Continue to

Nefyn This is another pleasant resort. Take the B4417 eastwards out of the little town along the coast, climbing up what has become known as The Saints' Road to Bardsey, which possibly links it to a pilgrims' route. At the junction with the A499 turn right and follow the main road to the hamlet of

Fourcrosses Turn left at the crossroads and take the B4354 back to

Llanystumdwy

Criccieth and

Porthmadog

70 THE MENAI STRAIT AND ANGLESEY

25 miles (40km) – Anglesey
Starting point: Bangor
OS sheet 115, Bartholomew map 27

Generally, Anglesey is rather flat, consisting of pleasant rather than impressive country, though the coast is wild and rocky with good seascapes. This short run gives a taste of both coast and country. Cyclists will certainly find the roads quieter than those near to the resorts of the mainland coast!

Bangor Follow the Holyhead signs that take you over the spectacular Menai Bridge. The distant hills of Snowdonia can be seen on a clear day. On leaving the bridge, follow the A545 which runs along the coast to

Beaumaris This is the 'capital' of Anglesey and its main point of interest is the castle which was built by Edward I in about 1295. Continue along the coast on the B5109, which soon turns inland. Follow the signs to

Penmon There is a ruined priory here, one of the earliest religious communities on the island (sixth century), which, like so many other religious houses on the west coast of Britain and Ireland, was destroyed by the Norse raids. Proceed to the coastguard lookout on the headland. The island just off the coast is Puffin Island, which is also known as Priestholm, again a name showing the influence of the Scandinavian invasions. Retrace to Penmon and take the road through

Mariandyrys and

Pentrellwyn where the coast is reached again. Take the hilly road to

Llanddona and, travelling south-west, cross the A5025 to

Llanfair PG The village is not inspiring, but has the claim to the longest name in the British Isles. In full it is Llanfairpwll-gwyngyllgogerychwyrndrobwyll-llantysiliogogogoch. Continue along the A5. There is a good view to the right between the two bridges across the strait – the railway and the road bridges. Recross the Menai Bridge to

Bangor

SCOTLAND

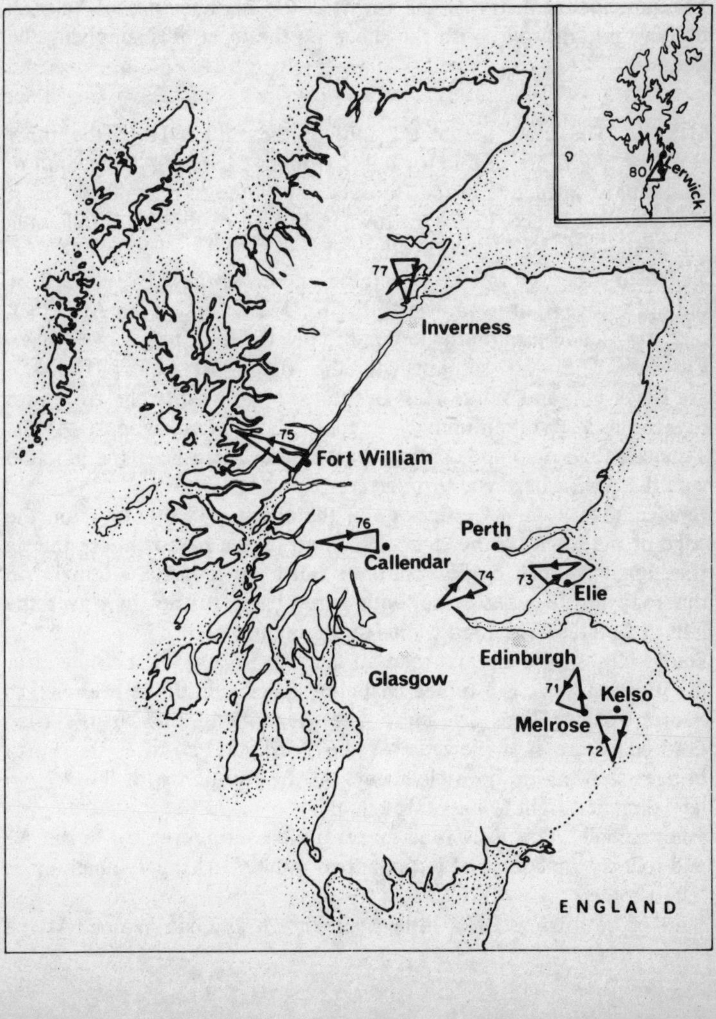
80
77
Inverness
75
Fort William
76
Perth
Callendar
74
73
Elie
Edinburgh
Glasgow
71
Kelso
Melrose
72
ENGLAND

The Borders

71 AROUND LAUDERDALE

45 miles (72km) – Roxburghshire and Berwickshire
Starting point: Melrose
OS sheet 73, Bartholomew map 41

Like so much of the Border region, the roads to the north and west of Melrose are traffic-free compared to most holiday areas of Britain. The principal industry of the towns is the manufacture of Scottish tweeds and knitwear, with the sheep on the local hills supplying the wool.

Melrose The town lies at the foot of the Eildon Hills, the three peaks of which are visible for miles around. Melrose Abbey, said to be the most attractive in the Borders, is reputed to contain the heart of Robert the Bruce. Leave the town in an easterly direction, following the signposts to Earlston. Pass through

Newstead then go left at a footpath and cross the River Tweed by the old bridge. Turn right on to the road, pass under the A68, then take the second turn on the left and follow the signs to

Earlston The two summits on the right just before Earlston are Black Hill and White Hill. In the town, go west to the A68, turn right on to it and then immediately left. There is no signpost. At the T-junction, go right and continue past Nether Blainslie to the junction with the A68, where you turn left to

Lauder Thirlestane Castle, one of the oldest in Scotland, is on the edge of the town on the right. It is more like a manor house than a traditional Scottish castle. Continue north on the A68. Remain on this road for 10 miles or so, with grand views to the right over the hills of Lothian. The road climbs to the summit of

Soutra Hill Take the first road on the left (B6368). Half a mile after the junction there is a ruined chapel or hospice on the left, known as Soutra Aisle. There are more fine views here, and as the road descends there is a view across the Forth to Fifeshire, the Forth bridges showing up on a clear day. At the junction with the A7, go left, then first right to pass through

Fountainhall This little road makes a pleasant alternative to the A7 and follows the course of a dismantled railway. At the T-junction, go left into

Stow The town is on a little river known as Gala Water. At the

crossroads, take the B6362, signposted to Lauder, then the first right while still in the village. Stay on the delightful little road to
Wooplaw At a crossroads, go right, signposted to Galashiels. Ride past
Langshaw Continue to the junction with the A6091 and go left to
Melrose

72 KELSO AND THE TWEED

50 miles (80km) – Roxburghshire and Berwickshire
Starting point: Kelso
OS sheets 73 and 74, Bartholomew map 41

With the grandeur of the Cheviot Hills away to the south-east, the Tweed slowly cuts its way through more gentle country, often missed by the tourist hurrying through to the 'playgrounds' of Scotland. This easy-riding landscape is rich in history, and there are still panoramic views of the Eildon Hills, favourites of Sir Walter Scott. Many cyclists find this area preferable for a short tour to the better-known Highland routes which are often traffic-choked.

Kelso Kelso is one of the most attractive of the Border towns. It has the advantage of having two rivers: the Tweed and the Teviot which merge on the south-west side of the town. The chief monument in the town is Kelso Abbey. From the abbey, leave the town in a southerly direction, crossing the Tweed, and go uphill to a sharp right-hand bend. Take the second on the left (B6352), signposted to Yetholm, and follow this road to
Town Yetholm Cross Bowmont Water, and in ½ mile
Kirk Yetholm is reached. This was for many years the headquarters of the Scottish gipsies. A cottage, once the gipsies' 'palace', still stands. Kirk Yetholm is the northern extremity of the Pennine Way which starts 250 miles away at Edale, in the Peak District. Retrace to
Town Yetholm Go south along the B6401 to
Morebattle The quiet village is right at the foot of the Cheviots and there is some splendid scenery. Continue west along the B6401, with Kale Water on the right, to the junction with the A698. Go right on to the main road and then immediately left, crossing the Teviot. There is a signpost at this point to Kirkbank station. Continue to a T-junction, where you go left to
Nisbet At the end of the village go right on to the B6400. There are ancient fortifications on the summit of the hill to the right, with tracks leading up. At the first junction, where there is no signpost, go right.

After 1 mile bear right again, then continue to the T-junction with the A699 and go left to
Maxton Continue on the A699 to a staggered crossroads on the A68. Proceed over and go right at a signpost to Bowden Church, then left at a T-junction and right at the next T-junction to
Melrose Visit the abbey, said to be the most attractive in this part of Scotland. The town is very attractive and a good place to halt for refreshments. Leave by following the Earlston signs, passing through
Newstead Go left at a footpath and cross the Tweed by the old bridge. Turn right on to the road and pass under the A68, then climb the hill and bear right to join the B6356. Continue on to
Scott's View This is a panorama of the River Tweed and the meanders east of Melrose, a popular spot with the novelist. Pass through
Bemersyde Proceed to the T-junction at the foot of the hill and go left at the signpost to Kelso. Continue to the junction with the B6404, where you turn left. Take the third turn on the right (signposted to Makerstoun Church) and go right again at the next T-junction, following the signs into
Kelso

The Lowlands

73 THE EAST NEUK OF FIFE

33 miles (53km) – Fife
Starting point: Elie
OS sheet 59, Bartholomew map 49

The East Neuk of Fife, bounded on the south by the Firth of Forth, is an area with picturesque little fishing and holiday towns, many showing a Flemish influence in the architecture. Inland, the country is quiet and there are some extensive views from the uplands.

Elie A small holiday town on the east side of a bay; on the west is Earlsferry, and the two make up a pleasant resort area with some excellent bathing. Leave the town by the A917, riding east along the coast. Divert right, as time permits, to any of these little coastal towns:
St Monance
Pittenweem
Anstruther Wester
Anstruther Easter All these places have interesting harbours. In each case, retrace to the A917 and continue to
Crail Take the minor road going east from the town to
Fife Ness This is the most easterly point of Fife, a rocky promontory which can be spectacular when the seas are being driven in by the gales. Retrace to
Crail Turn right on to the A918 then in ½ mile left on to the B940. Remain on this road, crossing the A921 and the A959 to
Lochty This hamlet is 450ft (137m) up and has fine views and a preserved railway line. Stay on the B940, crossing the A915 to
Peat Inn Turn left on to the B941 to
Largoward Go straight over the A915 and remain on the B941 to
Kilconquhar where there is a loch. Turn right along the shore of the loch and follow the signs round it to
Elie The route can be extended 8 miles or so by taking the A915 east from Largoward to Lower Largo, which is on the coast, and returning to Elie along the A921 and the A917.

74 AROUND THE LOMOND HILLS

35 miles (56km) – Fife
Starting point: Falkland
OS sheets 58 and 59, Bartholomew map 49

The area around the Lomond Hills provides easy riding in attractive scenery. This route also takes in Loch Leven, which is a nature reserve, and in summer a ferry can be taken to a castle on an island in the loch.

Falkland The Royal Palace, hunting residence of the Stewart kings, is open for much of the year, and there are many old houses of interest. The trading links with the Netherlands have had a strong influence on some of the architecture. Leave the town on the A912 travelling south-east, and after 2 miles turn right at a roundabout on to the A92, and 2 miles further on go right again on to the A911. Stay on this road to
Leslie Remain on the A911, past Auchmuirbridge to
Scotlandwell Directly opposite the T-junction is the well, a roofed-over spring which was known to the Romans. Go left on to the B920 and pass Portmoak Airfield, which is the headquarters of the Scottish Gliding Union. A mile after this point, go right and then right again along the south side of
Loch Leven to
Vane Farm This is a nature reserve run by the Royal Society for the Protection of Birds (small admission charge) which has displays of the water-birds of the area. There is also a nature trail and a picnic area. Continue on the B9097 to
Gairneybridge and go right on the B996 to
Kinross The gardens of Kinross House, on the shore of Loch Leven, are open during the summer. A ferry can also be taken from here to Loch Leven Castle during the season. At the north end of the town, go right on a minor road, signposted to Glenrothes, past the north side of the loch. There is an entrance through the trees for picnic spots and bathing. At the junction with the A911, go right on to the main road to
Wester Balgedie Go left near the top of the hill and take the road past Glenlomond Hospital. Keep left outside the hospital grounds on a sand and stone surface for ½ mile to Muirs of Kinnesswood. Soon the road becomes tarred and is then mostly downhill to
Strathmiglo Just before the little town is reached the remains of its castle can be seen on the flat ground. Go right on to the A912 and along the edge of the Howe of Fife to
Falkland If time allows, the two main summits of the area, East and West Lomond, give splendid views of the surrounding countryside.

The Highlands

75 LOCH EIL AND GLEN NEVIS

38 miles (61km) (plus the Glen Nevis section) – Argyllshire and Inverness-shire

Starting point: Fort William
OS sheet – Ben Nevis Tourist, Bartholomew map 50

The grandeur of the mountains around Ben Nevis, and the lochs, is justly famous, though the area is crowded in summer. This might be called one of the classic routes from Fort William, and its final section consists of a climb up Glen Nevis, say 8 miles or so, from where the road would have to be retraced. This section has been kept to the end of the ride, by which time the weather may well have made the decision as to whether or not it should be included or kept for another day!

Fort William The town is very popular in the season and it is usually necessary to book accommodation. There is a youth hostel in Glen Nevis. Visit the West Highland Museum in Cameron Square. Leave the town on the A82 going north to
Lochy Bridge This is 1 mile out of the town. Go left on to the A830 and continue along the northern shore of Loch Eil. The loch – a continuation of Loch Linnhe – is 10 miles long and the scenery is spectacular. At the head of the loch, turn left on to the A861 and make the return ride along the southern shore. Alternatively, if time allows, continue along the A830 after the head of the loch, to
Glenfinnan This is at the head of Loch Shiel and is famous for the statue of the Highlander mounted on a tall column, which marks the spot where the standard of the ill-fated Prince Charlie was unfurled on 19 August 1745. Retrace to the A861 on the southern shore of Loch Eil and ride the 10 miles to its eastern end, which is known as
The Narrows Here the road swings round to the right, and Fort William can be seen across the water. There is a ferry for anyone wishing to cut the ride short. Continue down the western side of the loch which is now part of Loch Linnhe, pausing after 6 miles at
Inverscaddle Bay Continue on to
Corran Here, across the narrow part of the channel, a ferry can be taken to the eastern bank. On landing, turn left and continue along the shore of the loch to
Fort William The entrance to Glen Nevis is at the northern end of the town. Turn right into the glen at the Bridge of Nevis, but do not cross the bridge. A mile above Glen Nevis House, on the summit of a hill, are the remains of the Forest of Dun Dairdill. The glen is extremely picturesque with the great mass of Ben Nevis dominating it on the left, and the river, the Water of Nevis, running through it. There are some spectacular waterfalls. Retrace to
Fort William

76 LOCH KATRINE AND THE DUKE'S PASS

50 miles (80km) – Perthshire
Starting point: Callander
OS sheet – Loch Lomond Tourist, Bartholomew map 48

An advantage on this ride, which is through a varied area of forests, lochs and open country, is that the 8 miles of the 'waterworks road' alongside Loch Katrine are closed to motor vehicles other than those on waterworks business but are open to cyclists and walkers. During the summer, a steamer, which carries cycles when space permits, sails along this loch, and this could be used to shorten the distance if desired.

Callander The little town is well endowed with boarding house and hotel accommodation, making it a good spot for a centre tour. Trossachs Youth Hostel is nearby. Leave the town by the A84, going west to

Kilmahog Turn left on to the A821, crossing a river, and follow the shore of Loch Venachar, with Ben Ledi the great summit on the right. Continue past Trossachs Youth Hostel to

Brig O' Turk where there is a convenient café. Continue to Loch Achray, pass the Trossachs Hotel and go straight on at the road junction to

Trossachs Pier Do not be put off by the large car park, but take the waterworks road along Loch Katrine. As mentioned above, there is unlikely to be any traffic on it, and it makes grand riding with the loch on the left and the great hills to the right. Many islands dot the lake, which is at its most beautiful at the eastern end. The steamer, if taken, goes from Trossachs Pier to Stronachlachar. At the head of Loch Katrine is

Glengyle Follow the road round to the south side of the loch to

Stronachlachar Go uphill at the junction and left on to the B829, passing Loch Chon and Loch Ard. There is grand scenery all the way, with plenty of forest. Continue to

Aberfoyle Go left on to the A821. A steep, winding climb leads to

Duke's Pass There is now a long, winding descent which makes exciting riding, and there are some grand views, finishing at

Loch Achray The outward route can now be retraced along the shore of Loch Venachar to

Callander

77 TOUR OF THE BLACK ISLE

50 miles (80km) – Ross and Cromarty
Starting point: Inverness
OS sheets 26 and 27, Bartholomew map 55

When the main roads around the well-known Highland beauty spots are congested in summer, the quieter ways of the area north of the city of Inverness, known as the Black Isle, make a pleasant change. The Black Isle is neither black nor an island, but a pleasant area of forest and glen with good coastal scenery.

Inverness This is the 'capital of the Highlands' and a good place from which to tour northern Scotland. From the centre of the town, follow the signs to the Kessock ferry, crossing the Caledonian Canal and ducking under the railway bridge. The ferry lands you at

North Kessock At the ferry landing, go left on to the B9161, bearing right with that road after 2 miles at the hamlet of

Artafallie Remain on the B9161, with Kessock Forest on the right, to

Munlochy Pause here to look at Munlochy Bay. Go right on to the A832, following the coast road with good scenery to

Avoch and

Fortrose There are the remains of an ancient cathedral here, containing the graves of some of the Highland chiefs. Divert to the headland, Chanonry Point, and retrace. From the town, continue right on the A832 to

Rosemarkie (good swimming), and then begin a stiff climb up a fine glen. Follow the main road along high ground with Cromarty Firth on the left and Moray Firth on the right. Descend to

Cromarty There are good views all around here. The geologist Hugh Miller was born here, and there is a museum devoted to his work. Leave by the B9163, running along the coast to

Jemimaville This little spot is the home of the author Jane Duncan. A mile after this point, fork right for

Cononbridge If desired, a diversion can be made to Dingwall, where there are cafés and shops. From Cononbridge, do not take the A9, which is very busy in summer, but choose the B9162 through the hamlet of

Tore where the A832 is crossed, to

North Kessock for the ferry and so back to

Inverness

NORTHERN IRELAND

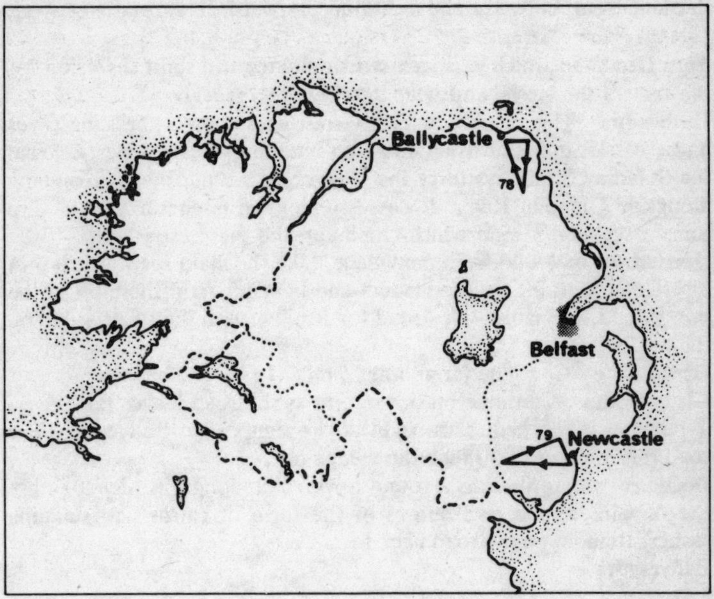

78 THE COAST OF ANTRIM

35 miles (56km) – Antrim
Starting point: Ballycastle
OS of Northern Ireland sheets 1 and 3

This north-east corner of Ulster is perhaps the most dramatic part of the country, with high, sheer cliffs from which the coast of Scotland can be seen. During the summer, ferries run from Ballycastle to Rathlin Island where, in a cave on the east coast, Robert Bruce hid after his defeat at Perth in 1306 and watched the spider 'try, try again' to spin its web, inspiring him to fresh endeavours which were to lead to Bannockburn, or so it is said.

Ballycastle This is a pretty and popular resort. Leave it on the A2, riding east and passing the golf course. After 2 miles, bear left at

Ballyvoy One mile further on, turn off on to a track which is signposted to

Fairhead This is a wild and beautiful spot and is firmly entrenched in Irish folklore. Here, a family of children, cursed by their step-mother, spent 300 years living as swans. There are two small lakes on the headland, though they are somewhat difficult to find. Retrace to the lane near Ballyvoy and continue eastward. The road twists on, past

Torr Head to which it is well worth making the short diversion for the sake of the views, and after 10 miles or so reaches

Cushendun This is another pretty spot with some interesting caves and a castle, much of the area being National Trust property. From the Standing Stone, north of the village, take a narrow lane running alongside Glendun River. It passes under the Glendun Viaduct and joins a secondary road which climbs up the picturesque glen. If the lane cannot be found from the village, take the main road, which is in a series of hairpins, to the viaduct and bear off right there on to the minor road. Remain on this road for 5 miles, with the river visible on the left, to

Orra Lodge Continue for another 5 miles to

Glens Bridge Continue on down, and as the road leaves the hills, a T-junction is reached. Turn right at the signpost to Ballycastle. The road runs due north through the village of

Doonans where there is a round tower. All along this high area are the remains of old civilizations in the form of cairns and standing stones. Remain on the road back to

Ballycastle

79 THE MOUNTAINS OF MOURNE

55 miles (88km) – Down
Starting point: Newcastle
OS of Northern Ireland sheet 9

Newcastle is the gateway to the Mourne country, where the mountains really do 'sweep down to the sea' as the song says. This route forms a figure of eight, with some retracing involved, in an attempt to include all that is best in the area, though that is really an impossible task in one ride. The route can easily be divided into two at several points; a week could be passed in this lovely district and some time should certainly be spent off the beaten tracks, with or without the bike.

Newcastle A pleasant coastal town with a youth hostel. Leave by the road going north-west which follows the Shimna River, and on reaching a T-junction after 2 miles, go left. To the left of the road is

Tollymore Forest Park This forestry area, on the northern fringe of the mountains, has a network of paths through the woods, linking streams and waterfalls. It is a good place in which to spend some time. The camping and caravan sites are placed so as not to spoil the natural beauty of the scene. Return to the road and continue west for 3 miles, turning left on to the road signposted to Kilkeel. This road bisects the Mourne Mountains. After 1 mile, you pass a youth hostel, and after a further 2 miles a reservoir is reached. The road is extremely beautiful, and after the summit the views improve again as the descent is made between Pigeon Rock Mountain on the right and Slieve Muck on the left. Do not descend directly to Kilkeel, but turn left 4 miles before that town on to the road to

Colligan Bridge This is a particularly beautiful spot where the reservoir in Silent Valley, to the north, discharges the Kilkeel River on its course southwards. If time permits, cycle north into the hills, and then retrace. This is also a point at which the route can be cut short and a return made to Newcastle (12 miles). Otherwise, continue south along the road following the course of the river for 4 miles to

Riverside Turn right into

Kilkeel There is a pretty harbour in this seaside resort, and a good beach. Take the road south-west where after 7 miles you reach

Greencastle (This section can be omitted if desired, going west instead from Kilkeel to Rostrevor to rejoin the route.) There is a ruined English fortress here, impressively situated on the headland. Retrace for 1 mile, then go left at

Whitewater Bridge The road follows the shore of Carlingford Lough and rejoins the Kilkeel–Rostrevor road. Go left on to this road, and shortly the mountains on the right will indeed be reaching down to the sea on the left. Follow on to

Rostrevor Leave the town by the road to the north signposted to Hilltown, but bear away to the right 1 mile north of Rostrevor and take the minor road over

Newtown Bridge This is the crossing point of the little Kilbroney River. The road stays on the right bank of the river, climbing into the mountains through forest scenery. Descend the other side and turn right on to the main road from Hilltown to Newcastle. Follow this back to

Newcastle If time allows, take the coast road south, where again the mountains rise up above the shore. The biggest of the summits is Slieve Donard (2,796ft; 853m), the highest in the range.

THE SHETLAND ISLANDS

(see map on page 193)

80 SOUTH FROM LERWICK

60 miles (96km)
Starting point: Lerwick
OS sheet 4, Bartholomew map 4

The discovery of North Sea oil has brought these remote islands into prominence, and with frequent sea and air services now available from the Scottish mainland (book well in advance), they provide the cyclist with something that is different from anything else in the British Isles. Be prepared for accommodation problems as the oilmen have taken much of what is available, but there is a youth hostel at Lerwick and a camp site on Knab Head. If you should go during the long winter, you might find interesting the festival of Up-Helly-Aa (last Tuesday in January), which marks the slow return of the sun. This is pioneering country for the cyclist, and you will find that few have left their wheelmarks there before you.

Lerwick This is the most northerly town in the British Isles, and closer to Bergen than any major British city. Many languages are heard in the streets – including Russian – as it is a cosmopolitan port for fishing vessels. Notice the 'lodberries' – houses built out over the sea which were convenient for unloading contraband. There is no cycle shop here, so carry some spares. Leave the town by riding south-westerly along the A970. This road runs right down the east side of the mainland peninsula. Turn off as time and prudence permit to visit this wild and rocky coastline. After 18 miles, take the first signposted road to
Sandwick From the pier, boat trips can be made (book the boat in advance) to the island of Mousa, which has a well-preserved Pictish Broch, that is a place of retreat or fortification, which is about 2,000 years old. Retrace from Sandwick to the A970, and then follow the road south for about 11 miles, again diverting along any interesting turns that attract you in this wild landscape, until

Sumburgh There is a busy airport here with helicopters flying out to the oilfields. At the end of the road is Jurlshof, a major archaeological site with dwellings from the Stone Age to a seventeenth-century castle. Return to Dunrossness Church (3 miles), turn left for
Spiggie left again at a hotel and then turn off for Bigton Farm and cross the isthmus to
St Ninian's Isle There is an early Christian chapel (pre-Viking) here, where a silver treasure was found. Return over the causeway and follow the B9122 to the A970 at
Channerwick and follow this road back to
Lerwick

(A grand two-day ride in the Shetland Islands is to take the A970 to Brae (25 miles), fork right past Sullom Voe oil terminal to Mossbank (another 6 miles), cross by the ferry to Yell (private youth hostel at Burravoe), take the B9081 and the A968 to Gutcher, and then cross by ferry to Unst. Ride on to Haroldswick (62 miles from start – there is a hotel). Climb Saxa Vord (tarred road to radar station). There are grand views of Muckle Flugga lighthouse and Out Stack, the northernmost point of the British Isles. Stay the night in Haroldswick or Burravoe and then return to Lerwick. Total distance: 120 miles.)

Bibliography

Ballantine, Richard. *Richard's Bicycle Book* (Pan Books, 1975)

Bowden, Gregory Houston. *The Story of the Raleigh Cycle* (W. H. Allen, 1975)

Crane, Nicholas. *Cycling in Europe* (Oxford Illustrated Press, 1984, Pan Books, 1985)

Crowley, T. E. *Discovering Old Bicycles* (Shire publications, 1973)

CTC Gazette (various volumes)

Cycletouring (various volumes)

Gausden, Christa and Crane, Nicholas. *The CTC Route Guide to Cycling in Britain and Ireland* (Oxford Illustrated Press, 1980)

Knottley, Peter. *Cycletouring in Britain and the Rest of Europe* (Constable, 1975)

Mackenzie, Jeanne. *Cycling* (Oxford University Press, 1981)

McFarlane, John W. *It's Easy to Fix Your Bike* (W. Foulsham, 1972)

Mecredy, R. J. and Wilson, A. J. *The Art and Pastime of Cycling* (1895)

Mee, Arthur (ed). The *King's England* series (various volumes) (Hodder & Stoughton)

Oakley, William. *Winged Wheel* (Cyclists' Touring Club, 1977)

Ritchie, Andrew. *King of the Road – An Illustrated History of Cycling* (Wildwood House, 1975)

Shaw, Reginald C. (ed). *The Raleigh Book of Cycling* (Peter Davies, 1975)

Watson, Roderick and Gray, Martin. *The Penguin Book of the Bicycle* (Penguin, 1978)

Whit, F. R. *The Restoration of Veteran-Cycles* Privately published. Undated

Wright, Robert. *Building Bicycle Wheels* (World Publications, 1977)

Acknowledgements

The production of this book has been made possible only through the help of cyclists and others throughout Britain. Members of the headquarters staff of the Cyclists' Touring Club, Godalming, Surrey, have been unstinting in the time and help they have given in advice and in the production of archive and other material. Cycle firms, too, both large and small, have given much assistance in providing up-to-date technical information and their help is gratefully acknowledged.

With such a wealth of help, it is difficult to thank everyone by name, and perhaps the following may be taken as representative of all those who have given their time and knowledge so generously: Alan Leng, Secretary of the Cyclists' Touring Club, Joan Bennett of the CTC headquarters staff, Alan Mepham, chairman of the Rough-stuff Fellowship, my son, Jeremy, for long hours spent in the darkroom, and finally to those cyclists who shared the miles and the laughter with me.

Simon Doughty drew the pen-and-ink illustrations in the routes section.

Appendix

Gear table for 26in wheels

Number of teeth on rear sprocket

Number of teeth on chainwheel	*12*	*13*	*14*	*15*	*16*	*17*	*18*	*19*	*20*	*21*
26	56.3	52	48.3	45.1	42.2	39.8	37.6	35.6	33.8	32.2
28	60.7	56	52	48.5	45.5	42.8	40.4	38.3	36.4	34.7
30	65	60	55.7	52	48.7	45.9	43.3	41.1	39	37.1
32	69.3	64	59.4	55.5	52	48.9	46.2	43.8	41.6	39.6
34	73.7	68	63.1	58.9	55.2	52	49.1	46.5	44.2	42.1
36	78	72	66.9	62.4	58.5	55.1	52	49.3	46.8	44.6
38	82.3	76	70.6	65.9	61.7	58.1	54.9	52	49.4	47
40	86.7	80	74.3	69.3	65	61.2	57.8	54.7	52	49.5
42	91	84	78	72.8	68.2	64.2	60.7	57.5	54.6	52
44	95.3	88	81.7	76.3	71.5	67.3	63.6	60.2	57.2	54.5
45	97.5	90	83.6	78	73.1	68.8	65	61.6	58.5	55.7
46	99.7	92	85.4	79.7	74.7	70.3	66.4	62.9	59.8	57
47	101.8	94	87.3	81.5	76.4	71.9	67.9	64.3	61.1	58.2
48	104	96	89.1	83.2	78	73.4	69.3	65.7	62.4	59.4
49	106.2	98	91	84.9	79.6	74.9	70.8	67.1	63.7	60.7
50	108.3	100	92.9	86.7	81.2	76.5	72.2	68.4	65	61.9
51	110.5	102	94.7	88.4	82.9	78	73.7	69.8	66.3	63.1
52	112.7	104	96.6	90.1	84.5	79.5	75.1	71.2	67.6	64.4
53	114.8	106	98.4	91.9	86.1	81.1	76.6	72.5	68.9	65.6
54	117	108	100.3	93.6	87.7	82.6	78	73.9	70.2	66.9

22	*23*	*24*	*25*	*26*	*27*	*28*	*29*	*30*	*31*	*32*	*34*
30.7	29.4	28.2	27	26	25	24.1	23.3	22.5	21.8	21.1	20.6
33.1	31.7	30.3	29.1	28	27	26	25.1	24.3	23.5	22.7	21.4
33.5	33.9	32.5	31.2	30	28.9	27.9	26.9	26	25.2	24.3	22.9
37.8	36.2	34.7	33.3	32	30.8	29.7	28.7	27.7	26.8	26	24.5
40.2	38.4	36.8	35.4	34	32.7	31.6	30.5	29.5	28.5	27.6	26
42.5	40.7	39	37.4	36	34.7	33.4	32.3	31.2	30.2	29.2	27.5
44.9	43	41.2	39.5	38	36.6	35.3	34.1	32.9	31.9	30.9	29
47.3	45.2	43.3	41.6	40	38.5	37.1	35.9	34.7	33.5	32.5	30.5
49.6	47.5	45.5	43.7	42	40.4	39	37.7	36.4	35.2	34.1	32.1
52	49.7	47.7	45.8	44	42.4	40.9	39.4	38.1	36.9	35.7	33.6
53.2	50.9	48.7	46.8	45	43.3	41.8	40.3	39	37.7	36.5	34.4
54.4	52	49.8	47.8	46	44.3	42.7	41.2	39.9	38.6	37.3	35.1
55.5	53.1	50.9	48.9	47	45.3	43.6	42.1	40.7	39.4	38.1	35.9
56.7	54.3	52	49.9	48	46.2	44.6	43	41.6	40.3	39	36.7
57.9	55.4	53.1	51	49	47.2	45.5	43.9	42.5	41.1	39.8	37.4
59.1	56.5	54.2	52	50	48.1	46.4	44.8	43.3	41.9	40.6	38.2
60.3	57.7	55.2	53	51	49.1	47.4	45.7	44.2	42.8	41.4	39
61.5	58.8	56.3	54.1	52	50.1	48.3	46.6	45.1	43.6	42.2	39.7
62.6	59.9	57.4	55.1	53	51	49.2	47.5	45.9	44.5	43	40.5
63.8	61	58.5	56.2	54	52	50.1	48.4	46.8	45.3	43.8	41.2

Gear table for 27in wheels

Number of teeth on rear sprocket

Number of teeth on chainwheel	*12*	*13*	*14*	*15*	*16*	*17*	*18*	*19*	*20*	*21*
26	58.5	54	50.1	46.8	43.9	41.3	39	36.9	35.1	33.4
28	62.9	58.1	54	50.4	47.2	44.5	42	39.8	37.8	36
30	67.5	62.3	57.9	54	50.6	47.6	45	42.6	40.5	38.6
32	72	66.5	61.7	57.6	54	50.8	48	45.5	43.2	41.1
34	76.5	70.6	65.6	61.2	57.4	54	51	48.3	45.9	43.7
36	81	74.8	69.4	64.8	60.7	57.2	54	51.2	48.6	46.3
38	85.5	78.9	73.3	68.4	64.1	60.3	57	54	51.3	48.9
40	90	83.1	77.1	72	67.5	63.5	60	56.8	54	51.4
42	94.5	87.2	81	75.6	70.9	66.7	63	59.7	56.7	54
44	99	91.4	84.9	79.2	74.2	69.9	66	62.5	59.4	56.6
45	101.2	93.4	86.8	81	75.9	71.5	67.5	63.9	60.7	57.9
46	103.5	95.5	88.7	82.8	77.6	73.1	69	65.4	62.1	59.1
47	105.7	97.6	90.6	84.6	79.3	74.6	70.5	66.8	63.4	60.4
48	108	99.7	92.6	86.4	81	76.2	72	68.2	64.8	61.7
49	110.2	101.8	94.5	88.2	82.7	77.8	73.5	69.6	66.1	63
50	112.5	103.8	96.4	90	84.4	79.4	75	71.1	67.5	64.3
51	114.7	105.9	98.4	91.8	86.1	81	76.5	72.5	68.8	65.6
52	117	108	100.3	93.6	87.7	82.6	78	73.9	70.2	66.9
53	119.2	110.1	102.2	95.4	89.4	84.2	79.5	75.3	71.5	68.1
54	121.5	112.2	104.1	97.2	91.1	85.8	81	76.7	72.9	69.4

22	*23*	*24*	*25*	*26*	*27*	*28*	*29*	*30*	*31*	*32*	*34*
31.9	30.5	29.2	28	27	26	25	24.2	23.4	22.6	21.9	20.6
34.4	32.9	31.4	30.2	29	28	27	26	25.2	24.4	23.6	22.2
36.8	35.2	33.7	32.4	31.2	30	28.9	27.9	27	26.1	25.3	23.8
39.3	37.6	36	34.6	33.2	32	30.9	29.8	28.8	27.9	27	25.4
41.7	39.9	38.3	36.7	35.3	34	32.8	31.7	30.6	29.6	28.7	27
44.2	42.3	40.5	38.9	37.4	36	34.7	33.5	32.4	31.4	30.4	28.6
46.6	44.6	42.7	41	39.5	38	36.6	35.4	34.2	33.1	32.1	30.2
49.1	47	45	43.2	41.5	40	38.6	37.2	36	34.8	33.7	31.8
51.5	49.3	47.2	45.4	43.6	42	40.5	39.1	37.8	36.6	35.4	33.4
54	51.7	49.5	47.5	45.7	44	42.4	41	39.6	38.3	37.1	34.9
55.2	52.8	50.6	48.6	46.7	45	43.4	41.9	40.5	39.2	37.9	35.7
56.5	54	51.8	49.7	47.8	46	44.4	42.8	41.4	40.1	38.8	36.5
57.7	55.2	52.9	50.8	48.8	47	45.3	43.8	42.3	40.9	39.6	37.3
58.9	56.3	54	51.8	49.8	48	46.3	44.7	43.2	41.8	40.5	38.1
60.1	57.5	55.1	52.9	50.9	49	47.2	45.6	44.1	42.7	41.3	38.9
61.4	58.7	56.2	54	51.9	50	48.2	46.6	45	43.5	42.1	39.7
62.6	59.9	57.4	55.1	53	51	49.2	47.5	45.9	44.4	43	40.5
63.8	61	58.5	56.2	54	52	50.1	48.4	46.8	45.3	43.8	41.3
65	62.2	59.6	57.2	55	53	51.1	49.3	47.7	46.2	44.7	42
66.3	63.4	60.7	58.3	56.1	54	52.1	50.3	48.6	47	45.5	42.8

General Index

A-poles, 55
About-town machines, 3–5
Adventure cycling, 62
Airline restrictions, 66–7
Alps, 72, 79
Alsace and Lorraine, 72
Aosta and Piemonte, 77
Ardennes, 73
Austria, 79–80
Autumn Tints, 63

Bed and breakfast accommodation, 59
Belgium, 73
Bernese Oberland, 76
Black Forest, 78
Blake, William, 28
Brakes, 12–13
Brazing, 9–11
Brittany, 70–71
Burton, Sir Richard, 31

Calabria, 78
California, 86
Campine, 73
Camping, 53–58
Canada, 87
Cape, 26–7, 36
Chain wear, 18
Channel ferries, 69
Clothing, 22–7
Colour coding, 43
Contour lines, 42–3
Côte d'Azur, 72
Cyclists' Touring Club, 59

Derailleur gears, 17
Distance estimation, 44
Dolomites, 77
Dordogne, 71
Dynamo lighting, 22

Eifel, 79

Family cycling, 60–62
Fellowship of Cycling Old Timers, 63
Fixed wheels, 16
Forty Plus, 63
Frame
  Hand built, 9
  Parts, 7
  Size, 5–7
France, 68–73
Folding cycles, 4

Gears
  Derailleur, 17
  Front changer, 17–18
  General, 14–19
  Hub, 18–19
  Ratios, 14–15
Gelderland, 75
Germany, 78–9
Gore-Tex, 25
Greece, 80
Grisons, 76–7

Handlebar bags, 21
Handlebars, 19
Headwinds, 37–8
Highway Code, 32–3
Holland, 74–6
Hubs, 11–12
Hungary, 83–4

Iceland, 84
Insulation mats, 54–5
Intersections, 32–3
Italy, 77–78

Junior cycles, 5–7
Jura, 72, 76

Kiddie seats, 60–61

Lights, 22
Limburg, 75
Loire Valley, 71
Lugwork, 9–10

Map-reading, 40–46
Massif Central, 71–2
Meuse Valley, 74
Mortlake, 29–31
Mountain Bike, 65

National Grid, 45–6
New England, 86
Normandy, 70
North German Plain, 79

Older riders, 63
Ordinary bicycle, 14
Overijessel, 75–6
Overshoes, 27

Pacific North-West, 86
Packing, 39–40
Panniers, 21–2
Paris, 73
Patterson, Frank, 63–5
Portugal, 81-2
Pressure stoves, 56
Provence, 72–3
Pyrenees, 73

Rail journeys, 68–9
Ridgeway, 47–8
Road surfaces, 33–4
Roadster, 4
Roughstuff Fellowship, 50
Roughstuff riding, 48–53
Roundabouts, 33
Rural rides, 34–7

Saddlebags, 20–21
Saddles, 5, 20
Safety, 32–4
Safety cycles, 15,
Sardinia, 78
Scheldeland, 74
Shoes, 24
Shorts, 24
Sicily, 78
Sidecars, 60–61
Silva Compass, 44
Sleeping bags, 53–4
Small-wheel cycle, 3–4
Spain, 81
Spoking, 12–13
Stoves, 56
Sturmey-Archer, 18
Sudgen, Amos, 49
Switzerland, 76–7

Tandems, 60–61
Ticino, 77
Time estimation, 44–45
Tools, 36–7
Touring, 37, 39
Touring machines, 6–7
Traffic-choked streets, 33
Training tops, 23
Training trousers, 23
Transporting a bike, 66–9
Tuscany, 78

United States, 84–7

Valais, 76

Wayfarer, 38
Wheels
  Building, 11–13
Winter riding, 38–9

Youth Hostels, 58–9
Yugoslavia, 82–3

Zeeland, 75

Index of Places in the Gazetteer

Abberley, 148
Abbotsbury, 106
Aberfoyle, 201
Abergwesyn, 182
Acton Scott, 153
Adlington, 161
Albury, 135
Alderminster, 145
Alderley Edge, 161
Alderton, 147
Alfriston, 122
Allerford, 104
Alsop en le Dale, 165
Alstonfield, 166
Alum Bay, 118
Ambleside, 173
Amesbury, 121
Ampleforth, 170
Anglesey, 191
Anstruther Easter, 197
Anstruther Wester, 197
Appleby, 167
Arden, 139
Arford, 133
Armscote, 146
Arne, 113
Arnside, 176–7
Artafallie, 201
Ashbourne, 165
Ashling, 116
Ashton, 97
Ashton under Hill, 147
Aveton Gifford, 102
Avoch, 201
Avonwick, 102
Axe Edge Moor, 167
Aynho, 144
Aysgarth, 171

Badger's Hill, 141
Bainbridge, 171
Ballaugh, 179
Ballycastle, 204
Ballyvoy, 204
Baltonsborough, 102
Bangor, 187, 192
Barley, 162
Beambridge, 153
Beaulieu, 114, 115
Beaumaris, 192
Beckford, 147
Beddgelert, 188
Beetham, 176
Bemersyde, 196
Berriew, 154
Berry Hill, 149
Bethesda, 187
Bettws Cedewain, 154
Betwys-y-coed, 190
Beulah, 182
Bewdley, 148
Beyton Green, 155
Bildeston, 155
Bisham, 128, 129
Bishop Monkton, 172
Bishop's Castle, 154
Bishopsdale, 171
Bishopsgate, 130
Black Isle, 201
Blackmoor, 133
Blackpool Sands, 101
Bladon, 145
Bledington, 143
Blencarn, 168
Bliss Gate, 148
Blue Anchor, 104
Boldre, 115
Bollington, 161
Bolt Head, 101
Bolton-le-Sands, 164
Borrowdale, 175

Borwick, 163
Bosham, 116
Bourne End, 128
Bournemouth, 112
Bourton-on-the-Water, 142
Boxted, 158
Bradfield St Clare, 156
Bradford Peverell, 108
Braithwaite, 176
Bramley, 134
Brays, 129
Brecon, 186
Brecon Beacons, 186
Bredon Hill, 146
Brenchley, 138
Brettenham, 155
Bridport, 106
Brig O' Turk, 200
Brighstone, 119
Brigsteer, 177
Broadplat, 127
Broads, 159
Brockenhurst, 115
Broncroft, 153
Brook, 118–19
Brookhouse, 164
Buckden, 171
Buckhorn Weston, 107
Bucklers Hard, 115
Bude, 97
Builth Wells, 183
Bulmer, 170
Bungalow, 179
Burchett's Green, 128
Bucks Green, 134
Burford, 142
Burton Bradstock, 106
Bury St Edmunds, 155
Butleigh, 102
Butt Yeats, 163
Buttermere, 176
Buttonoak, 148
Buxton, 166
Byland Abbey, 170
Bynorth Cliff, 97

Caernarvon, 189
Callander, 200
Cape Cornwall, 95
Capel Curig, 188
Cardington, 153
Carhampton, 104
Carisbrooke, 119
Carnforth, 163
Cassington, 145
Castle Howard, 170
Castlemartin, 185
Caton Moor, 163
Cawsand, 99
Cefn-coed-y-cymmer, 186
Cerne Abbas, 105, 108
Chainhurst, 137
Channerwick, 208
Charlecote, 145
Charlton, 141
Charminster, 108
Chatburn, 162
Chelmondiston, 157
Chelmorton, 167
Cheltenham, 146
Chepstow, 149
Cheriton, 120
Cherwell Valley, 143
Chichester, 116, 123
Chickerell, 106
Chilgrove, 124
Chipping Campden, 146
Church End, 140
Church Knowle, 109
Church Lench, 141
Church Stoke, 155
Church Stretton, 153
Clifton, 144
Clitheroe, 162
Clouds Hill, 110
Coast of Antrim, 203
College Green, 177
Colligan Bridge, 205
Combe Bottom, 135–6
Compton, 131
Cononbridge, 202
Constable Country, 157
Conway, 189, 190
Conway Valley, 189
Cookham, 129
Corfe Castle, 109, 113
Corley, 140
Cornwall, 94
Corran, 199
Cotswolds, 141
Cove, 177
Cowes, 117
Coxbridge, 102
Coxwold, 169

Crackington Haven, 97
Crail, 197
Cranbrook, 138
Cranleigh, 134
Crayke, 169
Creg-ny-Baa, 179
Cremyll, 99
Criccieth, 191
Croesywaun, 188
Cromarty, 202
Crondal, 125
Crosthwaite, 177
Cucklington, 107
Culgaith, 168
Culmington, 153
Cushendun, 204
Cut Mill, 132
Cwmystwyth, 181
Cwn Owen, 184

Dalham Tower, 176
Dartmeet, 99
Dartmoor, 98
Dartmouth, 101
Deddington, 144
Dedham, 158
Derbyshire Dales, 164
Derwentwater, 175
Devil's Staircase, 182
Devonport, 100
Dilwyn, 151
Dittisham, 101
Dodds Howe, 178
Dolgarrog, 190
Dolgellau, 182
Doonans, 205
Dorchester, 105, 108
Dorney, 127
Downham, 162
Drinkstone, 155
Drinkstone Green, 155
Drover's Arms, 183
Dufton, 168
Duke's Pass, 200
Dulcote, 102
Duncton, 123
Dunsfold, 133
Dunster, 104
Dorset, 168

Earlston, 194
East Bergholt, 158
East Clandon, 136
East Cowes, 117
East Dean, 123
East Mountain Gate, 179
East Neuk of Fife, 197
East Peckham, 137
Easton, 111
Eckington, 147
Eden Valley, 167
Elie, 197
Ellen's Green, 134
Elmley Castle, 147
Elstead, 124, 133
Englefield Green, 130
English Bicknor, 149, 150
Errwood Dam, 166
Erwarton, 157
Eton, 127
Evesham, 141
Ewhurst Green, 134
Exmoor, 103

Fairhead, 204
Falkland, 198
Far Forest, 148
Farnham, 125
Fenny Bentley, 165
Fernhurst, 124
Fifehead Magdalen, 107
Fife Ness, 197
Fifield 129, 143
Five Oak Green, 138
Fladbury, 141
Flatford, 158
Flaxton, 170
Forest of Arden, 139
Forest of Dean, 148
Fort William, 199
Fortrose, 201
Fortuneswell, 111
Fountainhall, 194
Fountains Abbey, 172
Fourcrosses, 191
Frensham Ponds, 133
Freshwater Bay, 118
Freshwater East, 185
Freston, 156
Frittenden, 138
Fritwell, 144

Gairneyridge, 198
Galmpton, 100

Gayle, 171
Gillingham, 107
Glastonbury, 103
Glen Nevis, 198
Glenfinnan, 199
Glengyle, 201
Glenridding, 174
Glens Bridge, 204
Glympton, 145
Glynde, 122
Godalming, 131
Godolphin Cross, 97
Godshill, 117
Golden Green, 137
Goodrich, 150
Goudhurst, 138
Goyt Valley, 166
Grange, 175
Grasmere, 173
Grately, 121
Great Barrington, 142
Great Comberton, 147
Great Green, 156
Greencastle, 205
Gressingham, 163
Grimstone, 108
Guildford, 134
Gumfreston, 184
Guthrie Memorial, 179
Gyffin Hill, 190

Hadleigh, 156, 157
Halton, 164
Hambledon, 133
Hampton Lucy, 145
Hardy Country, 104
Harkstead, 157
Harpsden Court, 126
Harrogate, 172
Hartington, 167
Harvington, 141
Haslemere, 123
Havenstreet, 117
Hawkes End, 140
Hawkhill Inclosure, 115
Haylotts Farm, 164
Headcorn, 138
Headley, 133
Heightington, 148
Helston, 96
Helvellyn, 173
Hempton, 144
Henley, 126
Hereford, 151
Heversham, 178
Higham, 158
Higher Bockhampton, 105, 110
Highgate, 154
Hillberry, 179
Hitcham, 155
Holbrook, 157
Honister Pass, 175
Hope, 101
Hopedale, 166
Hornby, 163
Horning, 159
Horsey, 159
Horsmonden, 138
Hovingham, 170
Howardian Hills, 168
Huby, 169
Hunsonby, 168
Huntington, 170
Hunton, 137
Hurley, 129

Idbury, 143
Idmiston, 121
Ilam, 166
Ilmington, 146
Inverness, 201
Inverscaddle Bay, 199
Iping, 124
Ipswich, 156
Isle of Man, 178
Isle of Wight, 117
Ivington, 151

Jacobstow, 97
Jemimaville, 202
Jenny Brown's Point, 177

Kelso, 195
Kent Orchards and Hopfields, 137
Kerne Bridge, 150
Kerry, 154
Keswick, 175
Kidlington, 144
Kilburn, 169
Kilconquhar, 197
Kilkeel, 205
Kilmahog, 200
Kingsand, 99

Kingsbridge, 101
Kingsley, 132
Kingston, 113
Kington Magna, 107
Kinross, 198
Kirk Michael, 179
Kirk Yetholm, 195
Kirkland, 168
Kirkstone Pass, 174
Knaresborough, 172
Knock, 168
Knowl Hill, 129

Lakeland, 177
Lamorna, 95
Lamphey, 185
Land's End, 95
Langham, 158
Langshaw, 195
Langstrothdale, 171
Langton Herring, 106
Langton Matravers, 112
Langwathby, 168
Largoward, 197
Lauder, 195
Lauderdale, 194
Laurel Street, 102
Lawford, 158
Laysters Pole, 152
Leominster, 151
Lerwick, 207
Leslie, 198
Levens, 177
Levens Bridge, 177
Lewes, 122
Little Comberton, 147
Little Marlow, 128
Little Salkeld, 168
Little Welnetham, 156
Llanddona, 192
Llanfachreth, 183
Llanfair PG, 192
Llanrwst, 190
Llanystumdwy, 191
Lleyn Peninsula, 190
Loch Achray, 201
Loch Eil, 198
Loch Katrine, 200
Loch Leven, 198
Lochty, 197
Lochy Bridge, 199
Lodsworth, 123
Lomond Hills, 197
Long Meg, 168
Long Mynd, 153
Long Sutton, 125
Longnor, 167
Lover's Leap, 167
Lower Hayton, 153
Lower Holbrook, 157
Lower Layham, 158
Lower Lydbrook, 149
Lower Slaughter, 142
Lower Swell, 143
Loxley, 145
Loyn Bridge, 163
Luccombe, 104
Ludham, 160
Ludlow, 152
Lulworth, 109
Luston, 151
Lymington, 115
Lynstone, 97
Lytchett Minster, 113

Maiden Newton, 105
Malborough, 101
Manafon, 154
Mapleton, 166
Marden (Hereford), 152
Marden (Kent), 138
Marhamchurch, 98
Mariandyrys, 192
Marlow, 128, 129
Marnhull, 107
Marshbrook, 153
Martham, 159
Maxstoke Church, 140
Maxton, 196
Melrose, 194, 196
Menai Strait, 191
Meon, 120
Meriden, 140
Merstone, 117
Mickleton, 146
Middle Aston, 144
Milburn, 168
Mill Street, 158
Millbridge, 132
Millbrook, 100
Milldale, 165
Millook Haven, 97
Millside, 178
Milnthorpe, 178

Milton, 185
Minehead, 104
Monkey Island, 129
Monks Eleigh, 156
Monmouth, 149
Montgomery, 154
Moorlands Nature Reserve, 169
Morebattle, 195
Morestead, 120
Morvah, 95
Mottistone, 119
Mourne, 204
Mousehole, 95
Munlochy, 201

Narrows, 199
Nayland, 158
Neatishead, 159
Needles, 118
Nefyn, 191
Nether Worton, 144
Nettlebed, 127
Neuadd Reservoirs, 186
New Forest, 114
New Mills, 154
Newbold on Stour, 146
Newbridge on Wye, 182
Newburgh Priory, 169
Newcastle, 204
Newchurch (Isle of Wight), 117
Newchurch (Pennines), 162
Newlands Corner, 136
Newlyn, 95
Newstead, 194, 196
Newton, 163
Newtown (Isle of Wight), 119
Newtown (Powys), 154
Newtown Bridge (Antrim), 206
Nisbet, 195
North Aston, 144
North Downs, 131
North Kessock, 202
North of Nidderdale, 171
North Wootton, 102
Nuffield, 126
Nunnington, 170

Oakhanger, 132
Ockley, 134
Odiham, 125
Offenham Cross, 141
Old Earswick, 170
Oldstead, 170
Orra Lodge, 204
Osborne House, 118
Oswaldkirk, 170
Oulston, 169
Over Whitacre Church, 140
Oxford, 144

Packington Park, 140
Paley Street, 128
Parkend, 149
Parwich, 165
Patterdale, 174
Paul, 95
Peat Inn, 197
Peaton, 153
Pembroke, 185
Penhalt Cliff, 97
Pen-y-Gwryd, 188
Pendle Hill, 162
Penlee Point, 95
Penmon, 192
Pentrellwyn, 192
Penzance, 95
Piddletrenthide, 105
Pilsbury, 167
Pin Mill, 157
Pittenweem, 197
Plymouth, 99
Polstead, 158
Pontrhydfendigaid, 181
Pontrhydygroes, 181
Poole, 111
Portesham, 106
Porthleven, 96
Porthmadog, 191
Portland (Isle of), 110
Portland Bill, 111
Porton, 121
Postbridge, 98
Potter Heigham, 159
Pott Shrigley, 161
Powerstock, 106
Prestbury, 161
Preston (Dorset), 105, 109
Preston (East Anglia), 156
Preston on Stour, 146
Princetown, 98
Puddletown, 105, 110
Pudleston, 152
Purbeck (Isle of), 112

Puttenham, 132
Pwllheli, 191

Queen Anne's Gate, 130

Raleigh's Cross, 104
Rame, 99
Ramsey, 178
Rhayader, 181
Richards Castle, 152
Ridge Lane, 140
Ridgeway, 184
Ripley, 136, 172
Ripon, 172
Riverside, 205
Robin Hill Country Park, 117
Rock, 148
Roewen, 190
Roof of Wales, 181
Rosemarkie, 201
Ross-on-Wye, 150
Rosthwaite, 175
Rostrevor, 206
Rousham, 144
Rudgwick, 134
Runnymede, 131
Rushbury, 153
Rydal, 173

Sabden, 162
St Briavels, 149
St Florence, 184
St Ives, 96
St John, 100
St John's, 179
St Just, 95
St Monance, 197
St Ninian's Isle, 208
Salcombe, 101
Sandford, 117
Sandford St Martin, 144
Sandwick, 207
Sarn, 154
Scotlandwell, 198
Scott's View, 196
Sea Palling, 159
Selborne, 132
Selham, 123
Selworthy, 104
Send, 136
Sennen, 95
Sennen Cove, 95
Shaftesbury, 107
Shakespeare Country, 145
Shalfleet, 119
Sheen, 167
Shelley, 158
Shelwick Green, 152
Sherbourne, 142
Shere, 136
Sheriff Hutton, 170
Sheriff's Lench, 141
Shorwell, 119
Shotley Church, 157
Shotley Gate, 157
Shotley Peninsula, 156
Shotley Street, 157
Silent Pool, 135
Silverdale, 176
Skelton, 169
Skirwith, 168
Slack Head, 176
Slapton Sands, 101
Sling, 149
Slingsby, 170
Snowdon, 187
Snowdon Ranger Youth Hostel, 188
Solent, 114
Somerset, 102
Somerton, 144
Sonning Common, 126
Souldern, 144
South Downs, 123
Southern Wye Valley, 148
Southwell, 111
Soutra Hill, 194
Spiggie, 208
Stackpole, 185
Stalham, 159
Staplehurst, 138
Starbeck, 173
Steen's Bridge, 152
Steeple Aston, 144
Strensall, 170
Stinsford, 105, 110
Stoke Fleming, 101
Stoke Tyo, 158
Stonehenge, 120, 121
Stour Row, 107
Stow, 194
Stow on the Wold, 143
Strang, 179
Stratford-on-Avon, 145
Strathmiglo, 198

Stronachlachar, 201
Studland, 112
Sulby, 179
Sumburgh, 208
Sutton Poyntz, 105, 109
Sutton St Michael, 152
Sutton St Nicholas, 152
Swanage, 112
Sydling St Nicholas, 108
Symonds Yat, 149, 150

Tackley, 144
Taf Fechan Reservoir, 186
Taynton, 142
Temple Guiting, 142
Temple Sowerby, 167
Tenby, 184
Thames Valley, 126–8
Thirlmere, 173
Thorncombe Street, 134
Thornton Rust, 171
Thorpe, 166
Thorpe Green, 156
Thorpe Morieux, 156
Thrang End, 176
Threlkeld, 174
Ticklerton, 153
Tilford, 133
Tillington, 151
Timberscombe, 104
Tissington, 165
Tichborne, 120
Toller Porcorum, 106
Tollymore Forest Park, 205
Tonbridge, 137
Torcross, 101
Tore, 202
Torpoint, 100
Torr Head, 204
Totland, 118
Totnes, 100
Town Yetholm, 195
Treen, 95
Tregaron, 182
Tregynon, 154
Tresparrett Posts, 97
Trossachs Pier, 200
Trow Green, 149
Tweed, 195
Two Bridges, 98

Ullswater, 174
Upper Lydbrook, 149
Upper Severn, 153
Upper Slaughter, 142
Upper Swell, 143
Upper Wye, 183

Vale of York, 168

Waddington, 163
Wainhouse Corner, 97
Walford, 150
Walliswood, 134
Waltham St Lawrence, 129
Wareham, 110, 113
Warren Row, 129
Warton, 163, 176
Wass, 170
Watchet, 104
Weare Street, 134
Week St Mary, 97
Wellow, 119
Wells, 102
Wenlock Edge, 152
Wensleydale, 170
Weobley, 151
West Clandon, 136
Westhope, 153
West Lilling, 170
West Pennard, 102
Wester Balgedie, 198
Weston, 111
Weymouth, 105
Whippingham, 117
White Horse, 169
Whitewater Bridge, 206
Widecombe in the Moor, 98
Widemouth Sands, 97
Winchcombe, 147
Winchester, 119, 120
Winder, 164
Windrush, 142
Windsor, 127, 130
Winter Hill, 130
Woking, 136
Woodend, 148
Woodstock, 145
Woolverstone, 156
Wooplaw, 195
Wootton Common, 118
Wootton Courtenay, 104
Worth Matravers, 112
Worton, 171
Wroxham, 159

Wyke Regis, 111
Wyre Forest, 147

Yalding, 137
Yarmouth, 118
Yealand Conyers, 176
Yelverton, 98
York, 168
Ysbyty Ystwyth, 181

Zennor, 96